A Journey Through

NEW MEXICO HISTORY

A Journey Through
NEW MEXICO
HISTORY

By DONALD R. LAVASH, Ph.D.
REVISED EDITION
Foreword by GEORGE A. AGOGINO, Ph.D

SUNSTONE PRESS

Santa Fe
New Mexico

Revised Edition
Printed in the United States of America

Library of Congress Cataloging-in-Publication Data:

Lavash, Donald R.
    A journey through New Mexico History / by Donald R. Lavash ;
  foreword by George A. Agogino. -- Rev. ed.
       p.   cm.
    Originally published: Rev. ed. Portales, N.M. : Bishop Pub. Co.,
  1980.
    Includes bibliographical references and index.
    ISBN 0-86534-194-X : $24.95
    1. New Mexico--History--Juvenile literature.   I. Title
  F796.3.L3 1992
  972--dc20   92-27191
                                                CIP
                                                AC

Published by Sunstone Press
       Post Office Box 2321
       Santa Fe, NM 87504-2321

DEDICATED
TO MY DEVOTED WIFE BOBBIE ANN
WHO CONSTANTLY ENCOURAGED ME
IN MY HISTORICAL LABORS
WHILE WRITING THIS TEXTBOOK
ON NEW MEXICO HISTORY

FOREWORD

It is more difficult to synthesize than to analyze, and it is more difficult to create a good middle school text than it is to construct a college text. Dr. Donald R. Lavash, in his textbook A Journey Through New Mexico History, shows a unique ability to synthesize accurately in compiling an excellent textbook. The book is a result of considerable research, careful selection of numerous photographs, and the necessary writing and rewriting of each chapter until the finished product is professional, interesting, and accurate.

I was impressed by the appealing narrative used by Donald Lavash. Too often, history is little more than a list of chronological events which fails to emphasize the fact that we are dealing with historical figures, not caricatures. Lavash's approach to the past, though, makes historical figures more human and understandable. This is so important at the junior high school level.

Lavash spent an entire chapter on New Mexico's state government. This is advantageous to an ethnically diverse state where even many adults do not understand, comprehend, or realize their individual roles, rights, and privileges within the state's system. Our democratic society, check and balance protections, and state electoral procedures, if understood, not only educate, but give strength to the state by producing citizens more willing to follow and accept an orderly and organized system of proper representation, the backbone of our democratic system.

A JOURNEY THROUGH NEW MEXICO HISTORY

I was particularly impressed with the complete chapter devoted to the American Indian, not only the contemporary Indians within our state, but the Indians of years past and their contributions, including a factual account of our state's Paleo-Indians, over 10,000 years of age and among the oldest representatives of American Indians anywhere. We must remember our Paleo-Indians beat Columbus to our continent by many thousands of years. A unit of equal importance deals with our state's Spanish period, a colorful and exciting era of pioneer conquest. Brave and dedicated men—Indians, Anglos, and Spanish-Americans—engaged in this period in a complex conflict with both the environment and at times with each other in molding the foundations and producing the rich ethnic heritage that makes our state so unique.

Not only are the major ethnic groups accurately and well represented, but the Black fraction of our state population is not neglected. These individuals, who were small in number in our state's historical past, have left their contributions as well. For years, a small group of fellow researchers, Donald Lavash included, and I have worked on the life story of a remarkable man, George McJunkin, a Black, who was responsible for the discovery of the Folsom-type site, the first widely accepted early-man site in the New World. Lavash includes this episode, as well as others concerning early Negroes in our state, in a manner which is both careful, accurate, and honest.

Perhaps the most colorful and romantic era in New Mexico's rich history is the Territorial Period. The period saw the first waves of non-Spanish or Indian exploration and exploitation. The earliest were the mountain men, wild and colorful as the Indians, as adventurous as the Spanish explorers, as rough and rugged as the mountains from which they derived their wealth. Later came a mixture of migrants, many motivated by greed, some seeking a better world in the West. Here, evaluated by chance, fortune, opportunity, and the wilderness of the West, some found the satisfaction of greed, others found glory, many had greatness thrust upon them, all too many died untimely and rest in unmarked graves. Some were true adventurers, seeking new frontiers, others were the

FOREWORD

world's flotsam and **jetsam,** **castoffs,** *the unwanted, the inadequate. The West brought out the most of their bravery or baseness.*

Political events caused conflict and war. External events brought on the Mexican-American War of 1848, internal pressures produced the Indian uprisings, while the shadow of an Eastern conflict resulted in a mini-sized civil war within the desert Southwest. From this mixture of conflict and conquest, exploration and exploitation, struggle, survival, and growth, a territory became a state.

Lavash, as he does elsewhere in his books, puts living flesh on historical bones in such a manner that the reader lives the adventure as he reads, and relives the saga of the Territorial Period of the state of New Mexico alongside the mountain men, the lawman, the soldier, and the territorial businessman.

Within the wonderful region of New Mexico is a rich heritage of multiple slags that forms the government. The area is unique in another respect. No group, Indian, Spanish-American, Black American, or Anglo, can claim dominance in numbers, since each group is in itself an ethnic minority when all the others groups are totaled together. You must realize and recognize that New Mexico is made up of a configuration of minority groups, each with its own rich historical past and contributions, that when molded together make up our contemporary population of our state. Whether this is our strength or our weakness depends on how we conduct ourselves at the present time and in the future.

The text, A Journey Through New Mexico History, *is enriched with several hundred well-selected photographs designed to make more understandable the shifting events and the landscape of a diversified land and a diversified population.*

Dr. George A. Agogino

Chairman Emeritus, Department of Anthropology
Director Emeritus, Paleo-Indian Institute and
Museums; Eastern New Mexico University
Portales, New Mexico

CONTENTS

ACKNOWLEDGMENTS

After much consideration I have written this New Mexico History textbook designed for use in the middle schools. Encouragement and assistance have come from many sources during the years of research for the preparation of this work. Special thanks go to Dr. George A. Agogino, Director Emeritus of the Paleo-Indian Institute, Eastern New Mexico University; Dr. C. Irwin Williams, formerly the Assistant Professor of Archeology, Eastern New Mexico University; Dr. Ira C. Ihde, former Chairman, Department of History, Eastern New Mexico University; Joe Walker, Chairman, Humanities Department, New Mexico Junior College; Eli M. Borden, Assistant Professor of English, New Mexico Junior College; Ray D. Bailey for the numerous pictures he supplied; Shirley M. Hooper who spent many hours typing the manuscript; Senator Mack Easley, a statesman and friend, who for years has helped me with New Mexico government facts; and to my friend Chris Gikas Professor of art, Eastern New Mexico University, who researched and then sketched the various scenes throughout the text. In addition, I want to express my gratitude and thanks to Arthur P. Lites, formerly of Stanford University, for the design of the book.

We are grateful to Dover Publications Inc. for permission to reproduce the circular Indian designs from *Decorative Art of the Southwestern Indians,* used throughout this book.

Grateful acknowledgement is made to Peter Hurd, nationally renowned artist of San Patricio, New Mexico for his assistance, help and support with artwork and graphics, contained in the book; George C. Paul, typographic consultant and technician; and to Maggie Bynum of the Albuquerque Public Schools and to Dr. David V. Holtby for editorial assistance; and to Jean Stouffer for proofreading.

Recognition is also due to the following colleges, commissions, and departments of the State of New Mexico which supplied vital information: Oil Conservation Commission; Department of Game and Fish; New Mexico State Highway Department; Department of Education; Commission on Indian Affairs; New Mexico Department of Agriculture; New Mexico Bureau of Mines and Mineral Resources; Department of Development; State Planning Office; Museum of New Mexico; State Library; *New Mexico Magazine;* State Supreme Court; Legislative Council Service; University of New Mexico; Eastern New Mexico University; New Mexico State University; and New Mexico Highlands University. Recognition should also be given to the New Mexico Municipal League, Los Alamos Scientific Laboratories, and Holloman Air Force Base.

My sincere thanks to Mrs. John Doherty for supplying information on George McJunkin; Marcello Povijua, former Governor of San Juan Indian Pueblo, for supplying information on the ancient village of San Gabriel; I am appreciative of the cooperation and information given on Indians by Dr. Bertha P. Dutton and George S. Janes, Ed Jeffers, and W. Bert Wayt of the Hobbs Municipal Schools for assisting me with the preparation of this book.

Finally, thanks and appreciation are due to all who have had a part in the progress of this work.

Donald R. Lavash, Ph.D.

A Journey Through

NEW MEXICO HISTORY

REVISED EDITION   By Donald R. Lavash, Ph.D.
Edited by David V. Holtby, Ph.D.

CHAPTER I
Land Formations and Early Life

CHAPTER II
Early Man of New Mexico

CHAPTER III
Indians of New Mexico

UNIT 1

BEFORE THE SPANISH ARRIVED

Land Formations and Early Life

Land Formations

What memory is to the individual, history is to the human race. Historians define history as the whole story of mankind. In this sense, history includes all we know about the activities of mankind. Therefore, to understand what man has done in the past, we must turn to his surroundings, his likes, and his dislikes to get a glimpse of the area that suited him best.

The study of the earth, both the surface and beneath the surface, has always been one of man's major activities. We seem to be driven by some inner force to know our environment, to improve it, and to apply our learning to practical ends for our own comfort.

Formation of the Earth

Geologists have divided the world into three separate divisions as it changed from its original state: eras, periods, and epochs.

(1) ERAS deal with the earth's estimated timetable of life. Most recent life is 70 million years old, medieval life 200 million years old, and ancient life 500 million years old. Older life is one billion, 200 million years old, and oldest life is more than 4 billion years old.

(2) PERIODS are subdivisions within the five eras. Those of major interest to the people of New Mexico are the Permian, Pennsylvanian, Mississippian, and Devonian of the Paleozoic Era (beginning 500 million years ago).

(3) EPOCHS are further subdivisions within the periods, such as Paleocene and Miocene of the Tertiary Period (70 million years ago). The Pleistocene (Ice Age) and Recent belong to a period called Quaternary (one million years

ago). Great geological structures from these epochs are seen today along the highways of New Mexico.

Land Forms

Traveling eastward from Santa Fe on Highway 85, one passes through some of the oldest formations in the state, estimated to be more than 3 billion years old. To the south of Santa Fe is Glorieta Mesa, thought to be more than 300 million years old. The Sangre de Cristo Mountains vary in age from middle or late Pennsylvanian to early Permian (250 million years ago). Moving eastward from Pecos Village about 18 miles (29 km.), one can see Bernal Butte. Geologists have estimated that this area is approximately 150 million years old.

Elsewhere in the state, one may see the steep slopes of the Canadian River Valley. On the west side of the valley is the Raton Mesa. Within this area, rock formations have been judged to be more than 40 million years old. Capulin Mountain in northeastern New Mexico is an example of the period when volcanos erupted, pouring out molten rock called lava, about 100 million years ago.

Still other places in the state, such as the San Juan Basin in northwestern New Mexico, are considered by many to be over 200 million years old, and are similar in age to the areas around Silver City in southwestern New Mexico. The Carlsbad Caverns in Eddy County (located in southeastern New Mexico) are an example of the activity during this period.

From the San Andres Mountains through Alamogordo to the Sacramento Mountains, the traveler will see various formations estimated to be 300 million years old. In eastern and southeastern New Mexico are the Llano Estacado or Staked Plains, which encircle the oil fields of the Great Plains Province. The Portales Valley of the Llano Estacado overlies an ancient stream bed which is about 30 miles (48 km.) wide. This valley is the remains of a Pleistocene drainage system (500,000 years ago) that developed from melting ice and increased rainfall.

Most of the formations beneath the surface of the Southern Great Plains of eastern New Mexico and western Texas are over 200 million years old. The more recent deposits, which can be seen on the surface along the slopes of the Llano Estacado, range in age from 10 to 20 million years. Many fossil plants and animals are found in the strata (layers of rock or earth material) laid down when the climate was humid. Journeying westward across the Pecos River, a visitor may notice that the country is free of any major geological barriers with the exception of the Manzano Mountains, located east of Albuquerque.

Glacial Period

The Glacial Period was born about 10 million years ago when the cooling climate forced conditions to change. Over a period of several million years, a great icecap was formed, which began moving southward about a million years ago. This period is called the Ice Age. According to many scientists, the Great Glacier did not reach New Mexico. However, smaller glaciers were formed, leaving their marks on various areas throughout the state. For example, Sierra Blanca, the highest peak in the White Mountains, located in Otero County, was the southernmost point in

Located in northern New Mexico are the grotesque shaped "Tent Rocks." The entire area is made up of soft volcanic ash as a result of the eruption of the Valle Grande during Pliocene and Pleistocene times.

the United States where such a glacier developed.

Slowly changing temperatures caused by the glaciers had a great effect upon all forms of life. Many creatures were destroyed by the great glaciers, while other life forms left the colder areas for more pleasant conditions in the south. The musk ox is an example of a form of life that moved southward in search of a warm climate. This animal has long since become extinct in New Mexico, but some remains have been found. According to scientists, many life forms crossed the Bering Strait land bridge during the late Glacial Period to seek a suitable place to live. Many animals that are seen today are their descendants—the fox, the racoon, the badger, the coyote, and the weasel. Man was part of this great migration to North and South America, although just exactly when he

came is not known, perhaps some day the answer will be found.

Mountains

Physical features (topography) of New Mexico vary from semi-arid deserts to great flat-topped mesas and to high mountains in the Sangre de Cristo Range, more than two and one-half miles above sea level. These huge mountains provide the shelter necessary for the many fertile valleys that are located throughout the state.

The Great Rocky Mountains that enter the state from the southern part of Colorado continue south along the east side of the Rio Grande, forming a long chain of mountains which extend to the southern boundary of Mexico and Texas. Chief among these ranges are the Capitan, Guadalupe, Sacramento, and White Mountains west of the Pecos River. To the north, the Los Pinos, Manzano, Organ, San Andres, Sandia, and Sangre de Cristo Ranges make up one of the major mountain groups in New Mexico.

West of the Rio Grande are the Jemez Nacimiento, and San Juan Mountains. In the center of the Jemez Group is Valle Grande, the largest volcanic crater ever found. Still farther west are the Chuska Mountains, located in San Juan and McKinley Counties. Lookout Mountain belongs to the Zuñi Range south of Bluewater Lake State Park. Mount Taylor, to the east, is part of the San Mateo Mountains. Traveling southward, we find the Gallinas, Mogollon, and Tularosa Mountains, which nearly surround the San Augustine Plains, followed by the Mimbres and Peloncillo Mountains located in southwestern New Mexico.

Forests

Seven national forests are located almost entirely within the state, providing not only timber, a most valuable resource, but also scenic beauty. These forests are the Apache, Carson, Cibola, Coronado, Gila, Lincoln, and Santa Fe. (Parts of the Coronado and Gila National Forests are in Arizona.) Long ago, primitive people lived in these forest areas, and many of their home-sites have been preserved so that man may see how his ancestors existed many hundreds of years ago.

The forest regions of our state cover more than 18 million acres, about 23 percent of all the land in New Mexico. The chief timber source in New Mexico is the ponderosa pine, which provides about 90 percent of all the timber taken from our national forests. The remaining 10 percent comes from the aspen,

The vast expanse of gypsum crystals stretches as far as the eye can see at White Sands National Monument.

Douglas fir and ponderosa pine make up the towering timber stands of the Lincoln National Forest in southern New Mexico.

Douglas fir, and spruce. Other trees include juniper, oak, and evergreen piñon pine.

About two million acres of private forests add to the great source of timber in New Mexico. The forest is managed for multiple use of timber, water, minerals, grazing, recreation, wildlife, and other resources.

Rivers

New Mexico is fortunate to have several valuable rivers, such as the Chama, the Gila, the Mora-Canadian, the Pecos, the Rio Grande, and the San

The Organ Mountains in southern New Mexico offer one of the state's scenic highlights. They are so named because claps of thunder reverberate through the craggy peaks like peals from a mighty organ. In the foreground of this picture is a yucca plant known as a Palmilla or Soapweed. Early Indians ground the roots to make soap and shampoo.

Aspens in the Santa Fe National Forest.

Juan. These rivers provide hydro-electric power, irrigation, and recreational facilities for surrounding counties and are widely known tourist attractions. Rivers such as the Alamosa, the Rio Chama, the Rio Puerco, the Rio Salado, and the San Jose flow in a general southeasterly direction and empty into the Rio Grande. The Chaco flows northward to join the San Juan River, and together they move westward to the Colorado River in Arizona.

The San Francisco and Gila Rivers originate in the Apache and Gila Forests, flowing in a southwesterly direction into Arizona. The Cimarron, the Hondo, the Mora-Canadian, and the Pecos flow east and southeast into Texas. The Corrumpa-Canadian, which has its source in the Sierra Grande Mountain, flows in an easterly direction into Oklahoma. Why these differences in water flow? The answer is the Continental Divide, a "ridge" or "fold" in the landscape of New Mexico. This imaginary line runs north and south

The Caballo Mountains of southern New Mexico stand as stern guardians over the southern Rio Grande Valley. During prehistoric times, huge animals roamed the vast lands around the Rio Grande.

into both North and South America, separating water drainage. Waters from the west slope will eventually reach the Pacific Ocean. Drainage from the east side will finally flow into the Atlantic Ocean.

Two major rivers in New Mexico that do not have their sources within the state are the San Juan and the Rio Grande. The headwaters of the San Juan are located in Colorado, and they flow westward across the northwest corner of New Mexico. The Rio Grande's source is in Colorado in the San Juan Mountains, from which the waters flow in a southerly direction, cutting New Mexico almost in half.

Geographical features of an area determine the places where people live. For example, the Pueblo Indians settled on or near the Rio Grande. Later, the Spanish, the Mexicans, and the Americans followed a similar pattern of settlement and established their home-sites near an adequate supply of water.

Climate

When we wonder about the weather conditions around us, we must consider three important factors that help us determine climate. They are:

(1) latitude (distance from the equator);

(2) altitude (height above sea level);

(3) humidity (the amount of moisture in the atmosphere).

Most of New Mexico is dry and sunny, and the yearly average precipitation (amount of rain and snow) is about 14 inches. A dry climate is a region that has less than 20 inches of moisture per year.

The amount of moisture that falls in New Mexico is small in comparison with the coastal areas of Oregon, California, Louisiana, southern Texas, and the coastal region of the New England states; these areas average from 90 to 180 days of rain and snow during the year. The frequency of **rain** and snowfall in New Mexico ranges from 30 days in the southern and central regions to about 100 days in the higher elevations of the Sacramento and Sangre de Cristo Mountains.

Since New Mexico lies within the temperate zone (moderate temperatures), many sections of the state do not drop in temperature more than 15 to 30 degrees below the freezing level (32 degrees Fahrenheit; zero Celcius) in the winter. In the higher elevations of Cloudcroft and Ruidoso in the Sacramento and White Mountain areas, however, winter temperatures may vary as much as 20 to 30 degrees below zero. This occurs because of the large Arctic air masses which invade New Mexico in the colder months of December, January, and February.

Many times the cold air masses produce high winds and heavy storms. In December, 1967, a crippling blizzard left a blanket of snow from Montana to the southern regions of New Mexico. The fierce Arctic snowstorm lasted for ten days, burying the Navajo tribe and much of the Southwest beneath a man- and cattle-killing seven-foot snowfall, the worst in the region's history. More than 2,000 Army, Navy, and Air Force men, Civil Air Patrol flyers, and Job Corps workers aided the state road and rescue crews. Missions such as "candy drop" (gifts for the 22,000 Indian boarding school students stranded during the holidays) and "Operation Haylift" (parachuting hay and feed to more than 500,000 horses, sheep, and cattle) helped to prevent further loss of life.

During early spring and summer, these Arctic air masses meet with the warm, moist air moving northward from the Gulf of California and the Gulf of Mexico, causing violent thunderstorms. Hail frequently accompanies these thunderstorms, and as a result, many valuable crops are damaged throughout the state. For example, in early spring of 1967, a violent hail

The entrance of one of the ice caves found in the "Malpais" or lava flow south of Grants, New Mexico. The ice in these caves does not melt even on the hottest summer days.

Climates of New Mexico

Modified after a map by Thornthwaite
(Courtesy State Planning Office)

- Arid

- Semi-arid

- Sub-humid/Humid (humid only in highest parts of mountains, not differentiated here)

storm destroyed many of the crops and caused considerable damage to homes and property in the Hobbs and Lovington area of Lea County. At times during this season of changing temperatures, the cold Arctic air mass and the warm, moist air from the Gulfs produce severe weather, resulting in many high winds and tornados. In the spring of 1969, these conditions caused considerable damage from Jal in southern Lea County, northward through Clovis, and into northwest Texas. In the San Juan Valley and the Rio Grande Valley during the spring and summer, flooding has been a serious problem. However, the Navajo Dam in San Juan County (along with Elephant Butte and Caballo Dams in Sierra County) has aided in controlling the flood conditions.

During the summer, temperatures are quite different throughout the state, partly because of the change in altitude. The altitude varies from 2,817 feet (845 m.) at the town of Red Bluff, the lowest point in New Mexico, to 13,160 feet (3948 m.) above sea level at the top of Mount Wheeler, the highest point in New Mexico.

Temperatures may vary from a high of 110 degrees (44 Celcius) in the semi-arid areas around Carlsbad (the county seat of Eddy County), and Deming (the county seat of Luna County), to highs of 60 to 70 degrees (16 to 22 Celcius) around Cloudcroft in the Sacramento Mountains. The average temperature in New Mexico, however, is usually around 85 degrees (30 Celcius) during the four summer months.

New Mexico has a lower average humidity than any other state in the Union. In some places in New Mexico during the hottest months of June, July, and August, the humidity is less than 10 percent. This is quite a difference when compared with the Eastern Coast Region. There, during the hot months of June, July, and August, the humidity is more than 70 percent. With 35 percent average humidity and a mild 85 degree (30 Celcius) temperature average, New Mexico provides a very healthful and enjoyable climate.

Early Life Forms

The earliest appearance of life was perhaps 500 million years ago (Penokean Period). These first moving things are referred to by scientists as invertebrates, or animals with no backbones, such as coral, starfish, and clams. Within the span of 200 million years, these simple creatures advanced to fish. Also, tiny plants of many varieties became trees; finally, forests were formed. During this time, fish developed backbones. Scientists refer to this group as the vertebrates. Many creatures learned to live both in the water and on the land.

A new age of life began with reptiles, 200 million years ago. They were small at first, only a few feet in length, but over the span of time they grew in size until they became the largest animals that walked the earth. These huge creatures, known as dinosaurs, ranged from 60 to 80 feet (18 to 24 m.) in length and weighed 50 to 60 tons. During the Age of Reptiles, they devoured many of the beautiful plants and trees. Numerous evergreens managed to survive, however, and new plant life came into being and flourished. During this period, new trees began to form, such as the poplar, oak, and maple, which shed their leaves in the fall and grew new ones in the spring; this new growth helped to increase the size of the forests. Plants which developed during this period included corn, barley, oats, and many kinds of fruits. As the Age of Reptiles ended, most of the large land and sea animals died, leaving modern man only their petrified remains. Some of these are on display in museums throughout the United States.

In New Mexico there are several museums to help us understand more about these animals of long ago. The museums at Santa Fe, the University of New Mexico, and Eastern New Mexico University—the latter museum is located some 10 miles (16 km.) north of Portales—will give us some information about these creatures that once lived in New Mexico.

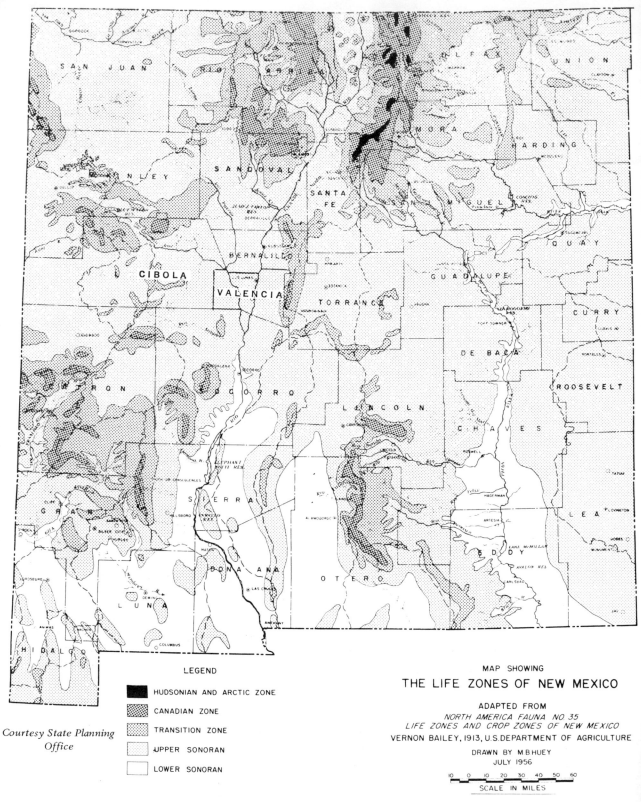

LEGEND

■	HUDSONIAN AND ARCTIC ZONE
	CANADIAN ZONE
	TRANSITION ZONE
	UPPER SONORAN
	LOWER SONORAN

Courtesy State Planning Office

MAP SHOWING

THE LIFE ZONES OF NEW MEXICO

ADAPTED FROM
NORTH AMERICA FAUNA NO 35
LIFE ZONES AND CROP ZONES OF NEW MEXICO
VERNON BAILEY, 1913, U.S. DEPARTMENT OF AGRICULTURE

DRAWN BY M.B. HUEY
JULY 1956

10 0 10 20 30 40 50 60
SCALE IN MILES

14

The Age of Mammals began, according to scientists, some 70 million years ago when warm-blooded animals appeared for the first time. Many descendants of these creatures live today in several parts of the world. It was during the late period of the Age of Mammals, perhaps 5 to 10 million years ago, that the great mountains, plateaus, and valleys were formed. Possibly through earthquakes and volcanic eruptions, the geography of New Mexico began to take shape. According to geologists, the Rocky Mountains are considered the most recent mountain formations in North America; yet, they are millions of years old. At any rate, by the time of the Ice Age (one million years ago), New Mexico as we see it today was formed. The Ice Age was, according to the scientists, separated into four periods, the last beginning about 50,000 years ago. An icecap, still detected around the North Pole, is a part of the fourth stage of the Ice Age.

Life Zones

Almost everyone is aware that life forms (both plant and animal) differ from one place to another. These changes occur because climatic conditions change the farther we are from the equator and the greater distance we are above sea level. We can see these changes in plant and animal life as we travel throughout the country. In our own state, we can see these changing conditions traveling along Highway 82 between Artesia and Cloudcroft. Another place would be along Highway 285 north into Santa Fe and Taos Counties.

Scientists have divided the earth into seven different areas where some form of life exists. New Mexico is gifted with six of the seven life zones. These are the Lower Sonoran, Upper Sonoran, Transition, Canadian, Hudsonian, and Arctic-Alpine zones. The seventh zone, not found in New Mexico, is the Carolinian Zone, called tropical climate.

The zone below 5,000 feet (1500 m.) is considered the *LOWER SONORAN ZONE*. This area, about 19,000 square miles (30,400 km.²), is warm, and farming can be carried on most of the year. Besides the valleys and mesas in the southern part of the state, the zone includes the Pecos and Rio Grande Valleys. It extends westward from the Rio Grande across the Deming Plains to the western part of the state. The Playas, Animas, and Hachita valleys are also part of this climatic zone, our most important agricultural area. The Lower Sonoran Zone is identified by mesquite, cresote bush, and black grama grass.

The *UPPER SONORAN ZONE* is the largest of all the life zones, containing more than 78,000 square miles (124,800 km.²). Lying between 5,000 and 7,000 feet (1500 to 2100 m.), it is very mild without extreme temperatures. This is the zone containing the piñon-pine, juniper, and blue grama grass. Most of the valleys, plains, and foothills lying above 5,000 feet (1500 m.) are included in this zone. The Upper Sonoran Zone embraces nearly all of the Llano Estacado and the plains north of the Canadian River. The San Juan, Zuñi, the upper Rio Grande, and the Gila Valleys along the San Augustine Plains in Catron County are included in this zone. Because of the new methods of irrigation, this zone provides rich soil for many kinds of fruits and vegetables, and as a result, a great deal of ranching is carried on here.

The *TRANSITION ZONE* lies at two different altitudes, depending on the amount of sunshine and heat received. On the northeast slopes, the altitude is from 7,000 to 8,500 feet (2100 to 2550 m.) On the southwest slopes, the altitude is from 8,000 to 9,500 feet (2400 to 2850 m.) In the high valleys, good farming can be carried on without irrigation. This zone is also good for grazing. The 19,000 square mile (30,400 km.²) area contains the chief timber tree of the state, the ponderosa pine. The Transition Zone covers broad mesas and extends along the sides of most of the higher mountain ranges.

The *CANADIAN ZONE* lies along the higher slopes of the mountains at altitudes of from 8,500 feet to 12,000 feet (2550 to 3600 m.). Although the most extensive area lies in the Sangre de Cristo Mountains, the White Mountains are also part of this zone. This area is a very wet zone, receiving the heaviest rain and snow and holding the snow until late spring. It contains an area of 4,000 miles (6400 km.²) and

is densely forested with aspen, fir, spruce, and pine.

The zone at 12,000 feet (3600 m.) is called the *HUDSONIAN ZONE*. This area of 160 square miles (256 km.²) is extremely cold most of the year, although the summer months are usually mild in temperature. It is a narrow zone along the timber line (normally 12,000 feet - 3600 m.) found high on the mountain slopes. This zone is marked by stunted growths of gnarled timber, mainly Englemann spruce, cork-barked firs, and foxtail pine.

The coldest of all the zones is the *ARCTIC-ALPINE ZONE*, covering less than 100 square miles (160 km.²) more than 12,000 feet (3600 m.) above sea level. It is treeless, and only hardy Alpine plants capable of surviving long, severely cold weather can exist. This area lies mainly within the Sangre de Cristo Range and is a storage place for moisture which flows down the slopes during the summer and provides needed water in the dry valleys below.

Wheeler Peak, the highest point in New Mexico, towers 13,160 feet (3948 m.) above sea level.

▼▼▼▼▼▼▼▼▼▼▼▼▼▼▼▼▼▼

REVIEW ACTIVITIES

1. From a map of New Mexico, compare the geography of your area with another section of the state. What are the similarities? What are the differences?
2. Describe the climate at the place where you live. How does it compare with the rest of New Mexico? Make a chart of the climatic conditions around the state.
3. What is your definition of history?
4. How old do geologists say the earth may be?
5. Where are some of the oldest formations found in New Mexico? Can you think of other places in New Mexico where unusual land formations may be found?
6. What is a glacier? What effect did the Great Glacier have on our state? Did any glaciers form in New Mexico during the Glacial Period? If so, where?
7. On a map name and locate the principal mountains, rivers, and forests in New Mexico.
8. How many National Forests are there in New Mexico? How many can you name? Which ones are located in your county?
9. Name the trees which produce most of the timber in our state. Which one is the "chief" timber producer?
10. What are the names of the two rivers in New Mexico which do not have their sources within the state?
11. What are the three important factors that help determine climate?
12. What are life zones? In which life zone do you live?
13. Explain the difference in climate, in vegetation, and in animal life among the life zones.
14. How could we make better use of our water areas in New Mexico?
15. What effect would air pollution have on the climate of New Mexico?

RECOGNIZE AND UNDERSTAND

eras	semi-arid
periods	humidity
epochs	arid
Glacial Period	temperate zone
extinct	Penokean Period
land bridge	invertebrates
topography	vertebrates
Continental Divide	Age of Reptiles
climate	Age of Mammals
geologist	

CHAPTER II

Early Man of New Mexico

Exactly when man first came to North America is not known, although tools of ancient man have been found which indicate he lived in this part of the world less than 11,500 years ago. Some archeologists, however, think that man lived in New Mexico over 20,000 years ago.

Scientists believe that some time during the last stage of the Ice Age man began to migrate to many different parts of the world. There are various ideas why he decided to move and settle many miles from his original home. One reason might be that food was becoming scarce, and since man was first a hunter, he needed to seek other areas for his food. He was not only trying to find food familiar to him, but he was also seeking a suitable climate for a new home. Perhaps wars and tribal skirmishes might be another reason for man's moving about from place to place. One source of conflict was the desire of each group to have enough land to be self-sufficient.

There seems to be little doubt, however, that the Great Glacier was the major cause for early man to settle in new lands. Whatever the reason may be, one thing is certain: man did come to North America many thousands of years ago.

Many geologists have agreed that the moving glacier cut deeply into the earth's crust and changed its surface. As it moved, the glacier drew water from the sea, resulting in the formation of new land areas. Other land areas came into being when the glacier lengthened the coastline. In places where the sea was shallow (such as the

Bering Strait), a land bridge was sometimes formed. This probably was the route that man first used to come to America.

Early Period

The first people who lived in the Southwest were big game hunters, as shown by the animal remains and tools of early man that have been found in areas known as "kill sites." These areas were places where large animals were killed for food or clothing. Many different kinds of ancient animals have been found at these sites, such as extinct forms of camel, horse, antelope, bison, sloth, mammoth, and mastodon. A few scattered, fragmented, or cremated human bones have been found at Paleo-Indian sites. But as yet archeologists are unable to reconstruct what these "first Americans" looked like.

Since dart points are the most outstanding artifacts (useful tools of early man), these tools have been carefully studied, classified, and named. Some of the points, being narrow, taper to a point with grooved areas on both faces. The base of the point usually has ground edges to prevent the cord which ties the point to the shaft from being cut. Besides spear points, scrapers and cutting tools have been found at the sites.

Sandia Period

What is thought to be the oldest dart point found is called Sandia. This point is leaf-shaped with a shoulder on one

Early man dart points. Top row (left to right): Clovis, Eastern Fluted, Sandia I, Sandia II, Folsom, Midland, Agate Basin, and Hell Gap (11,500 - 10,000 B.C.). Bottom row (left to right): Plainview, Meserve, Scottsbluff, Eden, Milnesand, Fredrick, Angostura, Browns Valley (10,000 - 7,500 B.C.).

side. Most of the points are not fluted. (See page 19.)

The spear point was found in the Sandia Cave, located at the north end of the Sandia Mountains near Albuquerque. Dr. Frank Hibben was the first professional archeologist to investigate the cave, which was discovered in 1936. Beneath the ochre rock (impure iron ore, usually red or yellow, used as coloring in paints), scientists found the spear points and several extinct forms of horse, bison, camel, mastodon, and mammoth. The points were first thought to be more than 20,000 years old. However, recent radiocarbon tests (carbon 14) by Dr. George Agogino, Director of the Paleo-Indian Institute of Eastern New Mexico University, place the points within the Clovis period, which dates around 10,000 B.C.

Folsom Period

In 1908, George W. McJunkin found bones of the pre-historic Pleistocene bison and a few spear points in an arroyo called "Dead Horse Arroyo," located west of the town of Folsom, New Mexico. It was not until 1926, however, that any digging was carried on at the site.

Events surrounding the early life of this well-known New Mexican seem uncertain. In the early 1880s McJunkin, who was in his late twenties, came to New Mexico with Dr. and Mrs. Thomas Owens. In 1885, they settled on the Pitchfork Ranch near the isolated village of Perico — a hamlet so far removed from other communities that it received its mail by pony express only twice a week. Even so, George McJunkin continued his self-education and this man, born into slavery, became an outstanding amateur historian and archeologist.

George McJunkin, when a young man. Courtesy Mrs. John Doherty, Folsom, New Mexico.

In 1926, two other archeologists, Howard Cook and J. D. Figgins, traveled to Folsom, New Mexico, to review the bones of the animals that had been found. Twenty-three remains of bison were found in the arroyo, along with several points, later called Folsom Points. In all, nineteen points were found in the area.

Using the same carbon 14 test, archeologists found Folsom points to be more recent than Clovis culture, and they dated them from about 9,000 B.C. Folsom points indicate that these people were fine craftsmen. Most of the points are two inches long. They have ears, usually a ground base, and well-shaped edges. An unusual feature of the Folsom Point is that both faces are grooved (fluted), so that the point could be easily attached to a wooden shaft. (See p. 19.)

Clovis Period

The oldest well-defined point in the New World was discovered in 1932 at

Blackwater Draw, located 7 miles (11 km.) north of Portales, New Mexico. This site is the oldest multicultural kill site ever discovered in North America. Studies by Dr. C. Vance Haynes, Jr., of the University of Arizona, and Dr. George Agogino indicate that mammoths at these sites were hunted and killed more than 12,000 years ago.

Blackwater Draw is in the Llano Estacado, or Staked Plains. Because many different periods of life were found at the site, archeologists call this area "the Llano Complex." The periods of life are estimated from 10,000 B.C. to the time of Christ. Folsom Points as well as several other types were found at more recent ground levels. Prehistoric Indians used this site for at least 11,000 years. Even within the historic period, Comanche Indians camped here and dug shallow wells.

Mammoth skull. Remains were found at Blackwater Draw archeological site. Huge animals were killed by man for food and clothing more than 10,000 years ago.

Ancient wells, estimated to be more than 4,000 years old, are also located near the site. These wells are considered the oldest wells in North America.

Bones of many extinct animals — the giant mammoth, camel, dire-wolf, four-horned antelope, straight-horned bison, and ground sloth — are found at Blackwater Draw.

Clovis Points vary from one inch to five inches long. They have grooved faces, fairly heavy points, and ground bases. Although these points indicate that the Clovis culture is the oldest, widely accepted culture recorded so far, archeologists believe that there are still older cultures yet to be found.

Cochise Period

Another important area of early man is located in southeastern Arizona and southwestern New Mexico. This area is called Cochise, named after the ancient Lake Cochise which dried up long ago. Although this culture lasted about 6,000 years, only a few bits and pieces of evidence have been found to tell us about the people. In addition to the tools discovered near the lake bed, several metates (flat stones hollowed out in the center used as grinding boards) and manos (hand tools used with the metates for grinding purposes) were found in the area. The method for grinding seed that identified pre-Columbian culture has continued to the present time.

Basketmaker Period

Approximately 2,000 years ago, the early people of the Southwest learned how to make fiber baskets and to raise corn. These people, who were called

Blackwater Draw Kill Site. Note how they kept the floor as untouched as possible by building wooden walk ramps. Artifacts are partially dated by relating them to the geological formation in which they are found. For this reason, care is taken to uncover one layer of deposit at a time.

Basketmakers, lived in crude, one-room houses made of logs and dried mud. They cultivated fields of corn, beans, and pumpkins. The numerous ruins of the Basketmaker settlements (located in New Mexico and Arizona) have yielded battle clubs, grinding stones, stone knives, and cloth from yucca fiber. According to the archeological remains, the Basketmaker culture existed in northern, central, and southern New Mexico.

Anasazi Period

There are three principal areas of pre-Pueblo Civilization in the Southwest: the Hohokam in south-central Arizona, the Mogollon in southwestern New Mexico, and the Anasazi culture in the "Four Corners" area where New Mexico, Arizona, Utah, and Colorado meet.

About 1,500 years ago, MOGOLLON CULTURE appeared in southwestern New Mexico. At first, these people lived in pithouses (circular holes dug in the ground with logs and mud or clay for covering); later they built houses of stone above ground. Remains of their pottery (usually white with black designs) have been uncovered, along with numerous arrow points, stone hammers, spears, knives, and stone axes.

The HOHOKAM in Arizona lived about the same period of time. They also made pottery, but with red designs. The Hohokam were an agricultural people, growing squash, corn, and beans, and even developing an irrigation system for their fields. The ruins have yielded many tools, some agricultural: hoes, picks, axes, knives, and stone hammers.

The most advanced culture of early Pueblo life is called ANASAZI. The earliest found so far was at Mesa Verde in southwestern Colorado. Excavations have revealed that the Pueblo people lived there as early as A.D. 700. Other areas were Aztec in San Juan County, New Mexico, and Pueblo Bonito located in Chaco Canyon in northwestern New Mexico. Pueblo Bonito is the largest pueblo ever found. Still other evidence is seen at Frijoles Canyon and Püye north of Santa Fe. The early Anasazi settlements were constructed beneath overhanging cliffs. Later, homes were built on the top of cliffs which formed the canyons. The buildings themselves were usually made of stone and plastered with mud, and each settlement contained numerous rooms, as at Mesa Verde.

The Anasazi people hunted with bows and arrows. According to archeologists, this ancient culture was the first to use this weapon in the New World. In addition to the bow and arrow, the Anasazi used an "atlatl" (a crude spear-throwing device) to provide greater distance when throwing a spear or atlatl dart. Other items uncovered include baskets, beads, needles, buttons, whistles, and brushes, as well as several different types of pottery, suggesting that each village made its own. The Anasazi people farmed, too—they raised corn, beans, berries, pumpkins, and cotton. Current research on classic Pueblo sites is being done by Dr. Jim Judge at Chaco Canyon and by Dr. Cynthia Irwin Williams at the Salmon site near Bloomfield, New Mexico.

Dr. Cynthia Williams of Eastern New Mexico University has uncovered recent information about Anasazi culture from an arroyo called En Medio, located northwest of Albuquerque in Sandoval County. The Arroyo En Medio shelter was discovered in 1965, and formal

Clovis point from Blackwater Draw

Mummy in cotton net bag which was hung originally from the roof of a cave. Estimated to be 1,000 years old, this mummy is thought to have belonged to the Mogollon culture.

excavation began the following year. It was occupied about 1,600 B.C., and the last inhabitants, identified as Basketmakers, left the area more than 1,200 years ago. From the ruins, the scientists uncovered hammerstones, choppers, scrapers, and grinding tools probably used for grinding seed. When additional information is released about En Medio, it will help us understand a great deal more about early Anasazi culture.

Recent Discovery

History is a living, constantly changing subject. With each bit of new information that is periodically uncovered, we get a glimpse of the past, which, in turn, teaches us a little more about mankind. For example, about 30 miles (48 km.) north of Silver City is another site of Pueblo culture called the Kwilleylekia Ruins, where work is being carried on by Mr. and Mrs. Richard Ellison of Silver City. The site is one of the many private diggings presently going on in New Mexico. The Ellisons believe the builders of this little settlement were the Salado stock of the Pueblo people who later, perhaps, became the Zuñi.

An interesting feature is that the Salado metates are cemented to the floors with adobe mud, unlike metates of other cultures, which were apparently free-standing. At the lower end of the Salado grinding plate is a bowl to catch the ground meal.

Although the Salado people usually cremated their dead, some human skeletons have been found. The Ellisons discovered a most unusual crema-

tion at the Kwilleylekia Ruins. Rocks had been arranged in the shape of a human body, and the dead person placed in the area and cremated. The remains were placed in a bowl and buried. No one yet has been able to explain this mysterious finding.

Another interesting and recent discovery is the town of Arizpe in the State of Sonora in northern Mexico. One of the most important garrisons in northern New Spain during the colonial period, today it is almost inaccessible and nearly forgotten. In 1780, though, it was the political and religious center north of Mexico City, with authority over the entire Southwest and north to Oregon.

The Church at Arizpe (center of photo) is the final resting place of the Spanish explorer and administrator Juan Bautista de Anza. He founded San Francisco, California, in 1776, and then served as governor of New Mexico from 1778 to 1788.

Dr. George Agogino, Chairman of the Anthropology Department at Eastern New Mexico University, preparing to throw a dart from an atlatl. The atlatl was first used by the Anasazi culture.

Gila Cliff Dwellings National Monument. The cliff dwellers built their homes within four large natural caves in the face of a 150-foot cliff above the Gila River.

Left: Mogollon red-on-brown, southwestern New Mexico (A.D. 900), and Hohokam red-on-buff southern Arizona (A.D. 700). Right: Navajo pottery, Gobernador area, northern New Mexico (1750).

Bandelier black-on-gray was developed in the northern Rio Grande valley of New Mexico about A.D. 1500.

∇∇∇∇∇∇∇∇∇∇∇∇∇∇∇∇

REVIEW ACTIVITIES

1. Make an oral report on one of the early cultures found in New Mexico. Did they use the atlatl or the bow and arrow? How do those two weapons differ?
2. Why are archeologists sometimes called "earth or historian" detectives?
3. On a map of New Mexico, locate the major sites of early man.
4. Describe the following dart points: Sandia, Folsom, and Clovis. According to archeologists, which one is the oldest? How were they able to prove this?
5. What are some of the reasons that early man decided to move to different parts of the world?
6. According to anthropologists, how did early man get to North America?
7. Since no remains of ancient man have been found thus far, how do we identify the early people of New Mexico?
8. Who are Dr. George Agogino and Dr. Frank Hibben? What contributions have these two men made in regard to ancient man in New Mexico?
9. Name some of the ancient animal remains found in the Sandia Caves, Dead Horse Arroyo, and Blackwater Draw.
10. Who was George McJunkin? Tell something about his life. What did he discover? Where?
11. Name some of the useful tools of the Cochise and Basketmaker Periods.
12. What are the three principal areas of pre-Pueblo Civilization in the Southwest? Which one is the most advanced culture of pueblo life? Name the most outstanding areas in New Mexico where this ancient pueblo civilization lived.
13. Name some artifacts found in the pre-Pueblo Civilizations.
14. Tell something about the recent discovery of early man that was found near Silver City, New Mexico.

RECOGNIZE AND UNDERSTAND

kill site	Cochise Period
artifact	Basketmaker Period
carbon 14	Anasazi Period
ochre rock	fluted
extinct	Blackwater Draw
Sandia Period	the Llano Complex
Folsom Period	Kwilleylekia Ruins
Clovis Period	atlatl
archeologist	anthropologist
matate	
mano	

CHAPTER III

Indians of New Mexico

History pervades all of New Mexico. In fact, many hundreds of years before the Spanish arrived, this region was a center of Indian culture. At first, many of these early inhabitants lived in caves which were cut deeply into the sides of the mountains. Later, the Indians migrated to the fertile valleys where they could plant and harvest their crops. Before the Spanish came to America, wandering tribes of Indians had invaded the Southwest and established their claim to portions of New Mexico.

The early people who lived in the cliff houses of Chaco Canyon, Bandelier, and Püye dug large circular pits called kivas (caves). Although kivas were later used for storing food, their original and primary purpose was religious. The people held their sacred ceremonies in the kiva. They believed that their ancestors came from inside the earth, and those who died before they reached the light became supernatural beings called "kachinas." When the kachinas reached the outer world, they taught the people how to plant, how to harvest crops, how to hunt, and how to fight.

On the walls and fronts of the cliff houses appear numerous pictographs (picture writing), which are the oldest ever found in the United States. Within the dwellings are remains of the metates and manos used to grind seeds. The cliff dwellers learned the system of grinding seeds from the earlier inhabitants of North America.

When the Spaniards arrived in the New World, all of the cliff dwellings had been abandoned. Perhaps severe droughts, diseases, or hostile tribes forced these people to leave their caves and move to the river areas of New

Mexico. Whatever the reason, anthropologists have determined that the cliff houses were abandoned sometime during the thirteenth century (probably around A.D. 1275), about 240 years before the Spaniards arrived on the continent of North America.

PUEBLOS

Pueblo culture is divided into two sections. The Desert Pueblos are Zuñi, Laguna, and Ácoma. The River Pueblos, such as Isleta, Jemez, and Zia, are located near rivers and fertile valleys. Most of the River Pueblos are located along the upper Rio Grande in Taos, Santa Fe, Rio Arriba, Sandoval, Bernalillo, and Valencia Counties.

See page 47 for a map of Indians in New Mexico.

The Indians who occupied the river valleys were called Pueblo Indians when the Spaniards arrived in 1540. Their homes were made of clay earth (adobe) and rock. The rich soil found in the river valleys provided excellent farmland for cultivation, while from the nearby forests came a rich supply of game for hunting, as well as wood for structures, fuel, and many tools that were hand-shaped. Animal hides became clothing, sometimes shelter, containers, thongs, and other items. Clays and other natural resources provided materials needed for the manufacture of fine pottery and utensils. The Pueblo Indians were experts in making earthenware vessels, baskets, clothes, and articles of decoration from shell and turquoise.

Whenever an Indian pueblo was established, it became a complete settlement. Pueblos have their own social organization and their own officers, and they are independent from all other pueblos or pueblo groups. Though the pueblos have from time to time formed allegiances among themselves, this does not form a tribe. A tribe is a group of people united by race and customs under the same leaders. In addition to forming independent towns, the Pueblo Indians speak several distinct languages. Those of New Mexico are Keresan, Tanoan, and Zuñi.

The Pueblo Indians were declared citizens of Mexico when that republic won its independence from Spain in 1821. Their rights were confirmed by the Treaty of Guadalupe Hidalgo (see New Mexico Bill of Rights, Article II, Section 5), signed by government agents of Mexico and ratified by the United States Senate on May 30, 1848. In recent years, several Pueblo groups have adopted constitutions patterned after those of the United States.

There are nineteen Pueblo groups located in the northern and western regions of New Mexico. They total about 36,000 people, according to the latest figures from the Indian Census Bureau. All but one group have pueblos in or near where the people dwell. The group that does not live in a pueblo is the Pojoaque people; they have not had pueblo organization for many years, and their homes are scattered over the Pojoaque reservation or elsewhere.

Keresans. Several of the larger Pueblo groups have more than one pueblo, located some distance from the main settlement. These communities, near good farm lands, have finally become permanent homes. By contrast, the Tanoan peoples located their pueblos on valley floors close to fertile lands;

CHART SHOWING GENERAL CLASSIFICATION OF INDIANS IN NEW MEXICO

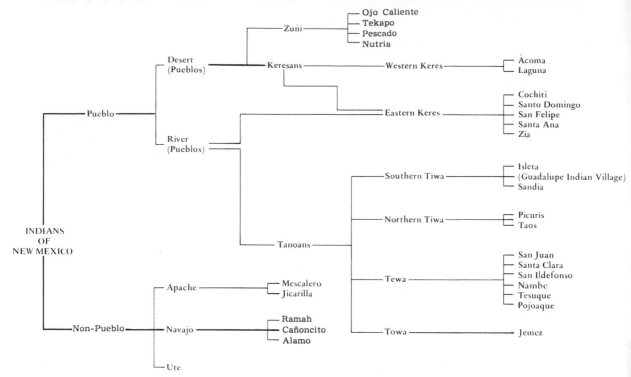

the Keresans, however, established their homes on rocky knolls, buttes, or mesas. Such sites were easily defended in days past and left the valley lands free for growing crops. With the peaceful conditions of modern times, defense sites became unnecessary.

The Western Keresans. The Pueblos of the western Keres groups, Ácoma and Laguna, amount to more than one-half of all the Keresan or Keres population. Ácoma (AH-koh-mah), some 50 miles (80 km.) westward from Albuquerque, is situated atop a great sandstone rock almost 400 feet (120 m.) high. More than 3,500 live at the pueblo, which is reached by a road (NM Highway 23) which leaves Interstate 40 at Paraje. Traveling to Ácoma,

12 miles (19 km.) south of the junction, one can see a famous landmark, the Enchanted Mesa, on the left. Many unusual rock forms add interest to the region. Ácoma is one of the oldest pueblos, Indians having established themselves at or near the present location as early as A.D. 900. Today, except for a few Keresan-speaking people that remain on the mesa, most of the Ácoma Indians live in two outlying communities. The men are primarily stockmen and farmers. Many of the women make fine pottery which, though thin and lightweight, is so well made that it holds water.

The feast of Saint Steven is observed at Ácoma annually on September 2, and the event is celebrated by traditional dancing. In mid-June, a Corn Dance is performed, and other ceremonial dances are presented at Easter and Christmas time. At Ácoma, kivas are built among the dwelling units.

Laguna (Lah-GOO-nah) Pueblo was built in a soft, yellow-white sandstone slope alongside Interstate 40, about 45 miles (72 km.) west of Albuquerque. The settlement was established around 1450 near the Rio San Jose, a western tributary of the Rio Grande. The present site of the pueblo dates from

Pictographs carved on the rocks near Faywood Springs, in southwestern New Mexico. Archeologists find them important sources for Indian religious and social life.

1699. The lands of Laguna are joined with those of the Ácoma. Since most of the region is good for grazing, the Lagunas became stockgrowers.

Outlying fields of the Lagunas led to permanent settlements. Mesita, one of the settlements, is the site of an electronics plant and a new housing project. Included in the pueblo are three small clusters of homes, the names of which are often rather startling to visitors — New York, Philadelphia, and Pittsburgh; they were named for eastern cities where Laguna students received training. Considered as a whole, Laguna is the largest of the Keres group, with a population of 5,978. It is a progressive pueblo, with recently erected community buildings where the governmental offices are located and assemblies are held. The people have modern homes and a kiva for religious ceremonies. Thus, certain of the old ways of life are present, along with the development of rich uranium deposits, fine grade marble, and other resources.

Another housing development is underway across the highway from the Ácoma-Laguna school on Interstate 40. Laguna has a scholarship fund to aid its young people in higher education.

Laguna commemorates the feast day of Saint Joseph each year on September 19. A great fair is held, with many of the Pueblo and Navajo Indians traveling

Arrowhead Ruins near Pecos, New Mexico, was once the home of an Indian people. Built of stone and adobe, these ruins were abandoned in the sixteenth century.

to Laguna to trade, to buy, or to sell products of their fields or of their skills. Sporting events and colorful dances are held at this time. Laguna Pueblo has the only V.F.W. (Veterans of Foreign Wars) Post in the United States that is made up entirely of Indians.

The Eastern Keresans. The Eastern Keres make up the remainder of the Keresan group. They are the Cochiti, the Santo Domingo, the San Felipe, the Santa Ana, and the Zia.

Cochiti (KOH-chee-tee), with a population of 914, is northernmost of the Keres groups. Located on the west side of the Rio Grande, the pueblo is reached by a paved road (NM 22) which turns northward from US 85, roughly midway between Albuquerque and Santa Fe. It is believed that the Cochiti people once dwelt upstream from their present reservation, in El Rito de Frijoles of the Pajarito plateau area, a region of unnumbered caves, cliff dwellings, and archeological remains. They settled at the present site after enemies had forced them to move from place to place. Today, some till their rich but limited valley lands, and graze animals in the higher elevations; many seek employment away from the pueblo. Part of their land is located in Bandelier National Monument.

Men and women work together in the performance of numerous tasks, including the making of jewelry and drums.

Ácoma Pueblo — New Mexico's "Sky City," as seen from the Plains. This pre-Columbian Keresan-speaking pueblo is said to be the oldest continuously occupied village in the United States.

Cochiti is well known for its double-headed drums that are fashioned from hollowed-out aspen or cottonwood and covered with leather that is tightly laced with rawhide thongs from end to end. Drums play a major roll in pueblo ceremonials, and their sounds may be heard for long distances through the clear, thin air of the Southwest. The Corn Dance on July 14 is Cochiti's annual feast day. Ceremonial activities center in two circular kivas, one of which pertains to each division of the pueblo, the Turquois people and the Squash people.

This Cochiti dwelling is typical of pueblo architecture in northern New Mexico.

Laguna Indian Pueblo, 50 miles (80 km.) west of Albuquerque, New Mexico, is the most recent of the 19 inhabited pueblos in the state.

While some Cochiti women produce pottery, others make soft, leather, moccasin-type "booties," as well as beaded ornaments for the tourist trade. A number of Cochiteños have become outstanding artists; others are known for their skilled craftsmanship.

About 7 miles (11 km.) downstream from Cochiti is Santo Domingo (SAHN-toh-doh-MEEN-go), with a population of 2,762, making it the largest of the eastern Keres pueblos. The people live as their ancestors did many centuries ago. One may reach it by a secondary road leading south from Cochiti, through the village of Sile (which the Indians say is a "silly" name, for its pronunciation is similar, SEE-lay). The best route, however, is along NM 22, which passes the railway siding of Domingo (which has no connection with the Indians), continues westward along the tracks,

33

and branches left into Santo Domingo. Located on the east side of the Rio Grande, this route is paved to the pueblo.

Many of the ancestors of the people of Santo Domingo, like those of Cochiti, formerly dwelt in sites on the Pajarito plateau. Others came from homes in the Galisteo basin.

The women of Santo Domingo, aside from being busy homemakers, produce a considerable amount of outstanding pottery. Jewelry is produced also—the shell and turquois types being tradition-al with the Pueblo Indians. There are a few silversmiths at Santo Domingo. The men are chiefly farmers.

Life here has changed little since the arrival of the white man. Great importance is placed on the religious organization, which is the heart of their society. One of the most dramatic of Pueblo ceremonies is the annual fiesta, presented at Santo Domingo each year on August 4. There are two circular kivas as at Cochiti. Other events occur throughout the year, especially during the Christmas-New Year season and at Easter.

Santo Domingo Indians are great traders. Some of them may be seen in nearby towns, or at considerable distance from the pueblo — perhaps at Laguna or Zuñi, in the Navajo country, or in Hopiland. If one stops at one of their roadside booths (ramadas), he may be able to trade for a piece of pottery or a rug, rather than to purchase it.

Approximately 7 miles (11 km.) south of Santo Domingo is another large Keres pueblo of the eastern division, San Felipe (sahn fay-LEE-pay). This pueblo, too, lays claim to ancestral homes on the Pajarito plateau. Its population today is 2,051. Having

The Pueblo Indians are a stoical race of people. A ceremonial dress is worn by this member of San Ildefonso Indian Pueblo.

Santo Domingo Church, New Mexico, 1899.

been driven from there by enemies, the people established a pueblo on the mesas overlooking the Rio Grande; the present pueblo on the west bank of the stream was founded during the first half of the eighteenth century. In recent years, some homes have appeared on the east side of the river.

The people of San Felipe live as their ancestors did many centuries ago and engage in beautiful ceremonies filled with tradition. A magnificent drama, the Green Corn Dance, which takes place each year on May 1 (the feast day of Saint Phillip), is without comparison. Hundreds of men, women, and children in symbolic dress participate in rhythmic dances throughout the day, to the accompaniment of great choruses of male voices. The plaza has been worn deep, like a huge bowl, by the action of many feet and the gusts of many winds through the centuries.

In order to reach San Felipe, one would travel Interstate 25 until he reached the turnoff that leads westward to the pueblo. The turnoff is located about 10 miles (16 km.) north of Bernalillo; this historic town was settled in 1698 by descendants of the Spanish historian, Bernal Díaz del Castillo, who accompanied Hernando Cortés in his conquest of Mexico.

Santa Ana pueblo (SAHN-tah AH-nah), thought to have been founded about 1700, is situated in a barren location on the north side of the Jemez River, which flows into the Rio Grande just above Bernalillo. Reservation lands extend into the Rio Grande valley, where good farming areas are located. Since argiculture is the chief economic resource of the Santa Ana Indians, they gradually established homes near their fields, giving rise to permanent settlements. These 510 people reside north of Bernalillo, on the west side of Interstate 25, and down along the river.

35

Santa Ana is located about 8 miles (13 km.) northwest of Bernalillo on NM 44. On that road, just west of the Rio Grande, is the Coronado State Monument, site of the pre-historic ruin of Kuaua. Among the features excavated are the remains of several subterranean, circular, and rectangular ceremonial chambers. On the walls of one of the chambers, archeologists found fragments of sacred paintings. These paintings are representations of people and some of the things Indians used some 500 to 600 years ago, the significance of which is still known only to Pueblo men well versed in their religious ceremonies. The ruin has been made safe and the "painted kiva" restored, allowing one to descend into it and see copies of the original paintings. A museum was established to exhibit the archeology and culture of the region, the old Tiguex province. Some of the Santa Ana people say that their ancestors formerly lived at Kuaua, which suggests that they spoke a Keresan tongue.

Unless one visits Santa Ana on its feast day, July 26, or when other ceremonies are being held, the pueblo may appear deserted. A few Indians are always there, however, guarding the pueblo; the entrance way is blocked because of vandalism which has been committed on occasion by non-Indians.

The Santa Ana Indians are the smallest group of those speaking Keresan, with a population of about 500. A few of the older men still weave attractive red textile belts and narrow bands that are worn by both men and women, especially during ceremonial events. Among the Pueblo peoples, weaving has always been a man's art. The woman's industry of pottery-making has about ceased at Santa Ana, although one lady continues to produce good vessels.

Another pueblo of the eastern Keres group is Zia (SEE-ah), also on the north bank of the Jemez River, 8 miles (13 km.) from Santa Ana along NM 44. This location was chosen around 1300, when the Zia Indians moved from a site farther up the Jemez. On its rocky knoll, the Pueblo is well camouflaged, blending with the landscape so that only sharp eyes note its presence until a road sign calls attention to it.

Most of the Zia acreage is suitable only for grazing sheep and goats; there is little farming land from which to make a living.

Zia women have long been recognized as makers of excellent pottery, which is artistically decorated, and the well-fired vessels are suitable for many household uses. An ancient sun symbol used by the Zia has been adopted by the State of New Mexico and appears in the design of the state flag.

A number of Zia men are outstanding artists in the field of watercolors, with some having become quite famous. Zia, which has a population today of about 750, observes its feast day on August 15 with a Corn Dance. Other colorful dance ceremonies occur during the year.

The western Keres people number about 9,500, while the combined eastern Keres groups number a little less than 7,000. This makes a total today of about 16,500, the largest group of the Pueblo Indians.

The Tanoans. Unlike those who speak the Keresan language, which is different from any other language of North America, the Tanoan tongues are related to the Axtec groups of Mexico. The origin of both is known as Azteco-Tanoan. In New Mexico, certain basic differences within the Tanoan family have led to several language subgroups, three of which are still spoken: the Tiwa, Tewa, and Towa. Today, altogether, about 5,500 Indians speak a Tiwa dialect; about 4,500, Tewa; and about 2,100, Towa. Each language subgroup has changed so far from its original form, however, that only those within the immediate group are able to understand the language. Even within the subdivisions, different languages occur. This is best described by the Tiwa-speakers, of whom Taos and Picuris are the northern representatives, and Sandia and Isleta the southern ones.

Taos and Picuris Indians converse together with ease, as do those of Sandia and Isleta. American Indian languages are very complex, changing many times through centuries of development.

The Southern Tiwa. In prehistoric

times, Tiwa (TEE-wah) pueblos dotted the Rio Grande Valley all the way from the region of modern Albuquerque down into Mexico near the Sierra Madres. Usually overlooked in accounts of the Indians of New Mexico is a Tiwa group dwelling near University Park at Las Cruces. This village is commonly known as Tortugas, but its official name is Guadalupe Indian Village. It is controlled by an Indian corporation, Los Indigenes de Nuestra Señora de Guadalupe. An impressive three-day celebration is conducted to observe the patron saint's day, December 12. The ceremonies, influenced by long association with the Roman Catholic Church, include religious singing, a candlelight procession, a trip to the summit of Tortugas Mountain, and dancing in front of the village church. All ceremonies are conducted under strict rules passed down by generations of Tiwa Indians, even though many Spanish customs have been adopted.

Thirteen miles (21 km.) south of Albuquerque, near the junction of NM 45 and Interstate 25, is the pueblo of Isleta (ess-LAY-tyh.) It is the largest of the Tiwa groups in population. The main settlement, which the residents call Shiaw iba, is on the west side of the Rio Grande. Two ranching colonies known as Chicale and T' aikabede have grown up on the east bank, slightly down river. Following the Pueblo Revolt of 1680 and the reconquest by Diego de Vargas twelve years later, Isleta was reoccupied (about 1709) by Indians who had scattered during the revolt. Most of the Isleta Indians had fled to El Paso, Texas, during the revolt and

An Indian woman in the pueblo of Isleta prepares the fall supply of corn.

Isleta Pueblo is located some 12 miles (19 km.) south of Albuquerque, New Mexico. There are no communal houses here, and the Indians live in separate dwellings built of adobe.

established a home site near the present city. Today, this community is a suburb of El Paso, also named Isleta.

A number of Indians returned from the Hopi country, some with Hopi husbands or wives and Hopi-Tiwa children. Around 1880, people from Laguna, accompanied by a few Ácoma Indians, received permission to establish homes at Isleta, in a location east of the railroad tracks. The move resulted from drought conditions, as well as religious beliefs that arose in the home pueblos.

As the history of the Pueblo Indian shows, many of the Indians who wish to keep the old ways may seek new locations where they can continue their chosen way of life. In every pueblo, some Indians strive to keep their traditions, while others seek to make changes. The new residents that arrived became part of the pueblo, with their area being called Oraibi, after that of the villages of the Third Mesa peoples in Hopiland. Including this group as a permanent part of Isleta, the pueblo now has a population of more than 3,100 people.

With fertile land, Isleta has based its economy on agriculture. The valley acres are bordered by grasslands and wooded regions. Too, Isleta lands join with Albuquerque, which provides revenue from lease agreements with several governmental agencies and business concerns. Employment in the city increases the income of some Isletans, as does the sale of the "tourist style" pottery produced by a number of the Oraibi women. The pottery is a red ware, decorated with red and black designs on a white background. Even though this is not traditional pottery, it does keep an ancient skill alive.

Ceremonial days have changed since Isleta adopted its constitution in 1947. Visitors to the pueblo are advised to seek information regarding ceremonies that may be observed with dances. The date of the annual feast day is September 4.

Located along Interstate 25 north of Albuquerque about 13 miles (21 km.) is the pueblo known as Sandia (sahn-DEE-ah). There population today is 297. Its native name, Nafiat,

The ancient Indian pueblo of Kuaua near Bernalillo, New Mexico, is now Coronado State Monument. The ruins of this village were excavated and partially restored in the 1930s.

meaning "dusty" or "sandy" place, is most appropriate. Established around 1300, Sandia was one of the pueblos visited by Don Francisco Vásquez de Coronado in 1540 and 1541, when he quartered his troops at the nearby pueblo of Mahi (Tiguex), now in ruin. Certain of the Sandia people say that their ancestors formerly lived at Kuaua (site of the Coronado State Monument).

At the time of the Pueblo Rebellion, the residents of Sandia fled to the Hopi country, where they remained until 1742. Some may have returned to the Rio Grande earlier, however, for there is no evidence of a gap in the cultural history of the pueblo.

On June 13, a Corn Dance is held at the pueblo, and other celebrations are observed during the year. Although the Indians of Sandia are primarily farmers, some are employed in nearby towns. Another source of revenue comes from rental of land for an aerial tramway to Sandia Crest.

The Northern Tiwa. About 75 airline miles (120 km.) separate the pueblos located closest to one another in the southern and northern Tiwa groups, Sandia and Picuris. Their relationships have been as remote as their differences in languages and other features.

Of the Tiwa pueblos, Picuris (Pee-kuhr-REES), hidden away in the mountains south of Taos, is the smallest in population with 221 residents. The pueblo lies at an elevation of 7,360 feet (2208 m.) in the valley of the Rio Pueblo, which flows through the Picuris range and, with other tributaries, reaches the Rio Grande. Important archeological excavations have recently revealed that Picuris was founded between 1250 and 1300 by Indians who moved from a large pueblo near Talpa on NM 3, now known as Pot Creek ruin. The Picuris reservation is small; its fertile lands are farmed, and livestock graze over the remainder.

Visitors to Picuris will find the Indians hospitable and ready to provide a guide to the ancient ruins of the pueblo, which may be photographed.

The Indians are proud of the new community building, decorated with pictures that keep the culture of the past before the eyes of the living. A few Picuris women make pottery from micaceous clay (mica is a group of minerals that separate into layers), which gives the vessels a pleasing sparkle. This ware differs from that made in the region before 1680, but it is well fired and can be used by Indians and non-Indians alike as cooking vessels and other utensils.

Picuris may be reached by various routes: NM 3, which branches from US 64 west of Taos; NM 75, leading eastward from US 64 through Dixon; or NM 76, which leaves US 64 at River side. On August 10, the feast day of San Lorenzo is celebrated with ceremonies that include a Corn Dance; other observances occur during the year.

Probably the most widely known of the pueblos is Taos (rhymes with "house"), northernmost of all those occupied today. With its multi-story dwelling units to the north and south of the plaza, through which Taos Creek constantly runs, this Tiwa pueblo expresses architectural forms that have been in this country for centuries. Mt. Wheeler, which has an elevation of 13,160 feet (3948 m.), provides a most spectacular scene.

In certain ways, the people of Taos appear the least typical of the Pueblo Indians. Their songs, chants, and beats, and some words relate to the Plains Indians, particularly the Kiowa. Linguists have established some relationship between the language of the people of Taos and the Kiowa. They also have borrowed other traits from the Jicarilla Apache, who dwell not far to the west of Taos, and with whom they have long been friendly. Thus, some aspects of Taos's culture differ from that of most other Pueblo peoples, and their ceremonial presentations are largely unlike those seen in the other pueblos.

Taos has a large reservation, with ample agricultural land and extensive grazing areas. They have good livestock, and even pasture a herd of bison, which one may sometimes glimpse in driving on US 64 from the town of Taos to the pueblo. Many of the Taos homes serve as shops in which local handicrafts and other items may be purchased. Signs indicate such locations. The men conduct a lively business in deerskin articles, the foremost of which are fine, authentic, Indian moccasins. The women make some micaceous pottery vessels similar to those of Picuris, and a few black or red pieces. One also may find toy drums, colorful corn, paintings, and miscellaneous items. The pueblo has been home to several excellent artists as well.

The Taos pueblo, with a population exceeding 1,850, presents colorful ceremonies. Taos dancers are widely known, and the rabbit hunts and racing events always attract visitors. On September 29, about sunset, the Sundown Dance is performed annually, followed the next day by the San Geronimo observances. The Corn Dances, the Eagle

Cultural contrasts are part of the charm of the Taos area of New Mexico. Taos Pueblo houses more than 500 Indian families less than three miles from the city of Taos, one of America's most famous art colonies.

San Juan Pueblo, north of Santa Fe. As shown in the photo, the Indians of this pueblo still live in the two- and three-story houses built hundreds of years ago. Here are a mother and her child climbing to the second story.

Dance, the Turtle Dance, the Horsetail Dance, and other presentations are well performed.

The Tewa. Between the northern and southern Tiwa people, an ancient group of Tewa (TAY-wah) Indians established themselves. Formerly, another Tanoan language, Tano (THAN-oh), was spoken in the Galisteo region, but those pueblos were abandoned in the late seventeenth or early eighteenth centuries, the residents joining those of other communities. Some of the Tano fled to Hopiland, where permission was given to establish a pueblo.

Those who dwell in this small village, called Hano, today speak Tewa and Hopi, a Shoshonean language. The Tewa Indians in New Mexico live in five pueblos on six reservations, all to the north of Santa Fe, with a population of 4,489.

San Juan (sahn-HUAHN) is located about 5 miles (8 km.) north of present-day Española. When Oñate arrived in 1598, the pueblo people of Yunguey-ungue permitted the Spanish to occupy their village, and the Indians moved to the San Juan Pueblo east of the Rio Grande. It was here on July 11, 1598, that the Spaniards named the pueblo "San Juan de los Caballeros" (St. John of the Gentlemen or Knights) because the Indians were so courteous to them. Later that month, the Spanish chose a site where the Indian settlement Yungueyungue was located, and they called that San Gabriel. It served as the capital for 11 years until a new and permanent location, La Villa Real de la Santa Fé, was established (presumably during the winter of 1609-10) at the prehistoric pueblo site called Kua-p' o-o-ge, or Oga-p' o-ge, by the Tewa Indians. Sections of the original wall of Kuap'ooge, four feet ten inches in breadth, are displayed in the Palace of the Governors Museum of New Mexico, Santa Fe.

Today, San Juan is the largest of the Tewa pueblos with a population of more than 1,780. It observes the feast of San Juan on June 24, and the residents present other colorful ceremonies, with beautifully costumed dance groups, several times a year. The women of the pueblo make skillfully decorated pottery, which is traditionally red or brown, but occasionally is black. Many of the men carve artful items of wood, such as the rasp sets used in the Basket Dance.

The Tewa group second in size is Santa Clara (SAHN-ta KLAH-rah), with a population of 1351. Their lands reach to Española and are in part leased to that community. The pueblo of Santa Clara, or Kapo, located on the west side of the Rio Grande, is on NM 30 south of Española. It is the home of noted painters and of several outstanding pottery makers, whose most characteristic ware is polished, black, heavy, and carved with simple, strong designs; red and polychrome varieties are also produced.

The Santa Clara people trace their ancestry to Indians who occupied the region of Püye (puh-YEH) on the Pajarito plateau, living there in cave homes in the rough cliffs and in pueblos built along the talus (rock debris at the base of a cliff) slopes and on the mesa tops. Püye was abandoned around the turn of the sixteenth century in favor of a valley location. However, the impressive ruins of Püye are brought to life for a weekend annually, in late July, when the Santa Clara people arrive for a public festival. Arts and crafts are exhibited and offered for sale, and excellent dances are performed. On August 12, the feast of Santa Clara is celebrated in the pueblo, and other observances are held there throughout the year.

San Ildefonso (Sahn eel-day FOHN-so) may be reached by coming downstream from Santa Clara on NM 30, crossing the Rio Grande at the Otowi bridge, and turning eastward on NM 4 for a short distance; or it may be

A line of Indians, led by a drummer, perform the Deer Dance at Santa Clara Indian Pueblo in northern New Mexico.

While much of the pottery made at San Ildefonso Pueblo in New Mexico is smooth and black, some potters specialize in pots with patterns. Isabel, the potter shown here, has developed many beautiful decorative schemes for pottery.

reached by NM 4 from east or west. It is a small pueblo but widely known because of the fine pottery made there. The most noted pieces are the black matte and burnished ware developed by Maria. Some members of the pueblo make pottery only for decorations. San Ildefonso is also the home of a number of recognized painters among its 503 residents.

The basic work of the pueblo is farming, but many of the Indian men and women work at the atomic energy center, Los Alamos, which has grown up on the Pajarito plateau a few miles west of San Ildefonso.

The pueblo organization has two rectangular ceremonial chambers—one for the North division of the pueblo and one for the South—and a circular build-ing used by the entire pueblo. Unlike the Pueblos who observe summertime feast days with Corn Dances, the feast of San Ildefonso falls on January 23 and is celebrated by special animal dance dramas. Other dances occur at different times throughout the year.

At the bridge across Pojoaque Creek, on US 64, one goes east on NM 4 approximately 5 miles (8 km.) to Nambe (nahm-BAY) Pueblo. A circular structure in the plaza is similar to a circular building at San Ildefonso. Nambe, largely Spanish in culture, with a population of 416, has lost many of its ceremonial features and most of its arts and crafts. Their talent for pottery making and weaving cotton belts has largely vanished. Farming is the main occupation of the villagers.

The Comanche Dance as performed by the Indians at San Ildefonso Pueblo in northern New Mexico. This is a winter dance and takes place on January 23 each year.

In recent years, Nambe has held a festival on July 4 at Nambe Falls on Nambe creek, above the pueblo. Dances and other events at this beautiful scene attract large attendance and the income from these celebrations goes for improvements in the pueblo. The feast day of the pueblo is observed on October 4 with colorful dances.

Tesuque (tay-SOO-kay), located off US 285-64 about 10 miles (16 km.) north of Santa Fe along Tesuque Creek, is the smallest and southernmost group of the Tewa. The pueblo today has 292 residents. While digging for sewer lines through the pueblo, workers found structures built there around A.D. 1250. Several of the present dwellings clustered about the plaza rise to two stories. The kivas at Tesuque have undergone changes so that the original settlement pattern is no longer seen.

The women do not make as much pottery as some of their Tewa neighbors. Emphasis is given, instead, to small vessels and figures molded of clay, painted with poster colors and oven-fired; these figures are frequently dressed in the clothes of their ancestors. Some kiln-fired, true Indian pottery is also produced. The men are primarily farmers. A Harvest Dance is held on November 12, and other ceremonies are seen throughout the year.

The Pojoaque reservation is situated between Nambe and Tesuque. Elderly residents of Tesuque Pueblo report having attended dances in the Pojoaque plaza as youngsters, but the pueblo of Pojoaque is now in ruins. Recently, the Pojoaque Indians have invited other Pueblo peoples to join with them in presenting dances. Its residents number 147.

Tesuque Pueblo Indians performing the Buffalo Dance, an ancient hunting ceremonial.

The pueblo of Jemez is located on Jemez Creek in northern New Mexico. The Jemez people speak Towa, a dialect different from that spoken in any of the other pueblos.

The Towa. Only one pueblo, Jemez (HAY-mez), remains of the many Towa-speaking Tanoans. A related people, once as many as two thousand, lived at the pueblo of Cicuye (see-koh-YEH), or Pecos (PAY-kohs). By 1838, though, only seventeen Indians had survived enemy attack, illnesses, and other troubles at Pecos. These were invited to take refuge at Jemez, nearly 50 miles (80 km.) west of New Mexico's capital city. Today their former pueblo is the site of the Pecos National Monument located about 30 miles (48 km.) southeast of Santa Fe. Their number is now counted with that of the Jemez population of 2,131. But, each year on August 3, the feast of Our Lady of the Angels, patron saint of extinct Pecos, is observed at Jemez by descendants of Pecos mothers. At that time, the old Pecos Bull Dance is performed, to the enjoyment of Indians and non-Indians who gather around the plaza.

On November 12, the feast of San Diego, or Saint James, is observed by the Jemez Indians. Large assemblies of dancers with powerful choruses perform before two rectangular kivas that dominate the plazas. The occasion is in the nature of an Indian fair, with people from other reservations and traders gathering to exchange goods and to enjoy festivities. The Indians of Jemez are widely known as excellent dancers, and any of the colorful ceremonies that they perform during the year are well worth attending.

Some Jemez women weave baskets of plaited yucca leaves; others make stylish pottery, but a few also make practical bean pots. A limited amount of fine weaving is carried on, and watercolor painting has received considerable attention and recognition. The Jemez men are primarily farmers, though their lands also are good hunting areas. Jemez is approached by NM 4 and NM 44. Both of the highways are paved and pass alongside the pueblo, 30 miles (48 km.) northwest of Bernalillo.

Zuñi. Besides the Keresans, the people of Zuñi (ZOON-yee) are the most nu-

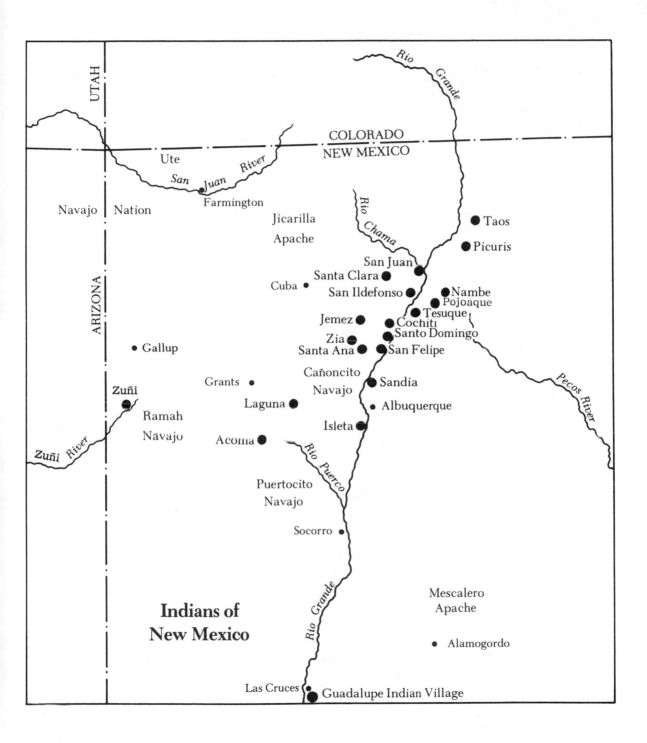

Indians of
New Mexico

Tesuque Indian Pueblo is the scene of one of the most authentic aboriginal rituals held annually by the Indians of New Mexico. Here an Eagle Dancer in full costume dances the famous Eagle Dance.

Their language is that of the Zuñian linguistic family, which may be very distantly related to Tanoan.

The Zuñi Indians engage in farming, and they are famous for their handicrafts. Zuñi jewelry of turquoise, silver, shell, and jet (a velvet-black mineral resembling coal) is known worldwide. Men, women, and youngsters work with this craft, which provides a good income. Very little pottery is now made; however, some attractive vessels are molded into the shape of bowls. Hand-woven woolen items are produced in limited numbers.

The Shalako ceremony, an incomparable religious celebration, is enacted at Zuñi each year in late November or early December.

Every month of the year visitors may observe Indian ceremonials in New Mexico. Many publications list the dates of these events. Also, there are many unscheduled events that may be seen at the pueblos. A unique opportunity to learn about the Pueblo Indians is to visit the Indian Pueblo Cultural Center in Albuquerque. Here are presented their history, dances, pottery, and craftwork.

merous of the Pueblo Indians, 7,143. Many ruins on and near the present reservation indicate Zuñi pueblos existed when Coronado and later Spanish explorers visited New Mexico. Today, the main populace is centered at Zuñi, on paved NM 53, about 40 miles (64 km.) south of Gallup. Other Zuñis reside in the outlying settlements of Ojo Caliente, Tekapo, Pescado, and Nutria.

Indian Pueblo Cultural Center, Albuquerque. Here the history, dance, crafts, art, and food of the nineteen pueblos are presented for all to learn about and enjoy.

Balancing an intricately decorated pot atop their heads is everyday work for these Indian women of Zuñi Pueblo.

These Zuñi Indians, who live in a remote pueblo south of Gallup in western New Mexico, plant corn, squash, and other vegetables in "waffle beds," which retain as much of the scarce water as possible.

The old Mission Church at Zuñi Indian Pueblo.

NON-PUEBLO INDIANS

Latecomers to the Southwest, the Navajo and Apache Indians preferred a nomadic way of life. They came in small bands at different times, but their first arrival was shortly before the coming of the Spaniards. The leader of each band selected a location for his people in an unoccupied area that provided good hunting—either the high plateaus or mesas with extensive grassland or the mountains where game was plentiful. Within this area, the people frequently moved about, usually camping or dwelling temporarily near good springs.

Although semi-nomadic, the Navajo and Apache Indians built comfortable, sturdy shelters. The Navajo lived in a hogan (Hoh-GAN), which was either round or octagonal and built of logs, adobe, rock, or any other available

materials. Doorways were toward the east, and an opening in the roof provided an exit for smoke from fires. The hogan was warm in winter and cool in summer. The Apache preferred a more movable shelter, and they built their wickiups or brush arbors of hides stretched over tall, slender poles in tepee form.

Both the Navajo and Apache were influenced by other Indian groups living near them in the Southwest. The Navajo, living close to the Pueblo Indians, eventually adopted many of their customs. They learned to raise crops and in time they became relatively settled. Navajo women learned from Pueblo Indians how to spin yarn and weave fine textiles on vertical looms. The sacred meal paintings of the Pueblos stimulated the development of sand painting as part of the Navajo religious ceremony.

The Apache bands dwelt at greater distance from the Pueblo Indians and took on fewer of their ways. Instead, they ranged over lands bordering those of certain Plains Indians, from whom they adopted habits of dress and shelter.

The Spanish also affected Navajo life. The sheep and goats introduced by the Spaniards to the Southwest appealed

A **Mescalero Apache camp on the huge Mescalero Indian Reservation, near Ruidoso in southern New Mexico. Each July 4th, the Apaches hold their "Devil Dance" near here.**

to the Navajo. After obtaining a few animals, they soon built up large flocks. Their nomadic life gave way to herding, and eventually they moved with the seasons—going from winter hogan to summer pastures and back again. As the Navajo became more settled, the horse (also introduced by the Spanish) was used to plow the fields, carry goods to market, round up cattle and sheep, and carry supplies from the Navajo summer home to the winter home. The Apache, on the other hand, were less receptive than the Navajo to Spaniards.

Neither the Navajo nor Apache changed completely under the influence of others. For example, the Navajo retained their individualism and did not live in communities like the Pueblos and the Spanish. Instead, hogans were for families at a given location, but these were not a village. Indian philosophy, particularly of the Navajo, has increasingly been studied because of its respect for nature and its emphasis on living in harmony and balance with the environment.

Apache. Some 4,900 Apache Indians live in New Mexico today; they are known as the Mescalero (mess-Kah-LAY-row) and the Jicarilla (hick-ah-REE-yah), names given them by early Spanish explorers. Because of their custom of eating mescal, a small cactus plant, one Apache tribe was named Mescalero. The Jicarilla was named because of the tribe's ability to make baskets suitable for drinking cups, or *jícara* in Spanish.

Mescalero. The Mescalero Apaches live on a reservation of 460,000 acres in the southwestern part of the state on each side of US 70, between Alamogordo and Roswell. The approximately 2,400 Mescalero live in modern homes, attend local churches, and send their children to public primary school on the reservation. High school students attend both Tularosa and Ruidoso public school.

The tribe's civic and commercial affairs are handled in government offices and business establishments.

Mescalero Indians have a federal charter, which makes them a federal corporation. They operate under a constitution and by-laws, and they are governed by the Mescalero Tribal Council, composed of ten members (men and women) elected by eligible voters. They have criminal and civil codes, police themselves, and administer their own government; additionally, they conform with non-Indian aspects of the culture about them.

Aside from being successful cattle-growers, Mescalero have been leaders in recreational and sporting enterprises, which their mountainous lands and clear streams encourage. Agricultural projects and timber also afford a good source of income. Few handicrafts are maintained.

At Mescalero, a four-day ceremony is performed annually at the beginning of July. The dramatic Gahan (gah-HAHN) or Mountain Spirits Dance is performed at night around a flaming fire, while other events occur during the daylight hours.

Jicarilla. The Jicarilla reservation of 2,500 residents is located in northwestern New Mexico. There are over 742,-000 acres which extend south from the Colorado border for approximately 65

miles (104 km.) from the agency headquarters at Dulce, on NM 17, to the vicinity of Cuba on NM 44. Many miles of improved and paved roads cross the Jicarilla reservation.

Jicarilla Apache men are good stockmen, owning mostly cattle, but also horses and sheep. Within the last few years, the Jicarilla improved their water and sewer facilities, built churches and many modern homes on the reservation,

The Mescalero Apache Gahan Dance. An important Apache ritual, the Gahan Ceremony introduces marriageable Apache girls to adult society.

Representatives of the two Jicarilla clans—the red and the whites—pass each other as they prepare for the relay race that is the ceremonial highlight of the annual celebration on September 15.

and remodeled a number of older ones.

Like the Mescalero, the Jicarilla operate by means of a council that follows an adopted constitution and by-laws. These laws provide that surplus money from businesses can be distributed on a dividend basis like that of a corporation. The Jicarilla are making plans to attract industries to the reservation. Funds of their corporation have been set aside for training of personnel and the construction of facilities to assist businesses that will provide the greatest economic benefit to the Jicarilla people. Education receives major attention.

The Jicarilla crafts have been largely neglected. However, the establishment of a factory, "Apache Indian Enterprises," is an operation that promises to employ many craftspeople doing their traditional work.

On September 14 and 15, the Jicarilla hold a two-day celebration at Horse Lake or Stone Lake where they have races and dances.

Navajo Nation. Today, the Navajo are more numerous than any of the other Indian groups north of Mexico. They are estimated at 150,000 to 160,000, and approximately one-third of them live in New Mexico. The majority, though,

Two types of Navajo hogans (houses) found in New Mexico.

dwell in Arizona, with a smaller number in Utah. Of those in New Mexico, certain Navajo groups live apart from the reservation, which covers 16 million acres of beautiful, but semi-arid, country. Lands for cultivation are limited; irrigation projects currently under development, however, may remedy this situation to some extent. Most of the reservation is suitable only for grazing sheep and goats, perhaps some cattle, and a few horses.

Smaller, separate Navajo reservations exist as well. About 1,500 Indians make up the Ramah-Navajo group. They live southeast of the Mormon-established town of Ramah on NM 53, east of Zuñi. Next in size is the Cañoncito group of 1,100 Indians, who live west of the Rio Puerco, about 25 miles (40 km.) west of Albuquerque, off US 66 (I-40). The third group is that of the Puertocito (or Alamo) Navajo, slightly less than 1,000, who live in lands some 30 miles (48 km.) northwestward from Magdalena on US 60. None of these groups have changed from the general pattern of Navajo culture. They are stockgrowers and farmers. The women do a little rug weaving,

Shiprock, the famous peak of northwestern New Mexico, stands guard over thousands of acres of range lands the Navajo Indians use for their sheep. Wool and mutton production are basic industries among these Indians, famed for their weaving. Shiprock is sacred in the legends of Navajo.

and a few baskets are made by the Ramah-Navajo. None of the Navajo make much pottery; it was not traditional with nomadic peoples.

In addition to the groups mentioned, some 18,000 Navajo live in a so-called checkerboard area west of the Jicarilla reservation and to the east of the main Navajo holdings — roughly between Chaco Canyon and Cuba. They are connected with the main agency.

Window Rock on the Arizona-New Mexico border, off NM 68 northwest of Gallup, is today the center of Navajo government and business undertakings. There, in a large council house and in nearby administrative quarters, the Navajo conduct a wide range of activities. They hold democratic elections, choosing, for four-year terms of office, a chairperson, vice-chairperson, seven judges, and seventy-four council members (both men and women). Those over twenty-one may register and vote by the ballot system. Various working committees are named. In the New Mexico state election of 1964, two Navajo men — Monroe Jymm from Gallup and James Atcitty from Shiprock — were elected to serve as State Representatives, the first to hold seats in the Legislature. Trained policemen maintain law and order, cooperating with state and federal officers.

The Navajo have gone into business on a large scale. They are operating sawmills and producing lumber; building motels and restaurants; establishing crafts centers; leasing vast tracts of oil, gas, coal, helium, and uranium; and engaging in banking. They are preserving prehistoric sites, conducting archeological excavations, and developing museums. The Navajo fairs, attended by many thousands of visitors each year at Window Rock and Shiprock, give testimony of the forward strides of Navajo culture in every area. Lately, an industrial park has been set aside by the Navajo east of Gallup (where the federal government employs an extensive staff to deal with Navajo and Zuñi matters), and several concerns are leasing this land and engaging in business activities that will promote the economy

of the region. Some Navajos engage in seasonal employment, working away from the reservation for a few months and then returning home for the rest of the year.

With industrial progress, the Navajo have come to realize the importance of education. Millions of dollars of Navajo money is set aside for scholarships for their young people, particularly those who wish to train for professions. The Navajo Nation has established a community college in Arizona. The Ramah-Navajo operate one of several bilingual schools for their children. Navajo people play an active part in the annual science fairs.

The old crafts—weaving of beautiful blankets and rugs and making of fine silver jewelry set with turquoise—which earned the Navajo worldwide recognition are slowly being abandoned. Individual producers are less frequently threading their looms and less frequently fashioning artful silver pieces with hand tools and simple forge. Most Navajo jewelry is now made by skilled workers in shops or trading posts, or by a few native craftspeople.

Navajo life is changing. Many have modern homes, wear stylish clothes, and often eat food purchased from a supermarket. Others are moving away from the reservation and finding employment in industrial areas both near and far from their homeland. Over 2,000 live

around Los Angeles and San Francisco; others are in New York, Chicago, Denver, Dallas, and, of course, Albuquerque.

The impact of non-Indian ways is evident on traditional ideals and religious ceremonies. As the Navajo medicine men die off, few are trained to take their place. This is because many of the young Navajos refuse to participate in the traditions of their ancestors. They are more interested in acquiring an education and in improving their standard of living to meet the challenges of a competitive society.

Navajo ceremonies are still held each year, particularly in more remote areas of the reservation. When a Night Chant, or Yei-bichei, a Mountain Chant, Squaw Dance, or some other ceremonial is scheduled, it is well worth traveling many miles to see. Most Navajo chants

Navajo Indians are famous for their intricate and beautiful sand paintings. This particular painting was made at the Gallup Inter-Tribal Indian Ceremonial.

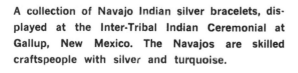

A collection of Navajo Indian silver bracelets, displayed at the Inter-Tribal Indian Ceremonial at Gallup, New Mexico. The Navajos are skilled craftspeople with silver and turquoise.

Strange contrast is presented by these Navajo warriors in their ceremonial dress, traveling to the Inter-Tribal Ceremonial at Gallup, New Mexico, in a brand-new bob-tail truck.

can be held at any time of the year, but the curing ceremonials are restricted to certain months. Cost of the ceremonies is usually paid for by the family; this frequently runs to hundreds of dollars, perhaps up to a thousand or more.

Ute. Very few Ute Indians now live in New Mexico. They once occupied lands in central and western Colorado, eastern Utah, and the upper San Juan drainage. They played an important role in the history of northern New Mexico and the surrounding regions. The Ute, like the Hopi, speak a dialect of the Shoshonean tongue. They are industrious and are making great cultural advances, seeking to free themselves from federal control.

Summary

New Mexico's Indians of today number around 99,000. They are industrious, talented, and skilled. They are law-abiding citizens who have lived along-side their neighbors for centuries. They are part of the culture that is characteristic of the State.

The culture of New Mexico is different in many ways, being shaped by the Indians, Spanish, and "Anglo" (those people who are non-Indian speaking or non-Spanish speaking, whether they are white, yellow, or black). The majority of Indians live on reservations that represent but a small part of the lands that were theirs before the coming of the Europeans.

In 1924, Congress declared that all Indians born in the United States of America territorial lands were citizens. However, the New Mexico Constitution excluded "Indians not taxed" from citizenship until 1948. At that time, the New Mexico Legislature made Indians citizens of the state as well as of the United States. Arizona took similar action at that time.

▼▼▼▼▼▼▼▼▼▼▼▼▼▼▼▼▼▼

REVIEW ACTIVITIES

1. Prepare a report on Indian art, religion, or farming.
2. Write a report on a particular tribe identifying their culture, government, religion, and so forth. How have they changed over the centuries? Identify the various cultural habits they have kept to the present time.
3. Make your own chart showing the general classification of Indians in New Mexico. Use outside reference material.
4. Why do we find Pueblo Indians living in the river areas of New Mexico?
5. What are the two culture sections of the Pueblo Indians?
6. For what reasons are the Pueblos not considered a tribe?
7. What are the chief sources of revenue of the Keresan Pueblos?
8. On what basis are the Pueblo Indians divided into different groups?
9. What is the main economy of the Tanoan Pueblos?
10. For what handicrafts are the Zuñi Indians famous?
11. In what ways have the Pueblo Indians retained some of their traditional customs?
12. For what reasons are the Tewa Pueblos known best?
13. Explain the basic difference between the Navajo and the Pueblo.
14. What did the Navajo learn from the Pueblo Indians?
15. What caused the Navajo to abandon their nomadic way of life?
16. From what sources do the Mescalero Apache receive their income?
17. Describe the governmental structure of the Mescalero.
18. Describe the governmental system of the Navajo.
19. How many Pueblo groups are there in New Mexico?
20. What Pueblo group has the only Veterans of Foreign Wars Post in the United States made up entirely of Indians?
21. In what ways have the Pueblos adjusted to modern times? The Apache? The Navajo? The Ute?

RECOGNIZE AND UNDERSTAND

kiva

pictographs

Apache Gahan Dance

talus

kachina

Enchanted Mesa

Taos Pueblo

San Gabriel

hogan

wickiup

"checkerboard area"

San Juan de los Caballeros

Ramadas

Ute

CHAPTER IV

Early Explorers of New Mexico

CHAPTER V

Invasion and Conquest of New Mexico

CHAPTER VI

Spanish Colonial Period

UNIT 2

SPANISH EXPLORATION AND COLONIZATION

Early Explorers of New Mexico

One of the most daring and courageous events to change the course of world history occurred in 1492. With three small ships — the largest reported to be 50 feet (16 m.) long by 18 feet (5 m.) wide—with crude instruments, and with unbounded faith, Christopher Columbus crossed the Atlantic Ocean in search of a water route to the East. Instead, he opened the door to the New World.

Havana, Cuba, became the first center for the expansion into the New World. From this city, Ponce de León explored the coast of Florida. Hernández de Córdoba captured slaves in Yucatan, Central America, and sold them in Havana in 1517. In 1519, Alonzo Álvarez de Piñeda left the West Indies to try to find a water route through the continents. He explored and mapped the Gulf Coast and became the first European to see a part of our Southwest, the coast of Texas.

When Córdoba returned from Central America, he brought tales of inland cities of gold. This news encouraged the governor of Cuba to send a military force to conquer the mainland. Hernando Cortés was chosen to lead the expedition.

In 1519, Cortés and 600 men set sail from Cuba. After a brief stop at an island off the Yucatan Peninsula, they embarked for the mainland coast. On the island, Cortés had rescued a Spanish priest named Aguilar who had spent seven years with the Maya and spoke their language. Once on the mainland at Tabasco, Cortés conquered an Indian tribe and also gained another translator—Doña Marina. An Aztec noble by birth, she had been sold in youth into slavery to the Mayas. Aguilar spoke to

Painting of Cortés after putting down the rebellion of his troops when the Spanish entered Tenochtitlán (Mexico City).

for the girl Doña Marina, and the legend of the Fair God, Quetzalcoatl. According to the legend, a god named Quetzalcoatl, a god of white skin, once ruled over all Mexico and had gone away to the east, promising to return some day to resume his kingship. Doña Malinche reminded the people of this legend and pointed to the white skins of the Spaniards, to their horses, and to their guns, which brought death at the Spaniards' bidding. The Aztecs believed that these people were indeed the children of Quetzalcoatl, the Fair God. And after several months of seige, the Aztecs surrendered.

The conquered land was called New Spain, and the Aztec city was renamed Mexico City in honor of the Aztec war god, Mexitli. All Indians throughout the new territory were now ruled by the king of Spain.

During the years that followed the conquest of Mexico, the Spanish were quick to take over the Indian ways that were useful in the new territory. In the hot weather of Mexico, the Spanish adopted the hammock for sleeping; throughout the new country, the Spanish settlers served beans and corn, and they drank the Mexican chocolate.

her in Maya, and in turn she interpreted to the Aztecs. She became Christianized and was a trustworthy member of the Cortés army. Many people, though, feeling that she betrayed her people, called her Doña Malinche (Traitor).

Cortés and his soldiers next sailed west along the coast to where Vera Cruz is located today. There they left their ships and began a two year expedition in which they conquered new lands and defeated the Aztec leader, Montezuma, and took over his capital, Tenochtitlan. That city must have been a marvelous sight for the Spanish. It was located in and over the waters of Lake Tezcoco and could only be reached by a great bridge. Beyond the bridge was the city which, the Spanish believed, contained the gold and jewels for which the expedition was searching.

This conquest of Mexico and its approximately eight million inhabitants by a small Spanish force might well have been impossible had it not been

Ta-ay-allona sacred mountain of the Zuñi. Near the mountain are the Zuñi pueblos (Seven Cities of Cibola) which hastened Spanish exploration into New Mexico. Adam Clark Vroman, 1899. Ward Ritchie Press, Los Angeles, California.

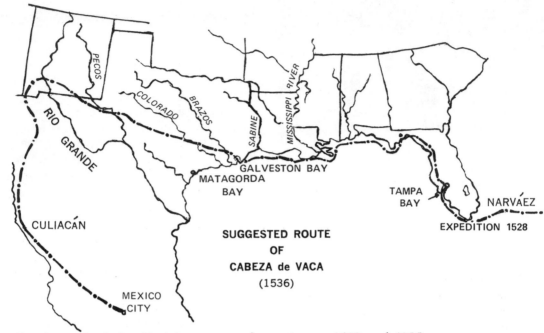

SUGGESTED ROUTE
OF
CABEZA de VACA
(1536)

By the end of the first ten years of Spanish occupation of Mexico, Mexico City did not have more than 2,000 inhabitants. These consisted of two classes, the settlers and the "soldiers of fortune." Most of the time the two groups were sharply divided. The more settled members of the city often became annoyed at the anxious fortune hunters who were always seeking ways to find the fabled "Golden Cities." Legends of wealth in the northern country prompted expeditions to find the treasures, but the hoped-for fortunes were never discovered. However, Mexico City soon became the headquarters for explorers, missionaries, and pioneers; soon these hardy adventurers would open the way for exploration and settlement of what is now the American Southwest.

Alvar Nuñez Cabeza de Vaca

One of the most amazing explorations of the North American continent was its crossing by the ship-wrecked survivors of the Narváez expedition be-

tween 1528 and 1536.

Don Pánfilo Narváez was in command of five ships and some 600 colonists and soldiers sent to conquer lands in Florida and to establish a settlement. One of the officers on the Narváez ship was Cabeza de Vaca, the treasurer and high sheriff of the expedition. After a stormy voyage in which Narváez lost some ships and a large number of men, he and the remaining members of the expedition landed on the coast of Florida near Tampa Bay.

The Spanish began exploring the country to determine whether the natives were friendly and to find food. For several months, scouting parties were sent out from the settlement at Tampa to seek friendly Indians and supplies. Some of these expeditions were attacked by Indians, who killed many of the soldiers. The Spanish village also was besieged, and several colonists were killed. Indian resistance to the Spanish resulted in the soldiers' decision to build boats and return to their settlements in New Spain.

The survivors of the colony built five boats from wood found in the area. Nails, saws, and axes were made from stirrups, spurs, bridle bits, and all other metal they could find. Hair from the horses' manes and tails was used as thread to sew the sails together; the survivors' shirts served as material for the sails.

When the boats were ready, the survivors began their voyage along the Gulf coastline of Florida, Alabama, Mississippi, and Louisiana in search of Spanish settlements.

One of the ships, commanded by Cabeza de Vaca, sailed southwestward past the mouth of the Mississippi River. There it dropped anchor on one of the small islands west of the river and waited for the other four boats. When the other ships arrived, the entire expedition set sail once more; however, the powerful current of the Mississippi River and a treacherous wind from the north cast the ships out into the Gulf Sea. All the ships were destroyed except the one commanded by Cabeza de Vaca. The survivors continued on their journey for several days without food or water, and in November 1528, Cabeza de Vaca and his crew were cast ashore on an island near Matagorda Bay on the coast of Texas.

De Vaca and Estevan, a Moorish Negro slave, built a raft and ferried themselves to the Texas mainland. By this time, all of the other survivors—except Dorantes and Meldonado—had

been killed by the Indians or had died of starvation. Cabeza de Vaca and Estevan later joined Dorantes and Meldonado, and the four of them traveled together on their long journey across the southwestern part of the United States.

The four survivors of the Narváez expedition endured many hardships in the eight years it took them to return to Mexico City. They were held captive by the Indians many times, but each time they managed to escape. They frequently suffered from thirst, hunger, and exposure.

At times, Indians suspicious of the Spaniards offered them their friendship as a pretext to conceal their true feelings. Other Indians, though, befriended the Spanish after de Vaca or his companions healed Indians who were sick or injured. These grateful Indians rewarded the Spaniards with many gifts, including some very valuable turquoise and gems. At times, the Spaniards re-

This foot trail winds its way up the mountain to the top of Sierra del Cristo Rey near Las Cruces in southern New Mexico. Near this mountain may have been the route taken by Cabeza de Vaca when he made his historic entrada or expedition into a still unconquered area.

ceived so many gifts that they could not carry all of them.

The long and painful journey that began in 1528 finally ended in Mexico City on July 24, 1536. Part of their journey had been through nearly a thousand miles of the vast expanse of Texas and southern New Mexico. De Vaca had kept records and maps of their wanderings across the continent. He also had heard stories from the Indians about seven cities of gold located some distance to the north.

Upon his return, de Vaca undoubtedly gave full account of their adventures to Antonio de Mendoza, the newly appointed viceroy of New Spain. The viceroy, a direct representative of the king, was eager to continue the search for the fabled "Golden Cities." Several more attempts were made to explore the northern country in pursuit of the gold and silver believed to be abundant there.

Fray Juan de la Asunción

Among the early explorers to travel north was Fray Juan de la Asunción. His mission was to review the conditions of the country, to locate the cities of gold for the glory of the Spanish Crown, and to Christianize the Indians for the glory of the Church. With these purposes in mind and with the viceroy's blessings, Fray Juan de la Asunción began his journey in 1538 from Culiacán, a Spanish outpost in northern Mexico. Traveling northwest, he made his way to the lower Gila River where it joins with the Colorado River in present-day Arizona. The Indians he met along the way appeared friendly; upon his return to Mexico City, he reported his findings to the viceroy. He was probably the first Spaniard to enter the land that today is the state of Arizona.

Fray Marcos de Niza

The news of friendly Indians in the northern area prompted Mendoza to assign Fray Marcos de Niza the task of leading an expedition to the land even farther north. Because Fray Marcos had knowledge of the natives and of navigation, Mendoza selected him. Fray Marcos, an Italian, had accompanied Francisco Pizzaro, conqueror of Peru. There he had established many missions and Christianized many Indians.

Fray Marcos left Culiacán on March 7, 1539, accompanied by the Negro slave, Estevan, who had come to Mexico City with Cabeza de Vaca and some Christian Indians. Traveling north, they found the Indians friendly, especially since Fray Marcos told them they would not be captured and made slaves. Some of the Indians spoke of the pearl islands to the west. They told of large settlements some four or five days inland where cotton was used for clothing. They also claimed that gold was used for ornaments and decorations.

Since Estevan had made friends with Indians and had heard about the seven cities of gold, he was sent by Fray Marcos to scout the area. He was told to blaze a trail, make friends with the Indians, and look for the golden cities. He was also instructed not to go into the cities if he found them; instead, he was to send a runner each day with a cross to identify what was found. If nothing was found, he was to send back a cross the size of a hand. If Estevan found anything of real value, he was to send a slightly bigger cross. When he found evidence of the golden cities, a very large cross was to be returned.

Within a few days, an Indian messenger returned with a cross as tall as a man. Fray Marcos was notified to come at once, because Estevan had

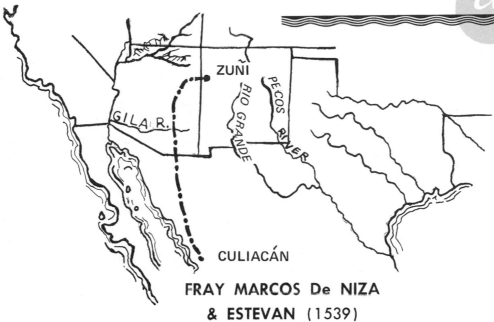

FRAY MARCOS De NIZA
& ESTEVAN (1539)

found people who knew about the golden cities. As soon as possible, Fray Marcos began his journey north, following the trail Estevan had left.

Estevan, meanwhile, had disobeyed the orders of Fray Marcos and entered Hawikuh, one of the Zuñi villages. He and all of his followers were captured and killed except two Indian guides who managed to escape. Several days later the two frightened Indians found Fray Marcos and told him of Estevan's death. The death of Estevan was a terrible blow to Fray Marcos, but he was determined to see for himself the wonderous cities that he felt confident lay before him. He journeyed a short distance to a hill overlooking the cities that were described to him by the Indians.

After seeing what he thought were the "Seven Cities of Cíbola," he erected a cross and claimed all the land in the name of Spain. What appeared to him

as golden houses may have been yellow corn drying in the sun on the roof tops of the buildings, but we have no way of knowing what he actually saw.

As quickly as he could, Fray Marcos prepared to leave the area, for he feared he might meet the same fate as Estevan. Within a few weeks, he was in Mexico City with his report of discovery of the fabled Seven Cities. The officials accepted this as true, although he brought back no gold for evidence.

Francisco de Ulloa

Besides these missions sponsored by Viceroy Mendoza, Cortés retained the right to authorize explorations. In July 1539, he ordered three ships under the command of Francisco de Ulloa to search for Cíbola by sea. Ulloa sailed from Acapulco to the Gulf of California. However, the viceroy of New Spain refused aid of any kind to Ulloa because there was a dispute as to whom the title of Cíbola would belong:

The site of the prehistoric Püye Pueblo commands a view of the Rio Grande valley stretching 100 miles (160 km.) from north to south. These dwellings were abandoned centuries before the Spanish arrived on the continent of North America.

Cortés or the viceroy. In the end, though, neither got it because Ulloa's explorations were unsuccessful.

Hernando de Soto

Another voyage was underway when Fray Marcos returned to Mexico. This one was under the command of Hernando de Soto, who received a commission by the King of Spain to conquer Florida. Landing near Tampa Bay, de Soto headed inland and picked up a survivor of the Narváez expedition who told de Soto about the golden cities somewhere inland. He crossed the present states of Georgia, North and South Carolina, Alabama, Tennessee, and Mississippi. He crossed the Mississippi River into Arkansas, where at one time he was only 300 miles (480 km.) from Coronado's expedition. The gold which they had been seeking was not found, and on the return trip, de Soto died or was killed by the Indians; he was buried under the waters of the Mississippi River.

Melchor Díaz

In 1540, Mendoza, viceroy of New Spain, sent Melchor Díaz on a scouting mission to check the route of Fray Marcos de Niza to ascertain the friendliness of the Indians. Díaz traveled north to the desert near the Gila River and returned with good news about the country.

LA HISTORIA GENERAL

y enojan : finalmente es animal feo y fiero de ro-
ftro, y cuerpo. Huyē de los los cauallos por fu ma-
la catadura, o por nunca los auer vifto. No tienen
fus dueños otra riqueza , ni hazienda., dellos co-
men, beuen, viften, calçan, y hazen muchas cofas
de los cueros, cafas, calçado, veftido y fogas: delos
hueffos, punçones: delos neruios, y pelos, hilo: de
los cuernos, buches, y bexigas , vafos: delas boñi-
gas, lumbre: y delas terneras , odres , en que traen
y tienen agua : hazen en fin tantas cofas dellos
quantas han menefter, o quantas las baftan para
fu biuienda. Ay tambien otros animales, tan gran
des como cauallos, que por tener cuernos , y lana
fina, los llaman carneros, y dizen , que cada cuer-
no pefa dos arrouas. Ay tambien grandes perros,
que

Early drawing of a buffalo from a Spanish manuscript. In that period,
Cíbola meant "Buffalo Cow" to the Spanish. Cabeza de Vaca and other
early Spanish explorers thought the buffalo looked like "shaggy cows."

Hernando de Alarcón

Another sea expedition the same year, under Hernando de Alarcón, was ordered. His mission was to sail up the Colorado River to meet the expedition of Coronado, but he was unable to locate the column. On the shore, however, were many unfriendly Indians; he recorded this, and upon his return to Mexico City he informed the viceroy.

Spanish Reasons for Exploration

Encouraged by the experiences of Fray Marcos de Niza and others, the young men and the old were drawn by various motivations to the New World. GOLD, LAND, SLAVES, CHRISTIANITY, AND THE THRILL OF ADVENTURE encouraged expeditions to the new frontier.

GOLD meant additional strength for the Spanish government and wealth to those who discovered it. This greatly inflamed the imperial ambitions in the already anxious Spaniards, especially the young nobles who did not share in the family's wealth.

LAND, which was the principal source of wealth, meant protection for Spain in the New World, because many countries in Europe were beginning to see the value of overseas expansion. Some countries had already sent men and ships to explore the northeast coast of North America.

In addition, LAND WITH AN ABUNDANCE OF INDIAN SLAVES provided an opportunity for the young to gain titles of nobility and enjoy the luxuries of life.

THE DESIRE TO SPREAD CHRISTIANITY, which had long been part of the Spanish culture, provided an additional motive. This vast land furnished a mission field for the priests to bring the Indians into the Christian faith. For this reason, many a priest became an essential part of every expedition. Missions were established, and the Indians were encouraged to become Christians.

To others, THE LOVE OF ADVENTURE AND CONQUEST was the reason for exploration.

REVIEW ACTIVITIES

1. Imagine you are traveling with one of the expeditions, and keep a daily record of what you saw and what you did for a week.
2. What conquest was made by Cortés?
3. What was one reason for the Spanish success against the Aztecs?
4. What three Indian ways were taken over by the Spanish?
5. What were the two classes of people found in Mexico City after the Spanish conquest?
6. What motives encouraged Spanish expeditions to the new frontier?
7. What was the reason for the Narváez expedition?
8. What materials did de Vaca and his men use to make rafts to sail from Florida to the Texas Coast?
9. Why were the Spanish leaders in Mexico City excited by the stories brought to them by Cabeza de Vaca and Fray Marcos de Niza?
10. How was Estevan to identify what he saw at Cíbola?
11. What happened to Estevan during the trip to Cíbola?
12. Describe an important event to New Mexico that took place on each of the following dates: 1519, 1528, 1536, 1539.
13. On a map of the Southwest, trace the routes of the following explorers: Alvar Nuñez Cabeza de Vaca, Fray Juan de la Asunción, and Fray Marcos de Niza.

RECOGNIZE AND UNDERSTAND

Hernández de Córdoba	Hernando Cortés
Aztecs	Tenochtitlán
Tezcoco	Doña Malinche
Montezuma	Quetzalcoatl
Mexitli	Cabeza de Vaca
Estevan	Antonio de Mendoza
Fray Juan de la Asunción	Fray Marcos de Niza
Hernando de Soto	Cíbola
Hawikuh	

CHAPTER V

Invasion and Conquest of New Mexico

The plans for invasion and conquest of New Mexico were being carefully prepared by the Viceroy Mendoza. The army would be made up largely of soldiers from Mexico who were seeking fortunes in gold, many of whom were sons of noblemen. Many of these men proved to be successful explorers and leaders.

Mendoza, a wise and able man, was concerned with who should lead the expedition. Jealousy ran high among the generals of New Spain. Each one sent a petition to the viceroy requesting permission to lead the military force into New Mexico. Among them was Hernando Cortés, the conqueror of Mexico. He felt certain the decision would be made in his favor, but his petition was rejected by the viceroy.

Don Francisco Vásquez de Coronado

In February 1540, the decision was made, and Don Francisco Vásquez de Coronado, about 28 years old, was selected to lead the expeditionary force. At this time, Coronado was governor of New Galicia, a northern province of Mexico and the present state of Jalisco. The general met his command at a place called Compostela, located on the Pacific coast of Mexico. On February 23, 1540, the huge force assembled, and from Compostela the entire army began its march to the north. Weapons, horses, and supplies were furnished in abundance by Coronado, Mendoza, and individual members of the army. The Spanish government advanced funds to anyone for the purpose of paying debts and purchasing equipment.

It must have been a splendid sight to

Cross-bows and armor were the accouterments of some of the infantry in the army of Francisco Vásquez de Coronado, who in 1540 made his epic entrada into New Mexico in search of the fabled Seven Cities of Cíbola.

see as the army passed in review before Mendoza. The 225 young nobles on horseback were dressed in their finest. Many had armor polished to shine like that of their commander. Each one had his own lance, a sword, and a shield with his coat-of-arms (emblems to identify nobility). Some of the 60 foot-soldiers carried the cross-bows, while others carried a sword and shield. As each group marched forward, their colorful banners were displayed before the cheering crowd. In addition, it was reported that there were about 1,000 Indians and 1,500 head of horses, mules, and cattle.

Spain required that each expedition be accompanied by at least one priest. But five went with this expedition; among them was Fray Marcos de Niza, who was the leader of the first expedition to seek Cíbola.

Entire family fortunes were invested in these expeditions. It has been estimated that this expedition cost about three million dollars. This, no doubt. was the grandest army ever assembled on this continent.

The journey northward was certainly not as the Spaniards had expected, even during the first few weeks of the venture. The army had to cross obstacles which they had not anticipated—swift rivers, deep arroyos, and steep cliffs. On one occasion, it took the main army three days to cross a single river located in a deep ravine—an almost impossible crossing. Unknown to Coronado, the desert ahead promised an even greater challenge, for this area afforded neither food nor water; therefore, the conditions became worse. Only a few Indians were met during the journey, but on one occasion during the march, one of the best officers was killed by an Indian who had hidden behind a tree. For this act, Coronado went to the nearby village, took several of the Indians and had them put to death.

In July, after more than four months of travel, the advance patrol of Coronado's army reach the Zuñi Pueblo. Later, the main army arrived and camped on a huge ridge overlooking the valley of Zuñi.

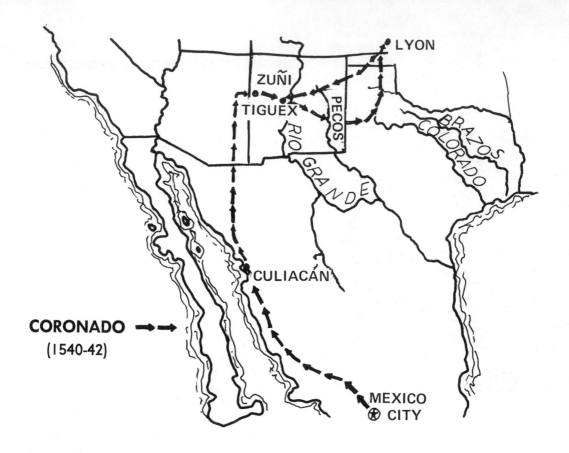

CORONADO ⟶
(1540-42)

The next day after arrival, Coronado ordered his troops to advance and capture the first Zuñi village, Hawikuh. The Indians had prepared for battle, but they proved no match for the Spanish. The battle ended almost before it started; Coronado was slightly wounded, but the pueblo was in the hands of the Spaniards. Within a few days, all the Zuñi towns had surrendered. Although Coronado and his command had conquered the pueblo, they were distressed and disgusted because the golden cities were nothing more than stone and adobe houses several stories high. The army was very angry with **Fray Marcos**, since he was the one who brought the news of the golden cities of Cíbola. He left rather quickly, heading south with an escort to Mexico City.

Don Pedro de Tovar. Because of his great disappointment at Zuñi, Coronado was determined to carry on further exploration. News had reached him through some Indians that, to the west, there were seven golden cities with houses of several stories. Don Pedro de Tovar was assigned to explore the area to the northwest where these cities were supposedly located. After a journey of several days, Tovar and his companions reached the Moqui or Hopi country in Arizona. The Indians were unfriendly at first, but after a short battle, they made peace with their invaders. The chiefs informed Tovar of a great river to the west and of the race of giants who lived along its banks. Returning to Cíbola, Tovar told Coronado· about the river and the giants.

Don Garcia Lopez de Cárdenas. Immediately, Coronado sent Cárdenas to discover the river and to find the giants who were living there. Cárdenas and his men arrived at the Hopi village where the Indians furnished the Spaniards with guides to explore farther west. Traveling over the desert, the Spaniards arrived at the banks of a deep canyon. The banks were so high and rugged that it was almost impossible to see the river below. Cárdenas and his men marched several days along the ridge of the canyon searching for

of the greatest scenic wonders of the world. He also had discovered the upper region of the Colorado River in Arizona.

Hernando de Alvarado. Before Cárdenas returned to the Zuñi Pueblo, a group of Indians came to visit the Spanish. They were led by their chief, whom the Spanish called "Bigotes" because of his long beard. Bigotes told Coronado about the country from which they had come, particularly of the buffalo, a picture of which was painted on the body

The crossbow was a powerful weapon used by Coronado's army in New Mexico from 1540-42.

an opening by which they might descend to the stream. At one point an unsuccessful attempt was made to get to the river. Finding no giants in the area and the river impossible to reach, Cárdenas returned to Zuñi Pueblo. He had discovered the Grand Canyon, one

In 1541, Coronado and thirty-five of his men headed for the treasures of Quivira located on the Arkansas River in Kansas.

of one of the Indians. This news interested Coronado, and he directed Alvarado, with Bigotes as his guide, to explore the regions to the east. After five days' journey, Alvarado reached the town of Ácoma, built on a mesa or rock several hundred feet high, with the only entrance being a narrow staircase cut into the cliff. At first the Indians were unfriendly, but they soon made peace with the Spanish.

Later, Alvarado rode eastward until he arrived at the town of Tiguex near the present town of Bernalillo on the Rio Grande. The Indians were very friendly toward the Spanish since Bigotes was with them; he was a powerful chief and greatly feared in that country. Alvarado was so pleased with the country that he sent word to Coronado recommending the area for a winter headquarters. Coronado accepted the suggestion, and Tiguex became the Spanish headquarters during the winter of 1540-41.

Awaiting the main army under Coronado, Alvarado made plans to continue exploring to the east. Traveling eastward for five days, Alvarado met an Indian from a village far to the east;

the Spanish called him "El Turco" or "Turk" because of his appearance. The Turk told the Spanish about other great cities and about the gold and silver that was to be found in this land to the east. Pleased with the information about the wealth in the east, Alvarado and the Turk returned quickly to Tiguex and found Cárdenas preparing the place for Coronado. Cárdenas needed a shelter; he therefore ordered all the Indians from one of the pueblos and allowed nothing to be taken with them except their clothes. This act angered the Pueblo people who had made friends with the Spanish only days before. Coronado arrived a few days later, and unaware of Cárdenas' deed, he ordered food and clothing for his men, but the angry Indians refused and barricaded their village. After several hours of battle, more than 200 Indians were killed, and the pueblo surrendered. It took many years for the people of Tiguex to be on friendly terms with the Spanish.

Quivira

Coronado talked to the Turk many times during their winter encampment. The Turk again assured Coronado of the

The Sandia Mountains form a massive backdrop for the Rio Grande as it runs near Albuquerque. About 15 miles (24 km.) north of these mountains, Coronado and his army camped at Tiguex during the winter of 1540-41.

great cities and of the fortune that was to be found in Quivira, a region to the east. In April 1541, Coronado and a part of his army began their march eastward with Bigotes; El Turco was to guide them. Also acting as a guide was a Wichita Indian woman, Big Eyes. They made their way to the Pecos Pueblo where Bigotes, who was the chief, was allowed to remain.

Leaving the pueblo, Coronado, the Turk, and about thirty-five horsemen headed in a southeasterly direction to a river, the Pecos near Puerto de Luna in Guadalupe County, New Mexico. A bridge was needed to cross the river, and one was completed in four days. The army crossed safely, and within a short time they came to the plains where they saw a great many buffalo but only a few Indians. At some time during this part of the trip, the guides led the Spanish several miles from their intended direction. To correct this, the Spanish changed their course and headed northeast to reach the place called Quivira, located on the Arkansas River in Kansas. Upon arriving at Quivira, Coronado erected a cross and claimed all the land for Spain.

There were no golden cities. The Turk confessed that he had lied about the gold and the great cities. To lay the blame elsewhere, the Turk also told Coronado that the people of Cicuye (Pecos Pueblo) wanted the Spanish to be led out into the plains to starve and perish. It was their plan that perhaps the few Spanish who did not die would easily be defeated in battle by the Indians. Subsequently, Coronado had the Turk put to death. Big Eyes escaped and later aided de Soto. Coronado then made ready for a return trip to his headquarters on the Rio Grande. After a march of forty-five days, he and his companions arrived at Tiguex ready to make preparations for the winter.

There were other expeditions sent out from Tiguex before Coronado and his army returned to Mexico. One group followed the Rio Grande northward to Taos Pueblo and, finding the Indians friendly, they then returned to Tiguex. Another group went south along the Rio Grande, passing many pueblos from the present two of Belen and San Marcial in Socorro County, where the Indians appeared friendly. Seeing this, the Spanish returned to their camp.

During the winter of 1541-42, Coronado and his men suffered terribly from cold and near starvation. They had few warm clothes, and their poorly constructed shelters did little to keep

Kuaua mural in the huge Kiva at Coronado Monument

out the cold weather. Food was scarce and becoming more difficult to find. The Indians, because they were no longer on friendly terms with the Spanish, refused to furnish them with supplies, and the officers and men were soon quarreling among themselves over the few supplies that were left.

Return to Mexico City

With the arrival of spring, conditions improved, and the men began to make preparations for the long journey to Mexico. Coronado, in the meantime, was hurt in a fall from his horse, and he remained near death for several days. By April though, Coronado had recovered and was ready to return to New Spain. Two priests, Fray Juan de

Padilla and Fray Luis Escalona, decided to remain with the Pueblo Indians. Fray Juan was anxious to return to Quivira to build a mission, and Fray Luis selected the Pecos Pueblo for his work. Guides and supplies were provided for their trip, which began the next day. They were never seen again. Later, reports from returning explorers indicated they were killed by the Indians.

Many horses and sheep brought to Tiguex by the Spanish, along with items too difficult to carry, were left behind. On the return trip they passed many Pueblo villages once visited by the Spanish, and from Zuñi they turned south, arriving at Mexico City two months later. It was a sad occasion for the army as well as the people of the city. Reporting to Viceroy Mendoza, a heartsick Coronado explained that he had found no trace of the rumored gold. He retired from the army and returned to his former job as Governor of New Galicia. Shortly thereafter, he disappeared from public life. Thus ended one of the greatest expeditions into North America.

Francisco de Ibarra

For the next forty years, there were no major expeditions to the Southwest. However, in 1563, a small expedition led by Francisco de Ibarra marched northward into the territory for eight days to a point overlooking a large settlement. This town may have been in the Gila Forest area, since Ibarra traveled east of the line followed by Coronado. Because of the unfriendly Indians, Ibarra and his soldiers returned to Mexico. The name *New Mexico* was first used to refer to the present State of New Mexico when Ibarra, reporting to the viceroy, said that he had discovered a "new" Mexico.

Settlements in Northern Mexico

Soon after the Coronado expedition, silver was discovered in northern Mexico. New towns sprang up, extending the frontier near the borders of the present states of Arizona and New Mexico. The Spanish government set up military posts in the new towns to protect the people from the Indians. These military outposts became the key cen-

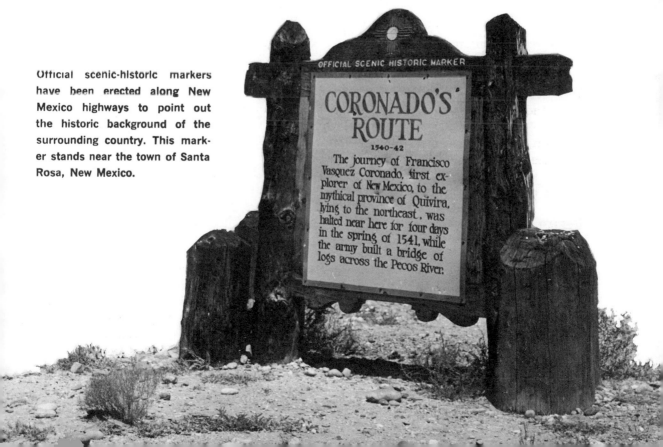

Official scenic-historic markers have been erected along New Mexico highways to point out the historic background of the surrounding country. This marker stands near the town of Santa Rosa, New Mexico.

OFFICIAL SCENIC HISTORIC MARKER

CORONADO'S ROUTE
1540-42

The journey of Francisco Vasquez Coronado, first explorer of New Mexico, to the mythical province of Quivira, lying to the northeast, was halted near here for four days in the spring of 1541, while the army built a bridge of logs across the Pecos River.

ters for explorations up the Río Grande by the end of the sixteenth century. As always, a church was set up in the center of the settlements, and a priest was always present to give aid in spiritual matters to miners, to their families, and to the soldiers. Another duty of the Church was to Christianize the Indians.

Fray Agustín Rodríguez

Forty years had passed, and during that time, almost everyone had forgotten the explorations of Coronado. People were more concerned with town life: building houses, working the silver mines, and farming. The Church, on the other hand, had provided missions for Indians who wanted to become Christians. Some of the Indians who came to the missions told about the many villages located in the north. Interest grew among the priests to seek out these cities and to Christianize the people.

Agustín Rodríguez was one of the missionaries stationed at the frontier town of San Bartolomé, located on the Conchos River and the headquarters for future explorations into New Mexico. Fray Rodríguez received permission from the viceroy and his superiors to look for the cities and to Christianize the Indians. Fray Rodríguez and two other priests, Francisco López and Juan de Santa María, and nine soldiers as an escort led by Francisco Sánchez Chamuscado, left San Bartolomé in June 1581.

The Rodríguez expedition traveled along the Conchos River to the Rio Grande; then turning to the northwest, they continued their journey, passing near the present city of El Paso, Texas, and the town of Mesilla, in Doña Ana County, New Mexico. They traveled for several more days, visited some of the pueblos, and finally arrived at the Puaray Pueblo (Village of the Worm) where they founded the "first mission" in the state on a bluff overlooking the Rio Grande in front of the present town of Bernalillo. Puaray was the principal pueblo settlement when Coronado had passed through the land. The church was known as the Mission of Friar Ruíz after Agustín Rodríguez. The priests decided to stay among the Indians, allowing Chamuscado and the soldiers to return to Mexico City to report their findings. Much later, news reached Mexico that Fray Santa María and Fray López had been killed by the Indians.

Antonio de Espejo

Franciscan officials, disturbed that the three missionaries had been left without protection, decided to rescue Fray Rodríguez, who they hoped was still alive. Antonio de Espejo offered to lead the expedition, which left San Bartolomé in November 1582. Following a route that took them to Tiguex, they learned there of the death of Fray Rodríguez. The main object of the journey had been completed, but Espejo decided to explore the region to determine whether the Indians were friendly. After several months of exploring, Espejo and his army returned to Mexico by way of the Pecos River and reported the news to the viceroy. In the records of Fray Rodríguez and Antonio de Espejo, the words "Nuevo Méjico" (New Mexico) were first used in print in reference to the place they had seen and explored; it continued to be referred to as New Mexico.

Gaspar Castaño de Sosa

After Espejo's return to Mexico, other explorers sent petitions to the king asking for permission to further explore New Mexico. Gaspar Castaño de Sosa, who had been refused a petition to explore New Mexico, was determined to go into the vast new territory. In July 1590, he and his command of 170 men, along with women and children, left Mexico to establish a settlement in the north. They traveled northward along the Pecos River and set up a camp site south of the present city of Santa Fe. Within a few weeks, a Spanish patrol found de Sosa and arrested him for having entered New Mexico without permission. He was put in chains and returned to Mexico City, and at a later date he died on the galleys in the Far East.

REVIEW ACTIVITIES

1. Review a map of Spanish expeditions and determine which one came close to where you live. Find out, if possible, the exact course it followed in your locality.
2. Make a time line showing the various Spanish expeditions in the Southwest.
3. Who was selected by Viceroy Mendoza to lead the expedition in search of the "Seven Cities of Gold"? Was the expedition a complete failure? Explain.
4. Name several conditions that made travel most difficult for the expeditionary force.
5. Who were the two priests that stayed in New Mexico when Coronado returned to Mexico City? Why did they decide to remain?
6. What part did the Church play in Spanish settlements?
7. Where was the town of San Bartolomé? How important was this settlement to the explorers who came to New Mexico?
8. What was the purpose of Fray Rodríguez's expedition into New Mexico?
9. Who first used the term "New Mexico" in referring to the present state of New Mexico? When were the words "Nuevo Méjico" first written in the records of the explorers? By whom?
10. Who founded the first mission in New Mexico? Where was it located?

RECOGNIZE AND UNDERSTAND

Zuñi Pueblo	Tovar
Cárdenas	Bigotes
Ácoma	Tiguex
El Turco	Quivira
Francisco de Ibarra	Gaspar Castaño de Sosa

CHAPTER VI

Spanish Colonial Period

In the early 1590s there were other unsuccessful attempts to colonize New Mexico. Many lost fortunes in their attempts to settle in the new land. The Spanish government supported the missionaries and sent a few supplies, but most of the expense of an expedition was paid for by wealthy individuals. The King gave grants of land and the tile of Governor to anyone who could afford such an undertaking.

Don Juan de Oñate

The viceroy of Mexico was instructed by the King to grant a license and a contract for colonization to the one who could provide the most money. In 1595, Viceroy Velasco accepted the propositions of Don Juan de Oñate and granted him a license to colonize New Mexico.

Oñate was rich and highly respected in Mexico. He was the great grandson of Hernando Cortés, conqueror of Mexico. Oñate was given the title of Captain-General of the expedition and governor of the territories to be colonized. He was granted unlimited powers.

The contract was signed by Oñate, and with the aid of his four brothers, he set about the task of recruiting an army. Soldiers and settlers, attracted by the favorable terms offered and the hope of wealth and fame in the north, came from all directions. There were great celebrations similar to those experienced by Coronado and his expedition in 1540.

Before the group left for New Mexico, though, a change in viceroys occurred, causing a delay in the march. Oñate had many rivals who were eager to lead this expedition, and with the help of the new viceroy, they prevented the newly formed expedition from leaving on schedule.

Don Juan de Oñate Coat of Arms

by the Spanish government. The reason for this inspection by the government was to make certain that Oñate met the requirements of his contract. In addition to the inspection, Oñate was required to secure a "performance bond" to make sure he complied with the contract. If he did not fulfill the requirements in the contract, Oñate had to forfeit the bond.

Everything having been in order, the army set out again for New Mexico. Progress with the wagons was naturally slow, but there were no major disasters along the way.

On the twentieth of April 1598, they reached the Rio Grande. They traveled a few miles up the river before setting

New petitions were sent to the King by Oñate's rivals. These petitions required less assistance from the Spanish government, most of the financing of the expedition would come from the one who organized it. The King decided to withdraw Oñate's contract and to review the more favorable ones he had received.

In January 1598, the king of Spain, agreeing that Oñate should go to New Mexico, finally renewed his contract. The army of 130 soldiers, their families, and several servants started northward from San Bartolomé, arrived at the Conchos River, crossed the stream, and made camp. There were 83 wagons and 700 head of cattle included with the expedition.

The Oñate expedition set up its camp site on the west bank of the Conchos River and prepared for final inspection

Oñate and his army as they might have looked preparing to leave for the frontier of New Mexico to establish a colony for Spain.

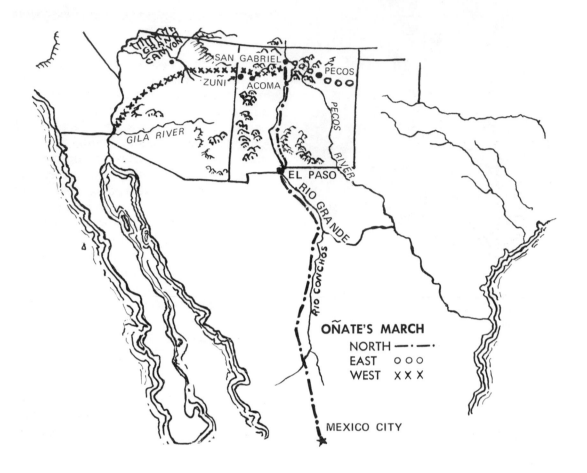

OÑATE'S MARCH

NORTH —·—
EAST ○○○
WEST ✕✕✕

up camp near the present city of El Paso, Texas. During their brief encampment, Oñate took formal possession of New Mexico and adjoining provinces for God, the King of Spain, and himself. That evening, a performance was given of an original comedy written by Captain Farfán. The subject of the play was the conquest of New Mexico. This was probably the first play ever performed by Europeans in New Mexico.

The next day, the army crossed the Rio Grande and continued its journey. During this part of the trip, several colonists died; for this reason, the area they traveled was called the Jornada del Muerto (Journey of the Dead).

Traveling several miles more, they arrived at the first group of pueblos. The Indians welcomed the Spanish in their town, provided entertainment, and furnished them with supplies of maize (Indian corn) and other foodstuffs. Because the Indians were so kind to Oñate and the colonists, he renamed the pueblo Socorro (help). At several convenient places along the Rio Grande, Oñate established missions and supply stations to assist other colonists when they came to settle in New Mexico.

The Spanish were told about two Mexican Indians who were left at a pueblo in the north by de Sosa. Oñate and a small search party headed north

Official scenic-historic marker near Bernardo, New Mexico, points out that U.S. Highway 85 follows the route of the Spanish conquistador Don Juan de Oñate.

and arrived at the pueblo of Puaray. They slept that night in the same room used by the slain friars, Rodríguez and López, seventeen years before. On the walls of the room of the pueblo were life-like pictures of these same friars, which the Indians had attempted to cover with whitewash. The next day, the two Mexican Indians, Tomá and Cristóbal, offered their services to Oñate as interpreters and guides.

Oñate and his party left the friendly pueblos and, traveling north, reached the Santo Domingo Pueblo a few miles south of present-day Santa Fe. From there Oñate sent his cousin, Captain Juan de Zaldívar, back for the rest of the wagons and the colonists.

Submitting to God, the Indians of Santo Domingo welcomed the Spanish and made friends with them. Oñate and the friars went from pueblo to pueblo

establishing the Spanish authority and religion. The friendliness which had been shown by several explorers who had come into the country since the expedition under Coronado helped Oñate in many ways in dealing with the pueblos. He was also assisted by the two Mexican Indians acting as interpreters.

A conference of the pueblos was held in July 1598, at which time they pledged their allegiance to the Spanish King. In September, a second conference was held to establish the religious missions of New Mexico, and the presidents of the missions were designated. Seven of the missionaries were commissioned to Christianize the Apaches and other wandering tribes. This was a dangerous task, and many lost their lives while performing their duty for God. It is remarkable how effective these priests were, given that the tribes themselves were almost at war. The priests knew nothing of the various Indian languages, and it was indeed an almost impossible task to convert the tribes to Christianity. Trusting in the power of God, they departed to their separate fields of work.

First Capital of New Mexico. In July 1598, the expedition traveled northward and arrived at the old pueblo settlement of Yungueyunge (YUGE-uingge) (The Village of the Ravine) on the west bank of the Rio Grande, north of the present town of Española. The people at the village welcomed Oñate, voluntarily gave up their town to the Spanish, and joined their pueblo brothers at Ohkey unge (OKE-uingge) (later called San Juan) across the river. For their courtesy in permitting the people of Yungueyunge to live at San Juan, the Span-

A scene in the fertile valley of the Rio Grande, near Bernalillo, New Mexico. The Sandia Mountains in the background were once landmarks on the trail during Oñate's journey into northern New Mexico.

ish named the village San Juan de los Caballeros (St. John of the Knights, or Gentlemen).

By the end of July 1598, besides occupying ancient Yungueyunge, Don Juan de Oñate built a city and named it San Francisco de los Españoles. Later the name of the town was changed to San Gabriel, and it was the first Spanish settlement in the Southwest and the first capital of New Mexico. Thirty-three years before Oñate settled San Gabriel, though, the Spanish constructed the town of St. Augustine, Florida, in 1565, which is the oldest city in North America.

The location of San Gabriel was an excellent site since there was a great deal of fertile land and good facilities for irrigation. Today, all that remains of the town is a monument, located on the west bank of the Rio Grande, identifying the site of the first capital of New Mexico.

Shortly after the Spanish settled at San Gabriel, the pueblo country was divided into districts, and a priest was assigned to each district. A mission was built in each district to identify the new faith. The labors of the priest were long and tiresome, for they did not have as many comforts as they had expected, and it was a very difficult matter for the priests to influence the Pueblo Indians to abandon the religion conducted in their kivas.

Oñate, however, was very confident of the eventual success of his project. He made several trips to pueblos in the outlying districts. He traveled to Pecos and other pueblos in that area, and he received oaths of obedience from the natives. He explored the country to the west near the great pueblo of Zia. He also journeyed to the Jemez Pueblo, and in his explorations he discovered the famous sulphur spring of that area. All the pueblos he visited eventually

Left—Aerial View of San Gabriel during University of New Mexico excavation in 1962.

Below—View of excavated wall of San Gabriel.

Bottom—Monument Cross of "Oñate's capital."

accepted the Spanish as their rulers.

In August of 1598, Oñate began work on the construction of a chapel and the building of irrigation and supply ditches for the settlement of San Gabriel. There were over 1,500 Indians who helped build the system. Despite the aid of the Indians, some settlers were disenchanted with their new life. There were times when some of the men were ready to give up the irrigation project, leave the town of San Gabriel, and return to Mexico. But with the strong will of Oñate and the determination of many of the colonists, the project of building the town was continued. On September 8, 1598, the church of San Juan Bautista was dedicated at San Gabriel; this was followed by an elaborate ceremony of festivities and sports which lasted for one week.

Early Expedition to the Hopi Villages

An expedition was sent in 1598 to explore the region to the west as far as the Hopi villages located in the present state of Arizona. During the trip west-

Zuñi Pueblo has not changed much in appearance since the time of Oñate.

ward. Oñate stopped at Ácoma Pueblo, and most of the natives welcomed the Spanish. One chief, Zutucapan, was opposed to submission to the Spanish, but he was overruled by others of more influence among the leaders of the pueblo.

From Ácoma, Oñate traveled to Zuñi, and soon this pueblo accepted Spanish authority. Here Oñate not only found the crosses that had been erected by Coronado more than 50 years earlier, but he also met the Mexican Indians left by him at that village.

They traveled to the Moqui (Hopi) villages, and from there Oñate sent out an expedition under Captain Farfán in search of mines and salt deposits. These were found several miles to the west. Oñate, feeling certain that the ocean was near, sent word to Don Juan de Zaldívar to bring thirty soldiers and join him in Hopiland.

Battle of Ácoma

Zaldívar started to join Oñate as he was commanded. Meanwhile at Ácoma, Chief Zutucapan still remained hostile and succeeded in gaining a following to resist the Spanish whenever they returned. When Zaldívar reached Ácoma on his way to join Oñate, the Indians came out to greet him. It appeared to Zaldívar that the Indians were anxious to assist them since they offered supplies and made every effort to show they were friends. Then, suddenly, there was a loud shout, and the Indians in a surprise attack caught their enemy off guard. A tremendous battle ensued and lasted for three hours; Zaldívar was killed during hand-to-hand combat with Zutucapan. Five Spaniards, driven to the edge of the cliff, leaped over; four of them escaped with small bruises. In all, nineteen survived the battle of Ácoma.

The messengers returned to San Gabriel and reported the incident. Once this news reached Oñate, he immediately set out for the capital city. As soon as Oñate arrived at San Gabriel, he called his best officers and the priests into council to decide what action should be taken against the Indians of Ácoma. The decision was made to attack the pueblo, to burn the town, to take prisoners, and to enslave all who resisted.

In January 1599, Don Vincente de Zaldívar, brother of the slain officer at

Ácoma, selected sixty soldiers, left the capital city, and camped on the plains near Ácoma. That night plans were made to attack the pueblo. The Spanish discovered that there were two ways to enter the mesa village. Zaldívar selected twelve men to enter a pass in one direction and sent the remaining force to attack the main entrance.

Early the next morning, the main army began its attack near the first entrance to Ácoma. During the attack, the twelve soldiers led by Zaldívar began their hazardous climb up the side of the cliff. As soon as they reached the top, Zaldívar and his companions maneuvered into position to assist the main army in the attack. Soon, reinforcements arrived, and the Indians were attacked from two sides. The battle lasted for nearly three days, and several hundred Indians were killed. During the third and final day of battle, the Spanish set fire to the pueblo. This act and the knowledge of many Indians who had fallen in battle caused the Ácoma chief to surrender. Only 600 Indians of the original 2,000 survived the battle.

The Spanish took several hundred of

Above. A narrow trail, cut In rock, leads up the sheer-sided mesa to Ácoma Indian Pueblo, New Mexico's famed "Sky City." The Spanish made their way through this pass during the battle and defeated the Indians.

Ácoma pueblo, as it probably looked during the Spanish occupation of New Mexico.

Ruins of the Mission Church of the now deserted Pecos Pueblo. This pueblo, one of the largest in the state when Oñate arrived in 1598, was occupied until 1837, when its few surviving inhabitants moved to the pueblo of Jemez.

the Indians as prisoners and made them slaves. As an additional punishment to the Indians, Oñate ordered the right foot of each male Ácoma Indian to be cut off. When the news reached other Indians about the defeat at Ácoma— the strongest fortress among the pueblos —the Indians felt further resistance to the Spanish was uselesss.

However, the Pueblo Indians never forgot the terrible defeat and suffering that occurred at Ácoma and in other pueblos. Many years later the pueblos banded together and drove the Spanish from their land.

Oñate in the East

When the report of Oñate's success reached the King of Spain, he immediately ordered the viceroy to give as much support as possible to the colony of New Mexico. Men and equipment were sent to Oñate to assist him in further explorations. The colonists seemed contented with the country as a home, and the priests were provided a field for their labors in the cause of Christianity. The colonists seemed happy with the new policy of good will in dealing with the Indians and were not particularly interested in exploration. Oñate, on the other hand, became somewhat restless and was anxious to begin new explorations.

In 1601, Oñate and a force of eighty men left San Gabriel and headed northeast over the plains. His route was similar to that followed by Coronado some 60 years before.

On his journey, Oñate visited the Pecos Pueblo and continued his march to the great plains near the Canadian River. He found a group of Indians whom he called Apache (enemy). These people lived in bell-shaped tents made of bright red and white tanned hides with flaps and openings. The tents were

90

huge, more than 9 feet (3 m.) in diameter at the base. To drag the tent poles, supplies of meat, and maize, the Indians used dogs since only the Spanish at this time had horses. The Apache were mostly hunters and moved about, often following buffalo.

A great battle was fought in the plains with a tribe of Escanjaques Indians. More than 1,000 of the Indians were killed, and many Spanish soldiers lay dead or wounded. Realizing that his force was too small to continue, Oñate decided to return to San Gabriel.

Upon his return to the capital city, he found it almost deserted, except for a few priests and some Indians from nearby villages. According to the priest, Friar Escalona, in his report to the viceroy, Oñate had taken all the supplies, and he did not allow any planting for support of the town. In addition there had been no rain, and everyone had been forced to live on wild seeds. Oñate was furious over the state of affairs and made plans to have the colonists returned to San Gabriel. Those who deserted were condemned to death, but none were ever caught. This conflict was the beginning of the frustrations and problems Oñate faced as governor and contributed to his eventual removal.

Oñate in the West

The prosperity of the colony gradually returned, and Oñate made plans to

Hopi towns, Shipolovi and part of Mishongnovi from the rock east of Mishongnovi, Arizona. Many Hopi Indians still occupy the five villages, and life continues much as it did during the days of Oñate in 1598.

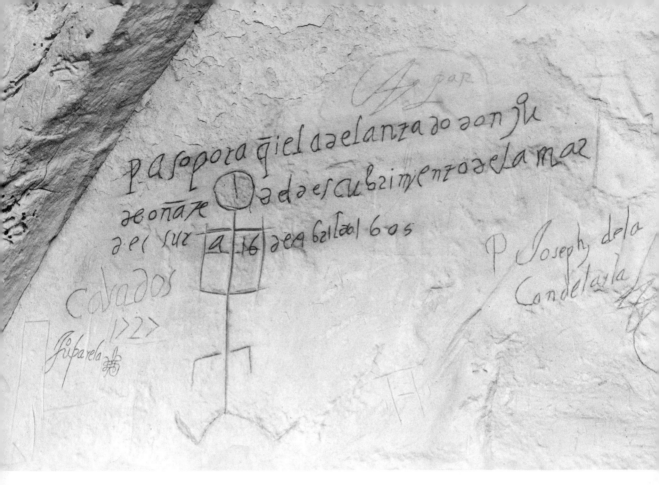

History is recorded on the cliffs of El Morro National Monument, often called Inscription Rock, in northwestern New Mexico. Such hardy adventurers of the 17th century as Oñate and deVargas have inscribed the dates of their encampment here. Dates inscribed on the rock extend back to 1605.

explore the west. On October 7, 1604, Oñate and thirty men headed for the west, stopping for a short time at the Zuñi Pueblo. From the Zuñi Pueblo, they traveled west to the five Moqui (Hopi) towns made up of 450 houses. These Hopi villages are located in the present-day state of Arizona. The people were dressed in cotton, and they farmed the nearby land.

Continuing their journey, the Spanish came in sight of the River Colorado Chiquito ("Little Colorado"). The river was so named because of its red color. The Indians informed them that the river flowed into a larger body of water, Rio Colorado, which finally reached the great ocean. The Spanish followed the river westward where it joined with the great river from the north. Turning south, Oñate and his companions followed the river which flowed into a very fertile and attractive country. This region was the home of a tribe of Indians who wore little crosses hanging from the hair on the forehead; the Spanish, therefore, named them the Cruzados.

The Indians told the Spanish that, many years before, a Franciscan priest had visited their lands. The priest taught them the meaning of the cross in making friends, not only to God, but with all white and bearded men who might one day appear. The Cruzados offered help and assistance to the Spanish, and some became guides.

Another tribe, called the Amajava (Mojave), became friendly with the Spanish as they traveled south along the Colorado River. The Mojave Desert, between Arizona and California, got its name from this Indian tribe.

In January 1605, Oñate and his men finally reached the mouth of the Colorado, which empties into the Gulf of California. Here he found a good harbor formed by an island in the center.

After his discovery of the "Sea of the South" (actually the Gulf of California), Oñate and his soldiers began their long march homeward to San Gabriel. During the journey to San Gabriel, Oñate stopped at El Morro, or "Inscription Rock" as it is called today, and carved his name on the side of the cliff. The inscription reads, "Passed by here the Governor Don Juan de Oñate, from the discovery of the Sea of the South on the 16th of April, 1605." The expedition finally arrived at San Gabriel on April 25, 1605.

Very little is known of Oñate's acts in New Mexico after he returned from exploring the west. In 1608 his son, Don Cristóbal de Oñate, was assigned as Governor until a new one was appointed by the King. In 1610, Don Pedro de Peralta was appointed Governor of New Mexico. By that time, more than 8,000 Indians had been converted to the Christian faith.

Founding of Santa Fe

La Villa Real de la Santa Fé de San Francisco, the oldest capital city in the United States, was founded between 1605 and 1610. Most authorities accept the date 1610 as the formal establishment of the present city of Santa Fe. Don Pedro de Peralta was the first appointed governor of the settlement.

In 1610, the Palace of the Governors was the first major goverment building erected in Santa Fe. For nearly three centuries this building was the seat of government for the Spanish, the Mexicans, and the Americans. The old Palace is now the Museum of New Mexico. During the Spanish period, the church of San Miguel was constructed, and it is probably the oldest continually used church in the United States. The oldest house in the city was originally built by the Pueblo Indians many years before the coming of the Spanish. A regular mission service was established in 1610, which opened a major route between Santa Fe and Mexico City.

In 1617, the governor asked for aid to help build the new seat of government. At this time, the friars had constructed eleven churches, converted more than 14,000 Indians, and prepared as many more for conversion. Only forty-eight soldiers and settlers in the town aided in the work of building and keeping peace with the Indians.

In 1620, a royal decree of the King of Spain required each pueblo, at the close of the calendar year, to choose by popular vote a governor, lieutenant governor, and other officials as needed to carry on the affairs of the pueblo. The decree stated that governors were to take their oath of office during the first week of the new year. A silver-headed cane (vara) was given to each pueblo governor as a symbol of his commission

The Palace of the Governors, which forms the northern side of the town plaza in Santa Fe, is the oldest public building in the United States. One of nine state monuments in New Mexico, the building was constructed in 1610. The Spanish, Mexican, and United States governments have all used it as the capitol building since that time. The building has housed the Museum of New Mexico since 1909.

and authority, with the cross on the silver mount symbolizing the support of the Church. The Franciscan mission of San Antonio de Isleta was established in 1621. Many towns, churches, and forts had already been established about the time the Pilgrims landed on the coast of Massachusetts.

By 1632, according to Friar Alonzo Benavides, there were about fifty priests serving over 60,000 Indians who had become Christians. These Indians lived in ninety pueblos and were grouped in twenty-five missions. The pueblos were easily controlled, and the inhabitants brought corn and cotton to support Santa Fe, then a town of 250 Spaniards.

Troubled Years

The next 15 years were filled with disagreement between the governors of New Mexico and the religious leaders. The main differences were over the civil laws, which many times conflicted with the laws of the Church. Religious agents were sent from Spain to settle the problem.

Governor Don Diego Peñalosa, in 1664, was relieved of his duties in New Mexico because of his conflict with the

San Miguel Mission, in Santa Fe, New Mexico, is the oldest mission Church in the United States. It was built by Spanish Franciscan friars in the early days of the seventeenth century and was one of the few missions to escape destruction during the Pueblo Indian Revolt in 1680.

Franciscan friars. He intended to explore in the north and east, but he was forbidden to do so by the Church. Instead, charges were brought against him; he was fined and imprisoned.

Religious difficulties among the Indians resulted in many outbreaks against the Spaniards. The first recorded outbreak was caused by the whipping, imprisonment, and hanging of forty Indians who refused to give up their native religion and become Catholics. The uprising was stopped soon after the hangings. Later, an uprising of the Jemez and Apache was crushed with twenty-nine Indians being caught and punished.

By 1650, conditions had grown worse, with the pueblos of Jemez, Isleta, San Felipe, and Cochiti, together with the Apache, intending to force the Spanish out of New Mexico. The plot was discovered, and nine of the leaders were hanged; others were sold into slavery. Soon after, plans for a general revolt were outlined at Taos on deerskin and circulated to the other pueblos. The plot failed because the Hopi refused to join. Many Taos Indians then fled to a pueblo in Scott County, Kansas.

The Spanish continued to use force to convert the Indians to Christianity. On one occasion in the 1670s, four Indians were hanged and forty-three were whipped and enslaved. A Spanish court claimed that the Indians had bewitched the superior of the Franciscan Monastery at San Ildefonso Pueblo.

In 1679, the worsening of relations was reported to the viceroy in Mexico City. The Apache were raiding towns and pueblos, destroying the settlements, and burning the churches. Many Spaniards and converted Indians were killed. Those who were captured were hanged or sold into slavery. The Spanish had provided very little protection for the pueblos and settlers. There were only five men for every frontier station, and these stations were sadly in need of arms and horses. Concerned about this grave situation, the governor of Santa Fe requested a force of 100 soldiers and additional supplies to be sent from Mexico City to stop the raids made by the Apache. By 1680, the relief column had assembled at Mexico City and prepared to leave for Santa Fe.

Pueblo Revolt. Meanwhile, a new threat to the Spanish was carefully being plotted in northern New Mexico by Popé, a San Juan Indian who had made Taos Pueblo his headquarters. He and his followers were preparing to destroy the Spanish settlements throughout the territory. Popé, who was called "Espejo" (Looking Glass) by the Spanish because he was able to predict the future, was an outstanding religious leader and prophet. He and his followers were preparing to unite the pueblos and begin a religious war against the Spanish. The Governor, Don Antonio de Otermín, was in a very serious position, and he felt certain that this new uprising would take place at any moment.

Popé was a man of great ability who demonstrated great influence over the Indians. He traveled over the country, speaking to the Pueblo Indians and telling them about the wrongs they were suffering. He told them that he

was commissioned by the Great Father and Chief of all the Pueblos to rid them of the Spanish and priests forever. He said he prayed in the great kiva at Taos, and the supernatural beings had told him to unite all the pueblos to fight their common enemy. He further informed them that he was to make a rope and tie in the number of knots that represented the number of days before the revolt would take place. The rope was to be taken to each pueblo, and each pueblo chief would then know when to prepare for battle. The day set was August 13, 1680. Everything was conducted with great secrecy, and steps were taken to prevent the Spanish from knowing their plans. Popé's own son-in-law, Nicolas Bua, governor of the San Juan Pueblo, fell under suspicion. Fearing he might inform the Spanish, Popé put him to death with his own hands.

Four days before the revolt, the Indians of San Lazaro, in south Santa Fe County, revealed the plot to the priest stationed there. The priest immediately informed Otermín, the Governor of Santa Fe, that the Pueblo Indians planned a revolt against the Spanish. Otermín sent messengers in all directions, requesting the settlers to return to the capital city. By this time, however, Popé had discovered that his plans were known to the Spanish and made ready his attack upon the scattered settlements in northern New Mexico on August 10, 1680, three days earlier than originally planned. The plan of Popé was to completely do away with all the Spanish in New Mexico. With this in mind, no man, woman, or child was to be spared. Those who

This ruin is all that remains of a large mission church built in 1617 by Spanish missionaries at the old pueblo of Giusewa. The pueblo and the mission were later abandoned in the face of attack by hostile Navajos. The ruins are set aside today as the Jemez State Monument, near the town of Jemez Springs, New Mexico.

did not find safety in hiding or escaping to Santa Fe were tortured and put to death.

The Indians began their seige of Santa Fe on August 15. They cut off the water supply, and after a series of vicious attacks which lasted for five days, the Spanish prepared to leave the city. With 1,950 men, women, and children survivors, Otermín left Santa Fe on August 21, 1680, and headed for Isleta Pueblo, located south of the present city of Albuquerque. The Indians entered Santa Fe, burning everything that was in sight, including the church. The only building left standing was the Governor's Palace, which was to be occupied by Popé when the Spanish were defeated. In the course of the rebellion, many colonists, Indians, and missionaries were killed.

When Otermín and the survivors of Santa Fe arrived at Isleta Pueblo, they found the village deserted. The next morning they left the town and headed south, where, several weeks later, they met the relief column near the town of Mesilla, south of Las Cruces. This was the supply train that was to provide support for the defense of Santa Fe. Before the end of September, the entire force had arrived at El Paso. It was determined in a special council that El Paso was to serve as the capital of New Mexico. From here, attempts would be made to reconquer Santa Fe. The reconquest, however, would not be accomplished for 12 years.

Some attempts were made to conquer Santa Fe. The first was under the leadership of Governor Otermín. Marching up the Rio Grande, he attacked the Isleta Pueblo. Within a few hours the pueblo was in the hands of the Spanish, and the Indians again accepted the Christian faith. When the Indians in the north received news of the Spanish invaders, they immediately gathered together an army and forced the Spanish to retreat to El Paso. The priests, on the other hand, were busy constructing missions in El Paso and nearby Indian villages. From here, new missionaries would be sent out to reestablish the lost mission field of New Mexico as soon as Santa Fe was recaptured.

French in the Southwest

Spanish plans to reconquer New Mexico were delayed in the 1680s by news of the French advance into Texas. The concern of Spanish officials in Mexico shifted from Indians in New Mexico to the French intrusion in the Southwest. For years, the French dominated the vast area of the Mississippi River northward into Canada. Now, since the Spanish were defeated by the Indians, the French felt it was the right time to establish a colony in the Southwest and gain complete control of the Mississippi River. French interest around the Mississippi caused great concern in Mexico City. Several expeditions were sent eastward in an effort to stop the gains of Spanish rivals. But, by 1684, the only Spanish settlements in present Texas were Ysleta, which was actually a relocated Indian pueblo, and El Paso, both considered to be in New Mexico.

Leading the French into the Southwest was René Robert Cavelier, Sieur de La Salle, a French explorer. He had established a fur-trading empire in the Great Lakes region, and now he was interested in further conquests. As early as 1682, he had traveled down the Mississippi to its mouth. Thinking that he was the discoveror of the Delta, he took possession of the river and its entire basin. He named the "Great Valley"

Louisiana in honor of his King, Louis XIV of France. He returned to France, hoping to make Louisiana a major shipping center for his fur trade.

While in France, he became acquainted with Peñalosa, a former governor of Santa Fe who had been relieved of his duties because of a conflict with the clergy. The Spanish government refused him any support for further explorations; therefore Peñalosa turned to the French for help. The French listened to the plan proposed by Peñalosa to explore the Southwest. However, the King of France decided to send La Salle to explore certain areas of the Southwest and establish a colony at the Mississippi.

La Salle set sail from France with 300 men on four vessels in late 1684. He sailed into the Gulf of Mexico, missed his bearing, passed the Mississippi River, and landed at Matagorda Bay, Texas. One disaster after another brought disorder to the new colony. In January 1687, La Salle set out upon an exploration to determine his location and find the Mississippi River. He took with him some of the colonists who, by this time, were filled with hatred toward their leader. At a point somewhere near the Brazos River, some of the men turned upon La Salle and put him to death. Several of the surviving colonists made their way to the Mississippi River and to the Great Lakes by canoe, finally arriving at Quebec, where they told of the disaster of the Mississippi colony. Those who were left at the colony were never heard from again.

The Spanish had received word about the French colony and sent an expedition to the east to drive out the invaders. By 1691, the Spanish had established a mission on the Trinity River in Texas, some 45 miles (72 km.) southwest of the present town of Nacogdoches. The mission was a failure, and the friars returned to Mexico. For the next 20 years, in the absence of any threat of French presence, the Spanish relaxed in their efforts to establish settlements in southeast Texas.

Spanish Reconquest of New Mexico

During the years from 1681 to 1692, the Spanish continued efforts to regain the territory of New Mexico. Every attempt by the Spanish, though, resulted in defeat by the Indians or lack of necessary supplies to carry on their campaigns.

Popé, meanwhile, was enjoying his new station among the Indians. He made tours throughout the entire country to see that everything was put in a proper state of defense to resist any attempt made by the Christians to return. At every pueblo he made certain that his laws were enforced. On his tour, dressed in full Indian costume, he wore a bull's horn on his forehead. At first he was received with great honor throughout the pueblos. Later, his rule became very harsh and oppressive, often resulting in death to those who disobeyed him. He told them they need have no fear of the Spaniards because he had stationed guards on the three roads leading to the capital city. He said he would build strong walls that reached from the earth to the heavens, and if they entered by any other road, he would surround them with darkness, take them without arms, and put them to death. These programs outlined by Popé never materialized, and the Indians grew more hostile toward their leader. Civil wars developed;

there was a severe drought; their gods did not give them aid when called upon; the wild tribes were no longer friendly and taking advantage of their perilous times, they began to raid and murder. Tribes were scattered, pueblos abandoned, and others moved to different areas. New leaders were chosen, and gradually Popé lost his power over the pueblos. Popé died in 1688, and a new chief, Tu-pa-tu, was chosen as ruler.

In 1690, Don Diego de Vargas was appointed governor of the province, and he immediately prepared for a campaign against the Indians in the north. All he could muster for the reconquest of New Mexico was 300 armed men, including Indians. The army, beginning its march in August 1692, was accompanied by four friars.

De Vargas marched quickly up the Rio Grande, passing all of the pueblos and finding them in ruins. He stopped only for necessary rest and sleep since he was determined to take the enemy by surprise and crush them before any defense could be made. The military force passed by the Santo Domingo and Cochiti pueblos, both abandoned, and on the morning of September 13, 1692 the army appeared before Santa Fe. The Spanish military force immediately surrounded the town and cut off both the water supply and all communications with the outside. The Indians refused to surrender, declaring they would rather die in battle than be punished by the Spanish. De Vargas, ably assisted by the priests, discussed peace agreements with the Indians and offered them full pardon for their crime of rebellion; that evening the Indians surrendered.

Late in October, an army was sent to Ácoma and Zuñi, west of Santa Fe, and the pueblos offered very little resistance to the Spanish. At Zuñi Pueblo, the friars were much impressed at finding that the Indians had preserved all of the property of the priests who had given their lives many years before in the cause of Christianity. This was the only pueblo that had preserved any respect for the teaching of Christianity. During the early campaigns in northern New Mexico, de Vargas brought all of the pueblos under the authority of the Spanish, without the loss of blood, except in the conflicts with the Apache.

The next year, de Vargas returned to Santa Fe with more than 1,600 settlers, including 18 friars and 100 soldiers. The Indians did not trust the governor, and they would not permit the Spaniards to enter the city. Shortly thereafter, de Vargas ordered his command to advance on the capital. The soldiers stormed the walls, smashed down the gate, and defeated the Indians; Santa Fe once more was under the control of the Spanish. Indian reinforcements appeared, but they were soon scattered by the Spanish cavalry. After the battle, 70 of the Indian leaders were executed, and 400 Pueblo women and children were made slaves.

The surrender of the Indians was shortlived, however, and for the next few years many bloody battles took place. The Indians of Taos, Jemez, Zuñi, and Ácoma carried on several campaigns against the Spanish, in which many on both sides lost their lives. Raiding their supply wagons and scattered settlements, the Ute and Apache were also a constant threat to the Spanish.

In 1695, 1,500 colonists were brought to Santa Fe to build additional homes and settle new communities. A permanent highway system was established between Mexico City and Santa Fe.

This historical event staged before the Palace of the Governors in Santa Fe reenacts de Vargas's conquest of New Mexico in 1693 and his reading of the royal proclamation in the plaza.

El Camino Real (King's Highway or Royal Highway) was established as a means to supply the new settlements and to bring new colonists to the frontier of New Mexico.

In 1696, because of a severe drought, famine occurred and the people were on the verge of starvation. Every kind of animal and herb was used for food. Supplies finally arrived in time to save the colony.

The term of office of de Vargas ended in 1697, and the king named Pedro Rodríguez Cubero to succeed him. De Vargas did not receive reappointment as governor of Santa Fe because the friars had accused him of neglect in his dealings with the Indians. They alleged his neglect had resulted in several uprisings and a famine. They further stated in their report to the king of Spain that they had warned de Vargas of an uprising of the Pueblo Indians because he had executed Indian captives in Santa Fe. These Indians were the leaders involved in the early battles before the pueblos finally surrendered. He was further charged with having sold a portion of the food supply in the south for his own private gain; this act contributed to the famine in 1696 and almost destroyed the com-

Don Diego de Vargas Zapata Lujan Ponce de León y Contreras, Marquis de La Nova de Barcinas, governor of the province of New Mexico. In 1692, he and his men marched up the Rio Grande and reconquered Santa Fe.

munity of Santa Fe.

The unfounded charges against de Vargas by the friars resulted in his arrest by Cubero, who kept him in jail for three years. Cubero also fined him 4,000 pesos and seized all his property — all without giving the man a hearing. Without a doubt, Cubero and other government officials united in a conspiracy against de Vargas, probably through spite and jealousy.

De Vargas was not even permitted an appeal to the viceroy, which was a privilege guaranteed by Spanish law to even the lowest commoner. But finally a priest, friend and *custodio* (prison confessor and protector), Fray Vargas — no relative of the ex-governor —

went to Mexico City and laid the whole matter before the viceroy. After discussing the matter with Fray Vargas, the viceroy reported his findings to the King. Several months later, the King ordered an impartial hearing and directed Cubero to permit the prisoner to go to Mexico City without bail to state his case to the viceroy.

After formal investigations were conducted by the Crown, de Vargas was pardoned by the King and reinstated to his former position as governor of Santa Fe. On a military engagement in the Sandia Mountains against the Apache, he became ill and died at Bernalillo on April 4, 1704. He was buried at Santa Fe.

REVIEW ACTIVITIES

1. Prepare a report on the daily life in a mission.
2. Write a report on the important differences between the expeditions of Coronado and Oñate.
3. How was the colonization of New Mexico financed?
4. Why was Oñate's expedition into New Mexico delayed?
5. Briefly describe Oñate's travels in New Mexico.
6. Where was the first town and capital of New Mexico located?
7. Describe the Battle of Ácoma. Why was the defeat of Ácoma Pueblo so important to the Spanish?
8. Why did the Spanish bring so many priests to New Mexico?
9. When was the Palace of the Governors built in Santa Fe?
10. What was the importance of the canes given to the Pueblo governors?
11. What were some of the problems in New Mexico that brought about the Pueblo Revolt?
12. What method did Popé use to inform the other Pueblo Indians when to begin the revolt?
13. What name did the Spanish give to Popé? Why?
14. What part did the French play in the Southwest?
15. How was de Vargas able to reconquer Santa Fe?
16. Describe an important event that occurred in New Mexico on each of the following dates: 1540, 1598, 1610, 1680, and 1692.

RECOGNIZE AND UNDERSTAND

Oñate	San Gabriel
Popé	pueblo
Otermín	Hopi
La Salle	Ácoma
Peñalosa	Zuñi
de Vargas	El Morro
Peralta	kiva
Cruzados	Taos
Apache	El Camino Real

UNIT 3
SPANISH TERRITORIAL PERIOD AND THE MEXICAN EMPIRE

CHAPTER VII

Spanish Occupation of the Southwest

By the end of the seventeenth century, nearly all of the Pueblos had submitted to Spanish rule. On certain occasions, there were small uprisings by the Pueblos with very little effect upon the Spanish in New Mexico. No longer was the principal enemy a band, town, or nation of Pueblos; however, groups of Apaches, Navajos, Utes, and the newly arrived Comanches became a more serious threat to the region. The presence of so many enemies helped to draw the Spanish and Pueblos together. The unity of the Spanish and Pueblo Indians provided the opportunity necessary to establish many towns throughout the territory. The friars were encouraged by this new development and continued to expand their mission fields in the Southwest.

Further explorations became necessary to establish trade routes to distant Indian villages and new settlements that had been established. Forts were erected as protective means against the French and the English, who by this time had a permanent foothold in the East.

Missions and Towns

Reconstruction of the old missions built before 1680 was achieved, and new ones built to accommodate the many converts throughout New Mexico. California, Arizona, and Texas became part of this great missionary enterprise. During the eighteenth century, Spain became the only European nation with established towns in most of the Southwest.

Father Eusebio Kino, a Jesuit missionary, directed the building of twenty-nine missions throughout the province of Sonora, in northern Mexico, and Arizona between 1687 and the early years of the eighteenth century. One outstanding mission, called San Xavier del Bac (White Dove of the Desert), still stands today as a landmark of Spanish missionaries in Arizona. Gold and silver were discovered near the southern border of Arizona, and soon many prospectors appeared and constructed a mining camp called Arizonac, which was abandoned a few years later. This town gave Arizona its name.

In 1706, the town of San Francisco de Alburquerque was established by Governor Don Francisco Cuervo. Later, the name was changed to San Felipe de Alburquerque in honor of King Felipe V of Spain and Governor Cuervo, Duke of Alburquerque. The first "r" in

Alburquerque has long since been dropped.

During Cuervo's rule in New Mexico, small garrisons were maintained at Santa Clara, Cochiti, Jemez, and Laguna to provide protection from the hostile Apache. A Spanish cavalry post was also established at the Zuñi Pueblo to prevent further attacks by the Moqui (Hopi) pueblos. The Moqui caused the Spanish much concern because they refused to be Christianized, and they occasionally made war on nearby settlements and Christian pueblos.

France was the only major foreign nation to cause any immediate danger

The Church of San Felipe de Neri at Albuquerque was established in 1706 by Francisco Cuervo y Valdez who succeeded Don Diego de Vargas as temporary governor of New Mexico. The church fell down in the 1790s and was rebuilt on the north side of the plaza at its present location.

to the Spanish. The French were busy with their fur trade along the frontier of New Spain, particularly in the Mississippi Valley. By 1700, they had established a colony at Biloxi, near the Mississippi Delta, and in 1718, they founded New Orleans. The French claimed all the territory northward to Canada and named it Louisiana. In 1762, after the French and Indian War, all of the French territory west of the Mississippi was ceded to Spain.

Missions and presidios (forts) were established by the Spanish throughout Texas. Martin de Alarcón founded the Presidio of San Antonio de Bejar in 1718, the second oldest town in Texas, the oldest being El Paso. Fray Antonio Olivares directed the construction of a mission near the fort. Later, in 1744, a chapel was built near the mission of San Antonio de Valero, which was to be known later as the Alamo.

Towns established in California during this period included San Francisco, San Diego, Los Angeles, and Monterey.

Spanish Plan for the Indians

The Spanish developed a program to make peace with the hostile tribes on the northern frontier during the eighteenth century. This plan included five major points; not all of them were used at the same time in a given region, and usually the results would vary. The principal points of the program were:

(1) To make agreements with nomadic tribes and encourage them to settle down to a peaceful life;

(2) To encourage the Indians to accept Spanish civilization through missionary efforts;

(3) To establish towns nearby the peaceful Indians to attract the warlike tribes and show them how to live in peace;

(4) To provide grants to both the settled and nomadic Indians from royal funds; and

(5) To depend largely on Indian soldiers for the defense of the frontier.

The program, used wisely, aided in the rapid growth of the Southwest. Although the Indians generally seemed to want peace, the Navajo, who at times were on friendly terms with the Spanish, never made a formal peace treaty with the Europeans. Certain

Many of the old ways are still evident at Isleta Pueblo. Here, as well as in other pueblos, the metate and mano are used for grinding seeds.

108

Apache tribes settled down and began trading with the Spanish towns. Other Apache tribes migrated to various parts of the Southwest and continued their nomadic way of life.

During the first half of the eighteenth century, several Pueblo groups began reconstructing their former pueblos or building new ones. Some of these included the Zia, Zuñi, Hopi, San Felipe, Sandia, and Jemez. In 1706, the Picuris returned from Kansas to the present site of their pueblo. Later, in 1718, the Isleta Indians began rebuilding their pueblo where it is located today.

The rebuilding occasionally was set back by natural disaster. In 1767, a great flood engulfed the Santa Fe area, causing much hardship among the pueblos in the vicinity. Many were left homeless, and many died of disease. The area recovered within a few months, but it next suffered the disaster of a smallpox epidemic of 1780, which took the lives of many Spanish as well as Indians.

Town Life

Life on the border of New Spain represented an effort to establish Spanish customs in the New World. Many of their customs were adjusted to meet the conditions of the new environment. During early frontier life, the Spanish

This is a typical northern New Mexico home located near Chamita, one of the oldest settlements in New Mexico. Chili is harvested as a staple crop by the Spanish-Americans, and is hung to dry and to cure in the sun.

Artist's drawing of typical landowner's home in New Mexico.

government provided supplies to the settlements and missions until they were able to take care of themselves.

As time passed, however, the settlements achieved a greater degree of independence; in fact, each mission and ranch within the province became very nearly a self-sufficient unit. Each had its own orchard and garden, its cattle and sheep, its shops and tools. Homes were usually constructed of adobe made from clay found nearby. Vigas (beams) cut from nearby forests were used to support the flat, dirt roof. Hard-packed earth floors were covered with skins and homemade rugs. Furniture was made of pine or oak, on which various designs were hand carved. Beds, which were spread on the floor at night, were rolled up by the wall in the daytime to serve as a kind of sofa.

Later, when travel was made easier and ships arrived more frequently, the wealthy Spanish imported many articles from Spain.

Within the home, the Spanish family, aided by the Indian craftsmen, made most of the necessities of life. Cattle

and sheep provided meat and hides, while the sheep provided wool which could be woven into cloth for garments. In addition, cowhides made leather available for boots and harnesses. The fat of these animals was used for making candles and for cooking. Pinto beans and corn ground into flour became the principal food, which was served in a variety of tasty dishes.

Horses and donkeys were the principal beasts of burden in New Mexico. Missions and larger ranches had hundreds of them, and those that escaped were caught by the Indians for their use. In 1806, horses were so plentiful that the settlers slaughtered 7,500 in one month.

Commerce in the eighteenth century was dominated by agriculture, stock raising, and barter (a means of exchanging items without the use of money). There were not enough minerals found to justify mining operations at that time. Manufacturing was rudimentary and consisted mainly of preparing skins for home use or for a southern market, the weaving of cotton in small quantities at some pueblos, the making of pottery at others, and weaving coarse woolen blankets by the Pueblo Indians. Agricultural products, mainly from irrigated lands, were beans, maize, and wheat. Some cotton, fruit for the home, and a poor grade of tobacco known as "punche" were raised in Socorro. In the south and in the El Paso district, the major agricultural products were fruits of many varieties, grapes, and wine; these agricultural products were also found near Bernalillo in northern New Mexico.

Coins were not available to the New Mexicans in the eighteenth century, and all trade was by barter. Each year, in July or August, the people met the Comanches and other Indian tribes at Taos, and a great fair was held to exchange many goods. In January, New Mexicans went to Chihuahua to exchange goods that had been acquired through barter at the Taos fair. They usually traded for cloth and groceries for the coming year. The amount of each year's exports was valued at more than $30,000.

Land ownership encouraged many settlements in New Mexico during its early stages of development. The earliest property deeds also included permission to govern the Indians living on and near the land. These grants of Indian labor (encomienda) meant that the Indians were the labor group who worked the land in exchange for Spanish protection and education. As the years passed, the landowners acquired the lands surrounding Indian villages, and in this way each enlarged his holding, called the "hacienda." In 1720, this type of land ownership was discontinued, and a new system — grants — lasting for many years was established.

The principal types of land grants were town ownership grants, community grants, and the "sitio" or ranch grants.

The town ownership grant permitted an individual to establish a new colony. He was to take at least thirty families to a given location, map out the town, distribute the farm land, build a church, and provide a priest.

In a community grant, the title was held by ten or more families who were granted a charter to establish a new village. The grant usually contained more than 17,000 acres. Instructions were included with the grant on how to build the town. The plaza was the first thing to be decided upon; then a church site was selected on high ground near the plaza. Homesites were laid out and distributed to the settlers, and as they erected their homes they were to follow specific rules as to style and proper ventilation. Near the village, pasture lands and wood lots were set aside to be used by the community. Farm lands were divided, each family receiving an equal share, and portions of the land were set aside for future settlers. Individuals and their heirs had title to the property.

The "sitio," or ranch grant, was approximately one square mile of land to be used for grazing. Most of this land was given to outstanding citizens and politicians. Ranch owners were very wealthy and had many luxuries not enjoyed by the townspeople.

The Church played an important role in community life in New Mexico, and often the priest was the only educated man in town. The settlers came to him for marriages, baptisms, and masses; they often had the priest read letters sent to them from Spain. A fiesta (feast or celebration) was held at the church in an attempt to integrate Spanish and Indian customs.

Rules and regulations under which the people lived were provided by the government. The King was represented by the viceroy, who appointed the governors of the various provinces of New Spain. Sometimes a lieutenant-governor was named to help administrate the laws in a large province. Under the governor were three types of local administrators. In the presidio (fort), the captain had complete control over the soldiers and laborers. The

The only presidio on the frontier of New Mexico was in Santa Fe—Palace of the Governors, 1870. Built by the Spanish in the early seventeenth century, the fortress was not changed from its original construction during the Territorial Period, 1851-1912.

rural areas were supervised by *alcaldes,* justices of the peace. They settled disputes, supervised the Indians, and issued orders from the governor of the community. Larger towns usually elected a town council, called a *cabildo.* The law provided that the cabildo should administer justice, direct public works, distribute irrigation rights, carry out the royal laws, and look after the welfare of the community. Laws made by the cabildo were subject to the approval of the governor. Generally, the alcalde and the cabildo were assigned to make sure that royal laws were enforced.

New Problems for the Spanish

During the years that New Mexico and other provinces in the Southwest were in the process of expanding, conditions in the East had reached the point of revolution. The thirteen colonies along the east coast of North America rebelled against the English and won their independence.

Spain entered the war hoping to gain its objective—the conquest of Louisiana east of the Mississippi. France sided with the colonies in an attempt to regain recent losses to the British. In the final treaty, Spain got all of Florida, but the newly independent colonies claimed all the territory from the Atlantic to the Mississippi. Spain now faced a new rival, the young United States.

New efforts were made by the Spanish to protect their empire. Forts were constructed, and new trade routes were opened in an attempt to establish lines of communication between the territory of Louisiana and the Spanish Southwest. In 1786, Pedro Vial, under authorization of the governor of Texas, started from San Antonio and explored a trail to Santa Fe by way of the Red River. In 1792, Vial traveled from New Mexico down the Canadian River, crossed over

to the Arkansas River, followed it eastward to the Missouri, and went down the river to St. Louis. The next year, he returned by following the Arkansas River farther west before crossing overland to Santa Fe. Although he had chartered the path for the later Santa Fe Trail, most of the settlements were not prepared for immediate trade with one another.

At the time of Vial's explorations, a second revolution was underway, this time in France. By 1792, the French were successful in their efforts to oust the King. However, their efforts were short-lived. A new form of government was established, and Napoleon became dictator of France. By 1800, Napoleon was in full command of France and quickly restored the territory of Louisiana to France by the Treaty of San Ildefonso. Then, in 1803, Napoleon sold the Louisiana territory to the United States to get money to carry on his war in Europe. Until 1819 the problem of establishing a boundary between the United States territory and Spanish possession was an open question. Near the coast, the lines between Louisiana and Texas had been settled for many years, but in the interior no boundary had ever been established. Moreover very little was known about the region.

The Americans claimed that the Red River was the west boundary of the Louisiana territory. The Spaniards regarded the Arkansas River as the limit to the territory. At the final settlement in 1819, the Spanish proposition was accepted, and the Arkansas River, from the mountains to the Red River, became the permanent dividing line.

Early Traders

Very little trade was carried on between New Mexico and Louisiana at the turn of the nineteenth century; however, extensive trade was going on with the Indians. In 1804, William Morrison engaged a French trader, Baptiste La Lande, to carry his goods to Santa Fe. La Lande was arrested by the Spanish, taken to the capital, and later released. La Lande received such good prices for the goods that he decided to settle in Santa Fe and neglected to return the money to Mr. Morrison. In 1805, James Purcell, a Kentucky trader, left St. Louis to discuss trade agreements with the Spanish at Santa Fe. After completing his job, he also settled at the capital city and became a carpenter.

Zebulon M. Pike. President Jefferson began sending expeditions to the West in an attempt to locate the boundary line of the newly acquired land. While Lewis and Clark were engaged in their journey to the far West, Lieutenant Zebulon Pike was sent with twenty-two men in 1806 to explore the Red and Arkansas Rivers. He was instructed to make friends with the Indians he met on the way, especially the Comanches. Traveling westward, he reached the Arkansas River. He journeyed up the river to the mountains and was to return by the Red River. Late in November, he reached a high mountain in Colorado which today bears his name—Pike's Peak.

For weeks he and his men struggled over the snow-covered terrain, and at the end of January 1807, suffering from cold and hunger, the expedition reached the Rio Grande, which they thought was the Red River. He built a fort and raised the American flag, and in February a Spanish force of 100 men came to investigate the explorers. Pike was informed that he was not on the Red River, but on the Rio Grande, and, after making apologies, he promptly lowered the flag.

The Spanish were very courteous and kind, supplying food and clothing to the weary travelers. The Americans were conducted under escort to Santa Fe to appear before the governor. The people were generally kind and hospitable to Pike and his men, who were in rags after their long journey. Their clothing consisted of overalls, Indian breeches, and leather coats; they had no coverings for their heads.

After discussing his case with Governor Joaquín del Real Alencaster, Pike and his men were transferred to Chihuahua. They left the capital in March after a dinner given by the governor in their honor. The route was by way of Santo Domingo and Albuquerque to a point below Isleta, where they met Lieutenant Don Facundo Melgares, who took charge of the party. Pike and his men were well treated by Melgares during their trip, and Pike had nothing but praise for the Spanish. The entire command arrived at Chihuahua in April, and Pike and his men were taken before General Nimecio Salcedo, Commandant of Chihuahua. Here General Salcedo treated them much as Governor Alencaster had done but insisted on keeping Pike's papers.

The Americans were finally sent home under escort, leaving Chihuahua at the end of April and reaching the United States outpost of Natchidoches, Louisiana, in July. Pike wrote a book published in 1810 about New Mexico and the Southwest. He was promoted to Brigadier General before losing his life at the Battle of Toronto in 1813.

Pike's description of the New Mexico

he saw in 1807 is the best we have of the country at that time. While on their journey from the fort in southern Colorado, they passed by many villages, one being Ojo Caliente (Hot Springs), which Pike described in his book: "The Village of Ojo Caliente is situated on the eastern branch of a creek of that name; and at a distance presents a square enclosure of mud walls, the houses forming the walls. They are flat on top, or with extremely little ascent on one side, where there are spouts to carry off the water of the melting snow and rain when it falls. From this village the Indians drove off two thousand horses at one time, when at war with

Lithograph of wagon train caravan of early traders arriving in Santa Fe.

the Spaniards. The stream (Ojo Caliente Creek) is permanent, running through a valley not over half a mile in width, and watering a long, narrow strip of irrigated land."

While at Santa Fe, Pike described the capital city as it was in 1807: "Santa Fe is situated along the banks of a small creek, which comes down from the mountains, and runs west to the Rio del Norte. The length of the town on the creek may be estimated at one mile, and it is but three streets in width. Its appearance from a distance struck my mind with the same effect as a fleet of flat-bottomed boats, such as are seen in the spring and fall seasons descending the Ohio River. There are two churches, the magnificence of whose steeples forms a striking contrast to the mis-

David Meriwether, one of the early traders who came to Santa Fe in 1819, became the territorial governor of New Mexico in 1853.

erable appearance of the other buildings. On the north side of the town is the square of soldiers' houses, 120 or 140 on each side. The public square (plaza) is in the center of the town, on the north side of which is situated the palace, as they term it, or government house, with quarters for guards; the other is occupied by the clergy and public offices. In general, the houses have a shed before their front, some of which have a flooring of brick; this occasions the streets to be very narrow, being, in general, about 25 feet. The supposed population is 4,500."

Pike further mentioned the fact that there were rich paintings in the church at Santo Domingo and that an excellent bridge had been constructed at San Felipe Pueblo.

Trading, Pike reported, was as it had been for many years. The caravans left Santa Fe for El Paso and Chihuahua to exchange their goods for other products. No coins were used in the transactions since barter was the only method of exchange. All exchanging of goods, which amounted to more than $125,000 annually, took place in the south.

At the beginning of the nineteenth century, the salaries of the officers and soldiers were paid in coins, but this did not furnish a medium of exchange for the needs of the country. There was very little industry except for agriculture and ranching. There were a few Spanish artisans in the country, but most of the work was done by the Indians. The population of New Mexico in 1800 was estimated at 34,000, including the Indians.

Only a few mines were worked, one being the copper mine at Santa Rita, discovered by Lieutenant Colonel José Manuel Carrasco in 1800. Pike referred to this copper mine west of the Rio Grande as yielding 20,000 mule loads of metal annually.

The government at this time was controlled by the military, the people having little to say. The pay of a regular soldier was $240 per year. Every man was liable for military service and had to supply his own horse, arms, ammunitions, and provisions. According to Pike, the Spanish were fine soldiers, excellent horsemen, and experienced Indian fighters

More Traders from the East. Pike's account of New Mexico interested many merchants and traders from the East who were convinced that they could make a large profit on their goods from the Spanish. In 1812, Robert McKnight, with a party of ten men, crossed the plains and arrived in Santa Fe during a period of political unrest; Mexico was on the verge of a revolution to be independent from Spain. The result was that his goods were taken from him; he and his men were arrested and sent to Chihuahua to prison. They were released in 1822 by the Emperor of Mexico.

Another trader who settled in New Mexico was David Meriwether, representing the American Fur Company. He entered Santa Fe in 1819, was arrested immediately and imprisoned. He was released and, much later in 1853, became the territorial governor of New Mexico.

The year preceding Mexican independence from Spain, Captain William Becknell, another trader from the East, arrived at Santa Fe. He and his four companions sold their small supply of goods and received a huge profit. He returned East and came again in 1822 with a larger caravan.

This was the beginning of many other wagon trains traveling over the Santa Fe Trail to New Mexico with all sorts of items that were produced in the industrial cities of the United States. It was a hazardous journey, especially through the Great Plains areas where the hostile Indians constantly raided the caravans. On certain occasions, entire families would travel with the wagon trains to settle in the new territory of Louisiana. More families later came to eventually settle in New Mexico and other parts of the Southwest.

REVIEW ACTIVITIES

1. Write a report and discuss with the class the economic and social life of New Mexico at the time of Lieutenant Pike's visit.
2. Find out about the Santa Fe Trail; the course it followed, the people who traveled it, the freight they carried, and the problems they encountered.
3. What were the main ideas in the Spanish plan for dealing with the Indians?
4. Describe town life during the Spanish occupation of New Mexico. What animals were the principal beasts of burden during this time?
5. Describe home life in the Spanish communities during this period.
6. How did the people of New Mexico get the things they needed without money?
7. What were the reasons for building missions and forts by the Spanish throughout the Southwest?
8. About how many people lived in New Mexico in 1800? Contrast that with the number of people living in New Mexico today.
9. How did United States army officer Zebulon Pike happen to travel through New Mexico? Describe his travel through the territory.
10. Why were so many United States citizens arrested in New Mexico in the early 1800's?
11. What was the major reason that caused the Spanish and Pueblo Indians to become unified?
12. What did the Spanish accomplish during this period?
13. What important event took place in New Mexico on each of the following dates: 1706, 1762, 1803, 1819, and 1822.

RECOGNIZE AND UNDERSTAND

Kino	encomiendas
San Xavier del Bac	viceroy
presidio	alcaldes
Apache	cabildo
Navajo	Vial
Ute	La Lande
Comanche	Napoleon
hacienda	Alencaster
sitio	Melgares

119

CHAPTER VIII

Rule by Mexico

CONDITIONS LEADING TO WAR

The revolution in Mexico had its beginning at the town of Dolores, led by the parish priest, Don Miguel Hidalgo y Costilla, in September 1810. The revolt unleashed long-standing economic, social, and political discontent with Spanish rule. At first he was successful, but Hidalgo was captured while trying to escape to the United States in March 1811. He was convicted of treason and was shot on July 31, 1811. A monument to his memory was erected in the city of Chihuahua, Mexico. The first attempt for independence caused little concern among the people of New Mexico since the province was so far removed from Mexico. It seemed the people of New Mexico were content to await the issue or were kept from knowing about the revolution by the royal officials.

Last Years of Spanish Rule. Facundo Melgares was the last of the Spanish governors at Santa Fe, serving from 1818 to 1822. On February 24, 1821, "The Plan of Iguala" was adopted by the Mexican revolutionary forces in an effort to free themselves from Spanish rule. It included the following statements: "All inhabitants of New Spain without distinction, whether Europeans, Africans, or Indians, are citizens of this monarch, with the right to be employed in any post according to the merit and virtues. The person and property of every citizen will be respected and protected by law." At this time, Agustín Iturbide was successsful in combining the various Mexican revolutionary parties and driving the Spanish army from the country, and he declared himself Emperor of Mexico in May 1822.

Before Mexican independence was assured, the United States and Spain ratified a treaty usually referred to as the Florida Treaty. In it the United

States acquired Florida and Oregon, and Spain retained the province of Texas. The disputed border zone was eliminated by agreement to a treaty line separating Spanish territory from that of the United States. The boundary was the Sabine River in eastern Texas, from there northward to the Red River and Arkansas River, then west along the Arkansas River to the Rocky Mountains. From the headwaters of the Arkansas, the line was drawn northward to the forty-second parallel and ran west to the Pacific Ocean.

On August 24, 1821, a formal treaty called the Treaty of Córdoba was signed between Spain and Mexico. The next month, on September 27, 1821, Mexico became independent of Spain, and New Mexico became a province of Mexico. The 6th of January, 1822, was set aside for a formal celebration commemorating Mexican independence from Spain.

Following Mexico's successful revolt, local government was largely un-

An early wagon train on the Santa Fe Trail. Wagon trains such as this one arrived in Santa Fe after a long and hazardous journey over the plains.

changed in the newly acquired provinces of Mexico. However, trade was opened to a large extent with the United States, and goods began to flow along the Santa Fe Trail.

Americans Come West. While Texas was booming with merchants, traders, and settlers from the southern United States, many others were heading west to Santa Fe and California. William Becknell, "Father of the Santa Fe Trail," brought the first wagons across the plains to Santa Fe. He left Missouri, crossed the Arkansas River, and turned southwest, arriving at Santa Fe; a similar route had been followed by Pedro Vial in 1792. Hugh Glen, Thomas James, Jacob Fowler, and Colonel Benjamin Cooper were some of the prominent merchants and traders who traveled the Santa Fe Trail and made huge profits in New Mexico and other areas of the Southwest. Robert McKnight, returning to New Mexico in 1828, made a fortune in the copper mines at Santa Rita.

The traders brought a variety of cotton goods, some woolen garments, and household items. On the return trip to Independence, Missouri, they took out

These deep ruts near Watrous, New Mexico, still visible after almost 100 years, were made by heavily-laden wagons on the Santa Fe Trail, a great trade route which ran between Independence, Missouri, and Santa Fe, New Mexico, during the period 1822-1880.

beaver skins, buffalo robes, horses, mules, gold, and silver. Horses and mules were first used to bring goods and settlers to the West. Later, oxen and mules were used, four pair usually to each wagon. Missouri became famous for its mules as a result of the trade along the Santa Fe Trail.

On March 11, 1824, the Bureau of Indian Affairs was established under the Department of War by the United States government. After that time, a military patrol accompanied the wagon trains over the dangerous trail through the Great Plains area. In 1829, William and Charles Bent, while traveling the western end of the Santa Fe Trail, were attacked by hostile Indians and had to be rescued by Ewing Young, another eastern trader at Taos. While at Taos, the Bents met an old friend, Cerán St. Vrain, and together they decided to build a fort and rest station on the trail. The "halfway house," or Bent's Fort, as it was called, provided some protection during the most dangerous part of the journey; it also served as a trading post for trappers and traders with the Indians. The fort was located near the present town of La Junta, Colorado, and the route followed was called the mountain route.

Later, after 1835 when Las Vegas, New Mexico, was founded, a southern route was established, and that town became the first Mexican village to be entered by the wagon trains from the East. In 1851, Fort Union was constructed for both military and civilian ventures in New Mexico on the southern route of the Santa Fe Trail.

Besides the regular traders who came to New Mexico, there were others of various nationalities seeking rich lands to farm and to graze cattle. Doctors, ministers, gold seekers, outlaws, and many others from all walks of life came to the Southwest. Gold was found first in the Sangre de Cristo Mountains near Santa Fe in 1828. Later that same year gold was found at Taos and Abiquiu. The fur trade, having been established earlier by the French in the north central United States and Canada, attracted another group who came to be known as Mountain Men. These hunters and trappers were fearless and rugged men. Dressed in buckskin, they carried the "long rifle" to pave new trails into the woodlands of the Rocky Mountains in search of adventures and furs. The sale of furs, especially beaver, was a great industry, and a great amount of money was made from these pelts at the Eastern markets. These men made Taos their headquarters for selling furs and losing their profits at the local gambling houses. These trail-blazers who preferred the vast wilderness to civilization did much to promote the opening and development of this country. Many Blacks were among the Mountain Men. By 1824, the streams were so thoroughly cleared of beaver that the New Mexico governor banned their further trapping in that area, and the men were required to go elsewhere to trap fur.

In 1826 a famous mountain man, Christopher (Kit) Carson, arrived in Santa Fe. He soon earned a reputation as a greatly skilled hunter, trapper, Indian fighter, trail blazer, and guide in northern New Mexico. He worked a short time for Robert McKnight in 1828 at the Santa Rita copper mine, located in Grant County, New Mexico. The next year he and Ewing Young opened up the fur trade along the Gila River in

Camp near the Old State House during the days of the settlement of New Mexico.

Arizona and returned in 1830 with pelts valued at $24,000. During his lifetime, he played an important role in keeping peace with the Indians, and he became one of New Mexico's outstanding figures.

Unrest in New Mexico. The years immediately following Mexican independence opened the way for hundreds of settlers and plantation owners to come to New Mexico and Texas. Texas was open territory with only a few scattered Mexican villages located in the south. New Mexico was heavily settled in the north because Santa Fe was the leading commercial center of the Southwest. During the early 1830s, the commercial promise of New Mexico

waned. Heavy import duties were placed upon shipments coming to New Mexico, and profits on trading decreased sharply. Eastern goods, which were preferred over the ones coming in from Mexico, were always in demand in Santa Fe.

The provisions in the Treaty of Córdoba were not carried out in New Mexico; therefore, many of the people in the provinces were turning towards the East for those things that Mexico could not or would not supply. During the twenty-five years of Mexican rule, governmental authority was very unstable in the departments (provinces) throughout the empire. The Mexican Constitution of 1824 provided little assistance

to the empire since it was never enforced. Riots and assassinations in Mexico brought about a military dictatorship during the 1830s.

A newspaper, *El Crepúsculo de la Libertad* (Dawn of Liberty), was established by Antonio Barreiro in 1834 in Taos. The newspaper, an attempt to explain the ideals of liberty and freedom during the shaky period of Mexican rule, lasted for one month. However, when the Americans arrived and occupied New Mexico, the newspaper *El Crepúsculo* was re-established as The Taos News.

By this time more than 20,000 settlers from the east had located in Texas. These people, accustomed to

freely exercising their rights, resented the social and legal restrictions under which they found themselves. On March 2, 1836, Texas declared its independence from Mexico; soon after General Santa Anna, President of Mexico, was on his way to that province to put down the revolt. He lay siege to the Alamo, a mission the Texans used as a fort. Many colonists died there including Davy Crockett and Jim Bowie. In April of the same year, Sam Houston defeated General Santa Anna at San Jacinto Creek and declared Texas a free and independent republic. Texas then requested permission to be admitted to the United States. However, Texas allowed slavery in the republic, and since strong opposition existed in the United States against admitting slave states, President Jackson denied the request.

In 1837, New Mexico had its revolutionary movement. It was, to some extent, a revolt against central authority, direct taxation, and the heavy import duty place on goods coming into Santa Fe from the East. The actions of Governor Albino Perez caused a great deal of discontent and hatred among the people. Some of his special acts, such as undue punishment of the Indians and settlers and laying new taxes, made him very unpopular.

On August 1, 1837, a mob released an Indian alcalde of a northern town who had been imprisoned on some unpopular charge. Soon after, a crowd composed largely of Pueblo Indians made plans to drive the Mexican governor out of Santa Fe. Word reached Perez at Santa Fe, and with about 150 soldiers and some friendly warriors from San Juan and Santo Domingo, he marched northward to meet the revolutionaries at the mesa of San Ildefonso. During the battle, Governor Perez and twelve of his companions were killed, and those who remained joined the rebels. José Gonzales, a Pueblo Indian of Taos (genizaro), was elected governor and occupied the palace at Santa Fe. Within a few days, an army from Mexico commanded by Manuel Armijo marched to Santa Fe. Greatly outnumbered, Gonzales fled the city and camped near San Ildefonso. Armijo entered Santa Fe and proclaimed himself acting governor. Reinforcements arrived from Mexico as added protection against the revolutionaries. The rebels, after they had assembled at San Ildefonso, were defeated in battle on January 27, 1838. Gonzales and several of his men were captured and shot. In recognition of his services, Armijo was appointed governor of Santa Fe, a position he held for eight years.

Besides the revolution of 1837, the only other important conflict of that period in New Mexico was the capture of the Texas-Santa Fe expedition of 1841. The Texans believed their territory extended to the Rio Grande, and they intended to exercise their right of authority over the people within the boundaries of Texas. The Texans set out for Santa Fe with 300 men under the command of Brigadier-General Hugh McLeod. Later, they claimed the expedition was not a military action but merely an attempt to open trade with Santa Fe and to make a treaty for friendly relations between New Mexico and the Republic of Texas. They left Austin in June, and in September, after a long and tiresome journey, they arrived on the New Mexico frontier.

Governor Armijo, having been warned of a possible invasion by the Texans, prepared an early defense. Troops were dispatched immediately under Don Demasio Salazar, who captured a large number of the intruders and confined them in prison. Later, they were escorted to Mexico under heavy guard; after several months of being chained and performing work duties, they were released by President Santa Anna.

War with Mexico

The period preceding the war with Mexico was a time of uncertainty for the people of New Mexico. Here, as in other Mexican departments, European society had been firmly established in foreign surroundings. After many years of continuous struggle, the local natives adopted some of these Spanish customs. The Spanish, on the other hand, acquired many ideas from Indians that became useful during the settlement of the Southwest. These two cultures, living side by side, had managed to survive under extreme hardships and many difficulties.

At the end of the eighteenth century, a different society based upon the principles of self-government emerged along the eastern coast of North America. Within fifty years new ideals of the United States had swept into the frontier provinces of Texas, New Mexico, and California. Manifest Destiny, a principle set forth by the American people to free anyone from the Atlantic to the Pacific Ocean and to provide free expression of thought under the law, was invoked to justify American aid to those living under Mexican rule. Moreover, liberal thought in the United States influenced many in the Southwest to demand political, social, and economic freedoms enjoyed elsewhere.

Charles Bent established one of the early trade routes to Santa Fe. In 1846, he became military governor of New Mexico and was assassinated during the Taos Rebellion.

The revolt in Texas arose from such claims.

The Mexican Constitution of 1824 in many ways contained similar ideals found in the United States Constitution, but these were never practiced in the empire. By 1842, Texas was a confirmed, independent republic, and New Mexico had just recovered from an unsuccessful revolution for independence. In 1843, Texas again entered New Mexico and attacked the town of Mora. The defeat of Governor Armijo's forces on the Arkansas River by the Texans, commanded by Colonel Jacob Snively, convinced the New Mexican officials that great political changes were near. Being convinced that the American government had far reaching ideas about New Mexico, the Mexican authorities began to do everything they could to maintain their power to the Arkansas River. Land grants were provided by the Mexican government for settlers other than Americans across the northern frontier. The grants of land, later known as the Tierra Amarilla, the Maxwell, the Mora, the St. Vrain, the Nolan, and the Montoya and Anton Chico grants, were made for the purpose of aiding and carrying out this policy.

Still claiming the lands east of the Rio Grande, Texas was finally admitted to the Union in 1845. While the annexation of Texas was in progress, the British and Foreign Anti-Slave Society, whose headquarters were in London, offered assistance to Mexico to regain the Republic of Texas. They promoted the building of several Mexican warships to plunder the Texas coast. Two outstanding British officers, Captain Cleveland and Captain Charlwood of the Royal Navy, were to command the vessels. They were permitted by the Mexican government to serve in the Mexican Navy. The ships were manned mostly by British seamen recruited from London.

Because of these startling events, President James K. Polk sent an army under the command of General Zachary

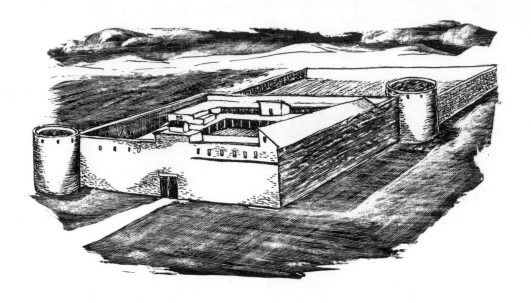

Artist's conception of Bent's Fort based on a historic description.

Taylor to the lower Rio Grande. The American government had formulated plans in the event of war with Mexico because, for nearly ten years, conflict had existed between the two countries. Now a new crisis had developed to hasten hostilities.

Meanwhile, General Taylor's forces were camped along the lower Rio Grande to defend the border in the event of an attack. Mexico claimed that this was an invasion of Mexican territory, and on April 24, 1846, General Taylor's troops were fired upon. Following this event, on May 13, 1846, sixteen of Taylor's men were killed and the United States government declared war on the Empire of Mexico. Volunteers were called for by the governors of several states, and the president asked Congress for authority to call for troops and appropriate funds to carry on the war.

The United States immediately put into action the plan of invasion of New Mexico, Chihuahua, and California. In June, 1846, a military force called the Army of the West under the command of Colonel, later Brigadier General, Stephen W. Kearny left Fort Leavenworth, Kansas, with 1,558 men and sixteen pieces of artillery. After a march of some 650 miles, they arrived at Bent's Fort in southern Colorado.

Shortly after the command arrived at Bent's Fort, a small force was sent to the Taos Valley to determine whether the Indians were friendly. The main army headed southward over the Raton Pass and camped near the town of Las

Vegas on August 15, 1846. The Taos force reached General Kearny soon after and brought several prisoners who told the general of Indians who were preparing to join the New Mexicans to halt the invasion. This report caused a great deal of concern to General Kearny and his men. As soon as possible, Kearny sent word to the villages along the invasion route, promising protection and no loss of life if they would not resist.

In the meantime on August 2, 1846, Captain Philip St. George Cooke, a soldier who knew the country very well, and James Magoffin, who operated a business in Mexico and had often visited Santa Fe, together with twelve men, left Bent's Fort for Santa Fe to discuss with Governor Armijo the surrender of that city. This was in advance of the main army which was to march on Santa Fe.

Before Captain Cooke and Magoffin reached Santa Fe, Governor Armijo issued a proclamation calling upon the people to take arms and to protect their homes against the Americans. Soon after the arrival of the two messengers, a meeting was held between Armijo, Magoffin, and Captain Cooke. Whatever was discussed at the meeting is not definitely known. However, soon after the Americans left Santa Fe, Governor Armijo recruited a small army and marched to Apache Canyon. Shortly after arriving in the area, Armijo dismissed his troops and escaped to Mexico. No one knows exactly why Armijo deserted his troops. Some say that Armijo and his commanders were constantly quarreling over the procedure of the battle and that the troops refused to obey the orders of the Governor of New Mexico. Others say that Armijo was a coward and that he

would not resist the American invasion of the territory.

When General Kearny discovered that the enemy had fled, he immediately began his march to Santa Fe, stopping at Las Vegas and San Miguel de Bado to proclaim to the people that they were to continue to live as they had been accustomed and that no immediate changes would take place. He promised protection to the new government.

On August 18, 1846, General Kearny and his army entered Santa Fe without firing a shot and were warmly received by Juan B. Vigil, the acting governor. The flag of the United States was saluted with thirteen guns. The next day the people of Santa Fe gathered at the plaza to hear a speech by General Kearny. He informed the people that they were no longer citizens of Mexico but of the United States. He further informed them that the Americans had come in peace and kindness to better their conditions and make them a part of the Republic of the United States. He promised to protect them and to help them in any way possible. A portion of General Kearny's speech is as follows: "New Mexicans: A change of government has taken place in New Mexico and you no longer owe allegiance to the Mexican government. I do hereby proclaim my intention to establish in this department a civil government, on a republican basis, similar to those of our own states. It is my intention, also, to continue in office those by whom you have been been governed, except the governor, and such other persons as I shall appoint to office by virtue of the authority vested in me. I am your governor—henceforth look to me for pro-

Christopher (Kit) Carson arrived in New Mexico during the early years of unrest in the territory. During the Territorial Period, he and his men were instrumental in the surrender of the Navajos. Later, he became an outstanding leader for New Mexico during the Civil War.

tection."

Most of the citizens accepted the situation and appeared satisfied. Since Governor Armijo had deserted his post at Santa Fe, Acting Governor Vigil answered Kearny with a fine speech. Part of his speech is as follows: "General: The address which you have just delivered, in which you announce that you have taken possession of this great

country in the name of the United States of America, gives us some idea of the wonderful future that awaits us. It is not for us to determine the boundaries of nations. The Cabinets of Mexico and Washington will arrange these differences. It is for us to obey and respect the established authorities, no matter what may be our private opinions. The inhabitants of this department humbly and honorably present their loyalty and allegiance to the government of North America. No one in this world can successfully resist the power of him who is stronger. How different would be our situation had we been invaded by Europeans! In the name then, of the entire Department, I swear obedience to the Northern Republic, and I render (surrender) to its laws and authority."

The first part of the plan of attack had been completed, and Kearny, placing Colonel Alexander W. Doniphan in command at Santa Fe, left the capital city to conquer California. He appointed Charles Bent as military governor of Santa Fe.

During the march to California, General Kearny received news that John Frémont, who had left Bent's Fort earlier, entered California from the north, and under his leadership most of California had achieved independence from Mexico. Meanwhile, Colonel Price had arrived in Santa Fe with about 1,000 troops, providing Doniphan, who had been stationed there, an opportunity to carry out his plan of attack.

Doniphan began his march south along the Rio Grande and encountered a Mexican army at Brazito, north of El Paso, Texas, under the command of Colonel Antonio Ponce. During the engagement, forty-three Mexicans were killed, while the Americans had only

seven men wounded. This was the only resistance Doniphan met in New Mexcio. After the battle, Doniphan continued his march south to take over the province of Chihuahua and eventually to join forces with General John E. Wool, who had left San Antonio for the town of Monclova, in the province of Coahuila.

On his march to meet General Wool, Colonel Doniphan engaged the Mexicans again in the town of Sacramento, north of the city of Chihuahua. After an hour of battle, Doniphan charged the city, killing 300 of the enemy and losing only one American.

During the early campaigns of Doniphan, General Taylor had successfully defeated the Mexicans at Point Isabel and Resaca de la Palma near the mouth of the Rio Grande; he continued his march southwestward to Monterrey, where he defeated the army of General Santa Anna. Several hundred Mexicans lost their lives during these two battles, and less than one hundred Americans were either killed or wounded.

Santa Anna retreated to the small Mexican outpost of Buena Vista, and again Taylor defeated him, but the battle resulted in severe losses to both sides. This encounter took place on February 21, 1847, and six days later, General Taylor was reinforced by the combined armies of Colonel Doniphan and General Wool, who had met Doniphan near the town of Parras, north of Buena Vista.

Back at Santa Fe, another army, called the Mormon Battalion, was marching south under the command of Captain Philip St. George Cooke. He was to follow the main army under

131

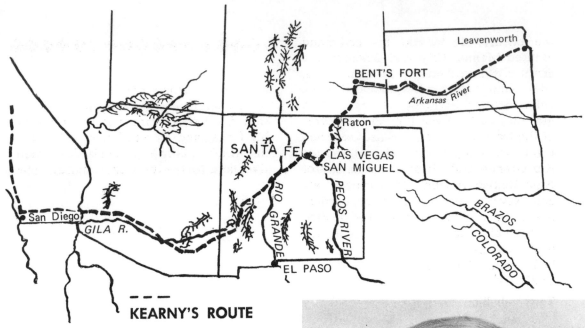

KEARNY'S ROUTE

General Kearny, mark a wagon trail to California and take possession of Tucson, Arizona. He engaged a Mexican army at Sonora, situated on the border of Arizona. He defeated the army and headed north to Tucson. Since the town had only a few armed men, the army commander at Tucson surrendered to Captain Cooke. From there, the two armies marched west to San Pascual near San Diego, California, and the last Mexican army in the northern provinces surrendered to General Kearny.

On March 9, 1847, General Winfield Scott landed 10,000 soldiers on the shore at Vera Cruz, the seaport of Mexico City. After several battles with

General Stephen W. Kearny led the Army of the West into New Mexico in 1846.

the enemy, Scott and his command entered Mexico City and defeated the army of Santa Anna on September 14, 1847. The Treaty of Guadalupe Hidalgo was finally ratified by the Senate on May 30, 1848. According to the terms of the treaty, the United States retained legal ownership of Texas as far as the Rio Grande and all of the territory of New Mexico, Arizona, California, Utah, and Nevada, as well as some borderlands. In return for this, the United States paid $15 million and cancelled many claims which American citizens had against Mexico; this amounted to $3,250,000.

Taos Rebellion

A general feeling of unrest was evident soon after Kearny and Doniphan left Santa Fe. Although the speech of Governor Vigil seemed to have voiced the feelings of most New Mexicans, there were some who did not share these ideas. A plot was formulated under the direction of Colonel Diego Archuleta to overthrow the new government. The revolt was uncovered by Colonel Sterling W. Price, who arrested several people connected with the plot. This did not end the unrest which had been carefully planned by Archuleta. The Pueblo Indians, who had been secretly organized, became violently hostile towards Governor Bent and the United States Army. In the north, at Taos and surrounding areas, the people were preparing themselves to carry out the ambitions of the revolutionaries.

On January 14, 1847, Governor Bent left Santa Fe to visit his family in Taos. While at Taos, he was warned of a possible revolt soon to take place in the area. Five days later, he was assassinated in his own home in Taos. On the same day of the assassination of Governor Bent, several other prominent

citizens met their death.

Colonel Price, accompanied by Captain St. Vrain, immediately organized his forces and marched north. A battle in which thirty-six rebels lost their lives and forty-five were wounded was

General Manuel Armijo, governor of New Mexico in **1846.**

133

The Taos Pueblo Indians organized a rebellion in 1847 to force the Americans out of New Mexico. The battle, which took place in an old mission near the pueblo, ended Pueblo resistance in the territory.

This D.A.R. marker, located near Deming, in southern New Mexico, commemorates the Mormon Battalion, which passed here in 1846 on its way to California. The route later became the Butterfield Stage Route.

134

fought near Santa Cruz.

The retreating force attempted to make a stand in a narrow canyon at Embudo. Once again the rebels were overcome by the advancing command under Colonel Price, and in this encounter the enemy's losses were twenty killed and sixty wounded.

The defeated army retreated north to Taos and fortified themselves in an old adobe church. Here, a fierce battle was fought. Several attempts were made to take the church. On February 4, 1847, Colonel Price and his men stormed the walls of the pueblo church, killing 150 of the enemy and wounding scores of others. Colonel Price lost seven men, and forty-five were wounded. This battle ended all resistance to the newly established government in New Mexico.

REVIEW ACTIVITIES

1. Imagine you live in New Mexico during the dictatorship of Santa Anna. Explain why he had so much unrest in the northern part of his territory.
2. Make a time line of the important dates of the era of the rule by Mexico from 1821 to 1846.
3. What was meant by the term Manifest Destiny?
4. Tell about the treaties of Córdoba and Guadalupe Hidalgo.
5. What part did the traders and trappers play in the building of New Mexico?
6. Discuss the conditions that brought about the war with Mexico in 1846.
7. What was the outcome of the Texas-Santa Fe Expedition?
8. What was the Army of the West?
9. Explain why General Kearny and his army were able to enter Santa Fe and claim the capital city for the United States without firing a shot.
10. What part did the Mormon Battalion play in the history of New Mexico?
11. Discuss the campaigns of the following commanders during the war with Mexico from 1846 to 1848: General Taylor, General Scott, General Wool, Colonel Doniphan, and Captain Cooke.
12. What was the Taos Rebellion? Results?

RECOGNIZE AND UNDERSTAND

Iturbide
Becknell
McKnight
Carson
Santa Anna
Perez
Armijo
Kearny

Vigil
Doniphan
Price
Frémont
Bent
St. Vrain
Young
Barreiro

CHAPTER IX

New Mexico Territorial Days

CHAPTER X

New Mexico in the Twentieth Century

CHAPTER XI

The Counties of New Mexico

CHAPTER XII

State and Local Government

UNIT 4

NEW MEXICO: A TERRITORY AND A STATE

SIMMS BUILDING

New Mexico Territorial Days

The Territorial Period in New Mexico began soon after General Stephen W. Kearny occupied the capital city of Santa Fe in August 1846. On September 22, 1846, Kearny gave to the people of New Mexico a set of rules and regulations known as the "Kearny Code." Colonel Alexander W. Doniphan and William Hall, a private, were responsible for the drafting of the laws. The document contained a combination of the laws of Mexico, the United States, and some of the laws of Texas and Missouri.

The Kearny Code

The Kearny Code provided for three separate branches of government. A legislative branch or General Assembly, as it was called, was to consist of a House of Representatives. Its members were to be chosen from each of the counties. A Legislative Council was made up of members to be elected from districts. The executive would be represented by a governor to hold that office for two years. The President of the United States could remove the governor at any time during his term of office. The judicial branch was to be called the Superior Court, consisting of three members appointed by the President. A Bill of Rights was attached, similar to the first ten amendments to the United States Constitution. Kearny appointed several people to various posts that were created by the code. When word reached Washington concerning the creation of a government by Kearny, President Polk several weeks later sent word back to Santa Fe declaring his disapproval of the new government. Congress also reacted in a similar manner. As it was, Kearny could not provide any political rights

James S. Calhoun, first governor of the Territory of New Mexico.

Hidalgo, ratified on May 30, 1848, New Mexico became a part of the United States. The southern boundary of the new territory was to be the Rio Grande, the Upper Gila, and a line uniting these two rivers just above El Paso, Texas. The people were given a choice to become citizens of the United States or of Mexico. They were to be given full protection for their person, property, and religious faith. The treaty did not provide for any immediate changes in the government of New Mexico. Officials were to continue in their present positions until Congress provided a territorial government.

Late in 1847, before the Treaty of Guadalupe Hidalgo was ratified by the Senate of the United States, a legislative assembly met in Santa Fe. It adopted a resolution to call another convention in February 1848. However, the convention did not meet until October 1848, four months after the acceptance of the Guadalupe Hidalgo Treaty.

During the meeting Colonel John M. Washington was appointed governor to succeed Donaciano Vigil. He was granted full authority as a combined military and civil governor. The convention adopted a resolution asking Congress for the immediate organization of a civil form of territorial government. Attached with this resolution was a statement protesting the claims made by Texas to New Mexico territory east of the Rio Grande. The resolution was sent to Congress, but very little was accomplished.

Another convention was held in September 1849, and this body elected

to people who, in fact, were not citizens of the United States. Since war had been declared on Mexico in May 1846, New Mexico was not and could not be regarded as a territory of the United States until after the war. The Kearny Code did not originate in Congress, but it did provide some measure of unity until New Mexico was admitted as a territory of the United States in 1851.

Early Efforts for Statehood

Under the Treaty of Guadalupe

Many of the early pioneers, settlers, and others who were heading for California to stake their claim in 1849 passed by this landmark at Wagon Mound, New Mexico, while traveling over the Santa Fe Trail.

Hugh N. Smith as a delegate to Congress. A plan of government was adopted by the convention. Smith was assigned the task of placing the document before Congress for adoption. However, the people of New Mexico were divided on the form of government. Some wanted statehood, while others wanted a territorial form of government. Governor Washington was opposed to the actions of the convention and refused to recognize the plan of government. Smith traveled to Washington, but Congress, by a vote of 92 to 86, refused to admit him.

On May 15, 1850, a convention was held in Santa Fe. Ten days later the convention adopted a state constitution and elected delegates to Congress to petition for statehood. Major Richard H. Weightman and Francis A. Cunningham were the first two delegates sent to Washington, D. C., to represent New Mexico in Congress.

Major Weightman's immediate plans were to take the new constitution to Washington. He hoped that it would be approved by the Congress. The constitution was similar to the constitutions of other states and had, among other things, a section prohibiting slavery in New Mexico. On September 9, 1850, a few days before the New Mexico delegate arrived in Washington, Congress passed a compromise bill (Compromise of 1850) admitting New Mexico as a territory. The act determined the northern and western boundaries of Texas. The United States paid Texas ten million dollars to give up its claim upon New Mexico. The new territorial government began operations in March 1851, and James S. Calhoun was appointed the first territorial governor.

One difficult question regarding New Mexico's request for statehood was the slavery problem. In 1850, the United States was divided into fifteen free states and fifteen slave states. Another "free" state would upset the balance. Therefore, Congress for this and other reasons denied statehood to New Mexico.

Gold Fever

As early as January 1848, before the Treaty of Guadalupe Hidalgo was signed, gold was discovered at Sutter's Mill in California. At first the discovery attracted only a few curious people to the site. Later that year, the rich returns brought miners from Oregon and Mexico by the hundreds. By March 1849, gold from California was brought to St. Louis, infecting the entire population with visions of wealth and prosperity. Shortly thereafter, the Atlantic coast received news of the gold strikes, and within a few weeks the people headed for California.

Hundreds upon thousands left their homes and jobs, piled all that they could in their wagons, and headed west. Some went by ship around the tip of South America to California. Those who traveled overland followed the Santa Fe Trail into New Mexico. From here,

some went northwest through Utah and Nevada and on into California. Still others took the southern route through El Paso and followed the trail established by the Mormon Battalion in 1846. Many left Santa Fe and traveled the Old Spanish Trail in an attempt to arrive first to stake their claims. In less than two years, over 93,000 people had come to California.

There were others less fortunate who never reached the precious gold fields. Sometimes a single wagon train would be completely destroyed during an Indian attack on the Great Plains. At other times, sickness would overtake the pioneers, and some of the passengers died enroute.

The buffalo was the main source of food and clothing for the Indian. The mass slaughter of the great herds nearly caused them to be extinct, but today they are found in many states.

The Ute Indians signed a peace treaty in 1855, and they were placed on a reservation in northern New Mexico under the Indian Agent W.F.M. Arny (center-back).

The gold rush of 1849 brought many travelers to New Mexico and other parts of the Southwest. These hearty pioneers, although interested in gold, sometimes were unable to continue their journeys west. They then often decided to settle in various areas in the territory. Gold strikes located in southern Colorado near Pike's Peak also helped to bring hundreds of settlers to New Mexico.

But the statement that prosperity brings evils was true for New Mexico. Millions of dollars in gold, wagons loaded with many valuable goods, people traveling alone with their riches—these conditions attracted gamblers, outlaws, and thieves from every part of the United States. The men began wearing guns to protect themselves and their families. The military units provided some protection for civilians. Most of the time, though, the army was too far away and too few in number to give immediate help.

During the gold rush of 1849, the army started a pony express service from Fort Leavenworth, Kansas, to Santa Fe. This service provided mail once a month to the people of Santa Fe and other small towns along the trail. A stagecoach line, established that same year, made scheduled trips from Independence, Missouri, to Santa Fe. There were only a few trails from Santa Fe heading west to California, but there were no good wagon roads. With so many people in the West and thousands more yet to come, a good roadway between Santa Fe and the Pacific coast had to be found. In 1871 the U. S. Congress gave a charter to the Texas and Pacific railroad company to build such a line across the Southwest. A railroad line was not finished, though, for another decade.

First Years as a Territory

The first New Mexico territorial legislature assembled at Santa Fe on June 2, 1851. In his message to the assembly, Governor James Calhoun favored the establishment of a public school system. A penitentiary and a police force, or militia, were also called for to provide some means of protection from the Indians and the outlaws. The territory was divided into counties, and justice courts were established. Forts were built, and a volunteer army was organized in order to control the Indians throughout the territory. David Meriwether became governor in 1853. During his administration, he arranged treaties with several Indian tribes. Many of the treaties were not approved by Congress.

Gadsden Treaty. A treaty was concluded between the United States and Mexico by James Gadsden in 1853.

St. Francis Cathedral as Archbishop Lamy intended it to look.

John B. Lamy, Archbishop of the Territory of New Mexico in 1875. The Territory achieved archdiocesan status that same year.

Under the treaty, the United States purchased a strip of land on the southern border of the present-day states of Arizona and New Mexico. The treaty, known as the Gadsden Purchase, provided a route for a stageline, and later, a railroad.

Indian Uprisings. The westward movement of the United States meant Indian lands were often sought by the new settlers. Tribes were forced to make room for unwanted newcomers. Not all Indians were willing to find new homes, though, and they fought to protect themselves and their lands. Some Indians at this time became very dangerous and active in their raids on the people in the territory. Utes, Navajos, and all the Apache tribes were attacking settlers, especially in remote areas that had little protection. Finally, after a long campaign by the military, led by Lieutenants David Bell and John W. Davidson, the Jicarilla Apache wanted to stop fighting. A treaty of peace was signed in July 1854. By May 1855, the Utes were defeated in a decisive battle by Colonel Thomas Fauntleroy.

The Apache tribes in the south were a constant threat to travelers and settlers. The bands causing most of the trouble between 1853 and 1857 were the Mescalero, the Mimbres, the Mogollon, and the Gila Apache. Those years saw many battles, engagements, and skirmishes with these Indians.

In 1855, Captain Richard S. Ewell and Captain Henry W. Stanton engaged the Mescalero in the Sacramento Mountains. Within a few hours the Apaches surrendered. Many died on both sides during the battle, including Captain Stanton. A treaty was concluded, and the Mescalero were moved to a reservation near Fort Stanton, renamed for the slain captain. By 1857, separate treaties were made with the Apache tribes; some were kept, but others were not.

The Navajos were the most difficult of all the Indians to manage. They caused the military more trouble between 1850 and 1860 than all the other New Mexico Indians combined. In 1850, there were more than 10,000 Navajos who occupied the northern part of New Mexico. There were several treaties made, each lasting only a short time. During the raids, the Navajos would steal cattle, sheep, and anything that was available. They were not as destructive as other tribes though. They simply raided the settlements, being careful not to destroy things, since they wanted farming communities to continue raising crops for them to harvest.

In 1860, the Navajos boldly attacked Fort Defiance in the nighttime, but they were driven off without serious loss. This was the only instance since the American occupation that enraged Indians in New Mexico ever attacked a strongly garrisoned post. It would be several years before the Navajos signed a lasting peace treaty.

Between 1847 and 1861, the government spent an average of three million dollars a year to control the Indians of New Mexico. Unfortunately, little had been accomplished by this expenditure. If anything, the Indian was stronger than he had been before the Americans arrived. The basic weakness was the policy of fighting the Indians with guns in one hand while holding a peace treaty in the other. The Indians grasped the peace treaty when it was to their advantage, only to fight as soon as the military force moved elsewhere. This was by no means a one-sided affair. The white man would alter or change a peace treaty when it suited him best. In most cases, the Indian was never informed of the change until it was too late.

By the end of the first decade of territorial government in New Mexico, relations between Indians and whites were becoming more peaceful. But before long Indians were raiding, burning, and killing along the frontier. The leaving of federal troops for active service in the East was a signal for some tribes to demand and enforce their power.

Pre-Civil War Problems

There were other problems in New Mexico before the Civil War. Quarrels between the civil and military authorities caused a great deal of confusion in the heavily populated areas. Laws made by the territorial legislature always

took second place when federal orders were sent to New Mexico. The federal orders, of course, were enforced by the military commanders stationed there. Consequently, the legislature achieved very little in the way of law making during this time.

The clergy of the Church were constantly arguing among themselves. Many left their missions in the pueblos and retired to social life in the towns

St. Francis Cathedral as it now looks.

and villages. Protestant denominations were being introduced to the territory by the people from the East who came by wagon train to New Mexico. When Mexico won her independence from Spain in 1821, the Crown recalled priests and officials. Some of the priests stayed in New Mexico but did not perform their duties as they had in the past. The people of New Mexico were not without religious services, though. For about a century, a religious group called The Brothers of Light, popularly called Penitentes, had been present in New Spain.

After 1821, the Penitentes became the guardians of the faith. They sought to nurture Catholicism and to keep it alive in New Mexico. The official church was temporarily replaced by the Moradas, Penitente churches. Church hymns gave way to the sacred songs of the Penitentes, the Alabados. The Moradas became the central meeting place in the local community for social gatherings, for providing for the welfare of those in need, and for worship.

The Penitentes continue to survive in the isolated towns of northern New Mexico. Their major religious celebration today, as it was in the nineteenth century, is during Easter Week. Throughout their history, Penitentes have been hard working citizens, and oftentimes public officials.

Their contributions to local and state affairs are many, but the Penitentes have not always been well-received. Not until 1947 was a conflict between them and the Catholic Church settled. In this agreement, the Penitentes were permitted to use the Moradas, provided they follow certain religious guidelines set down by the Catholic Church.

This conflict between the Church and the Penitentes dated from 1851. In that year Jean Baptiste Lamy, a French clergyman, was assigned to New Mexico and established his headquarters in Santa Fe. Jean Baptiste Lamy came to the United States from France in 1839 and began his 12 years of mission work in Ohio. In 1850, because of his outstanding work in the East, he was assigned to the mission field in the Southwest. He was the first priest in New Mexico sent from the United States. There were only fifteen priests in New Mexico in 1851. One of these priests held services only once a year.

In 1853, Lamy was appointed as Bishop of Santa Fe to reorganize the Catholic Church in New Mexico. In order to do this, Bishop Lamy supplemented the regular clergy throughout New Mexico with European priests. Lamy believed it was necessary to do away with the Penitentes if Catholicism was to be revived in New Mexico. He made many reforms to be rid of the Penitentes. He introduced teaching orders and assigned Jesuit priests the task of instructing the people of New Mexico in the Catholic faith.

During the years Bishop Lamy spent in New Mexico, he founded schools and colleges, built hospitals, and established forty-five churches throughout the territory. An example of his building program is St. Francis Cathedral, which was erected in Santa Fe as he originally planned it, except for the steeples.

In 1875, he was appointed Archbishop of the new diocese of New Mexico. Because of his efforts, the Catholic Church regained its strength.

A serious condition in New Mexico that caused widespread unrest and bloodshed was the question of property rights. In the early days of Spanish and Mexican occupation, land ownership presented few difficulties. After the

Only adobe walls remain of Fort Selden, a military outpost established in New Mexico in 1865 to protect travelers and settlers against raids by the Gila Apaches. The ruins of the fort lie near the town of Radium Springs on U.S. Highway 85 in southern New Mexico.

war, this vast territory was in the hands of the United States. The Treaty of Guadalupe Hidalgo stated that property rights were to remain as they had been under Mexico. But since the territory had not been surveyed, it was difficult to determine who had legal title to the land.

When the Americans came to settle, they also laid claim to certain portions of the land in New Mexico. Some families might claim land as far as they could see to a cliff or mesa. Others claimed all the land they could ride around in one day. Whatever they claimed, they were determined to hold their land, regardless of the consequences.

In 1854, William Pelham was ap-pointed by the Congress as a surveyor-general for the territory. With the use of a compass and transit, he was able to measure small portions of the land for the people of New Mexico. Soon after the land was surveyed, many claims were brought to court. Congress established the Court of Private Land Claims, which settled many of the disputes. However, some claims on land in New Mexico are still being adjudicated in the courts of the United States.

Early Roads. After the war with Mexico in 1848, thousands of people came west and settled in many parts of the new lands that had become part of the United States. Shortly thereafter, it became necessary to find new and better communication routes to the South-

The ruins of old Fort Union, near Las Vegas, New Mexico, stand today like a spectre from the past. It is now a National Monument, preserved from further decay by stabilization measures. The fort was established as a U.S. Army outpost in 1851, five years after General Stephen W. Kearny took possession of the western territory for the United States. Ft. Union served as a stop on the old Santa Fe Trail; it was abandoned in 1890.

west. In 1853, the government sent out surveyors to locate the best routes for trains to the West. A. W. Whipple was the man selected to find a path for a road across New Mexico and Arizona. He surveyed a route west from Albuquerque to Flagstaff, Arizona, and finally to California.

Since this part of the territory was so dry, an idea was brought to the attention of the government. Jefferson Davis, the United States Secretary of War, initiated a plan to provide the army with camels. In 1855, Congress authorized funds for the camel expedition, which was to begin its journey two years later. The army sent an expedi-

tion from San Antonio, Texas, to El Paso and Albuquerque in 1857. It then proceeded west along the survey line established by Whipple. The leader of the expedition, Lieutenant Edward F. Beale, reported that the camels performed well and requested that the army get more of them. But events in the East soon resulted in war and prevented further interest in camels. Many of the camels died soon after; some were sold, and others were left to roam the desert.

About the same time, a stagecoach line was promoted by the federal government. The Congress offered six hundred thousand dollars a year to anyone who would establish a mail route to California. John Butterfield of New York secured the contract. The 2,750 mile (4,400 km.) Butterfield Overland Mail Route started in St. Louis. From there it went through Fort Smith, Arkansas, El Paso, the southern portion of New Mexico and Arizona and on to San Francisco, California. It stopped at many other towns and cities along the route. The new stageline carried mail, passengers, and freight to California in only 20 days. With the finest horses and Concord coaches, the Butterfield Overland Stageline provided another means of travel from the East to the Pacific coast. Even though it was a hazardous trip, the stagecoach was the

fastest and best method of travel in those days. Villages and towns along the way grew and prospered. But when the Civil War began in 1861, Congress required Butterfield to use his stagecoaches on the Santa Fe Trail.

Fort Union

Following the Mexican war and to protect the settlers and to keep open the trade routes, New Mexico was organized into the Ninth Military Department. Many forts were erected as bases of operation with the headquarters designated as Fort Union in 1851. The fort was constructed by the

Post Commanding Officer's quarters, Fort Union (N.M.), c. 1884. Original in the Arrott Collection, New Mexico Highlands University, Las Vegas.

Post Officers' Row, Fort Union (N.M.) c. 1876.

department commander, Colonel Edwin V. Sumner. He moved his headquarters to the west bank of Coyote Creek, near the dividing point of the Santa Fe Trail. Three separate units of forts were constructed. The last section was built in 1863 by General James H. Carleton, the Federal Commander in New Mexico. Other forts were established as they were needed. These were located near the Indian tribe that was currently causing trouble.

The value of goods hauled over the trail rose from $15,000 in 1821, when the Santa Fe Trail was opened, to five million dollars in 1855. In 1858, 1,827 wagons crossed the plains with nearly ten thousand tons of merchandise, much of it for the army. The merchandise was received at the Fort Union Quartermaster Depot.

Fort Union offered travelers a place to rest before continuing their journeys. Soldiers from the post patrolled the trail as far east as the Arkansas River in times of Indian danger. Military escorts were often sent from the fort to accompany mail coaches and gold shipments in the dangerous areas along the trail. Fort Union was the guardian of the Santa Fe Trail and the Southwest

for forty years, from 1851 to 1891.

In addition to protecting the Santa Fe Trail, Fort Union troops sought out and punished Indians who were causing serious problems in the territory. Later between 1860 and 1861, successful campaigns were conducted against the Kiowas and Comanches menacing the eastern borders of the territory. Today the ruins of Fort Union stand as a memorial to the men who won the West. During the years the fort was in operation, it played a major roll in shaping the destiny of the Southwest. Fort Union was the largest United States military post guarding the southwestern frontier in the last half of the nineteenth century. In April 1861, Fort Union took on new importance. With outbreak of the Civil War, an immediate Confederate invasion of New Mexico was expected.

The Civil War in New Mexico

Soon after the Civil War began in the East, the newly formed Confederacy turned its attention to the West, particularly New Mexico. In New Mexico in 1861 some people favored the Southern position. Others, who were mostly descendants of the original Spaniards and who had been United States citi-

150

Fort Craig during the Civil War. General Sibley's field guns were unable to penetrate the fortress.

zens only since 1848, did not know much or even care about the Union. They simply considered that this was not their war. The major portion of the people, however, were Union men. They were loyal to the cause and to their conscience. When the danger of invasion was evident, the people of New Mexico joined together to protect their land from Confederate intruders.

Texas, a "slave state," had joined the Southern cause with the idea of regaining the territory east of the Rio Grande. The Confederacy, however, was more interested in the gold supply shipments of the Santa Fe Trail. The trail was the most important supply route connecting the East with the West. Fort Union, the main outpost on the trail, became the key target in the plans for invasion of New Mexico by the Confederates.

The plans to attack New Mexico were laid by various military commanders who once had served the federal forces in the territory. By 1861 they had abandoned their duties, left New Mexico, and joined the Confederate States of America. One of the officers was Major H. H. Sibley, who had served in New Mexico territory

during the early Indian campaigns. He was promoted to general and appointed to head the Confederate expedition. The army, consisting of more than 2,300 officers and men, began its advance from San Antonio, Texas, in November 1861. The plans for invasion were the boldest and most extensive of any of the military schemes of the Confederacy.

Before Sibley and his men reached Fort Bliss in El Paso, the Confederates had already begun their operations. Colonel John R. Baylor, commander of Fort Bliss, had marched up the Rio Grande and taken possession of the plaza of La Mesilla. This was located south of the present town of Las Cruces, New Mexico. The commander of Fort Filmore, Major Isaac Lynde, surrendered his forces and turned over more than $17,000 in government funds to Colonel Baylor. On August 1, 1861, Colonel Baylor proclaimed himself governor and established the territory of Arizona in the name of the Confederacy. La Mesilla was made the capital city of the new Confederate territory.

The territory extended as far north as Socorro in New Mexico. The western boundary line of Arizona was the Colorado River, which separated California from the Confederacy.

During this time, General E. R. S. Canby, newly appointed Union commander in New Mexico, reported to Fort Craig. This fort was north of La Mesilla in Socorro County. Once there he proceeded with the organization of volunteers to defend the garrison. He requested additional funds and equipment from Washington, but aid was never sent. However, some help was

BATTLE
OF
VALVERDE,
NEW MEXICO
(at time of Confederate charges)
FEBRUARY 21, 1862

0   Yards   600

Old Channel of Rio Grande

MAIN CONFEDERATE ATTACK

RAGUET

Rio

McRAE'S BATTERY

2d N. M. VOLS.

SELDEN   CARSON   DUNCAN

HALL'S BATTERY

Grande

2d N. M. VOLS.

MESA DEL CONTADERO

received from the people of New Mexico because of arrangements made by the chief quartermaster, Major James L. Donaldson. Governor William Gilpin of Colorado promised assistance and organized an army of volunteers. These troops rendered great service to the saving of New Mexico from the Confederacy.

On January 1, 1862, General Sibley, brother - in - law of General Canby, marched northward on the east bank of the Rio Grande. His goal was to take Fort Craig, the stronghold in the south. Sibley, very confident of success, sent a proclamation to the people. He asked them to lay down their arms and join the Confederate States of America. Governor Henry Connelly, who was appointed by Abraham Lincoln to replace Governor Abraham Rencher, a Southern sympathizer, called upon the people of the territory to resist the

invaders from Texas. Two companies of volunteers were organized by Colonel Kit Carson and Colonel Cerán St. Vrain to reinforce Fort Craig.

In February, General Sibley advanced on Fort Craig. However, the fort was too strong to be stormed. The light Confederate artillery could not be used for an effective bombardment. At this point General Sibley ordered a company of cavalry, under the command of Captain George M. Frazer, to advance northward. They were to bypass the fort, and to determine a place to cross the river. Since Captain Frazer was somewhat familiar with the territory, he was charged with the duty of leading the Confederate Army over the hazardous terrain to Valverde. There the river was shallow and easy to cross. He was to select an adequate position to defend in the event of a Union attack from Fort Craig. Sibley calculated

▼▼▼▼▼▼▼▼▼▼▼▼▼▼▼▼▼▼▼▼▼

the fort and destroy the garrison. However, with supplies dangerously low perhaps just ten days' rations left to feed the men, General Sibley decided to continue the march northward. The captured towns along the way would provide the necessary supplies for the army. Meanwhile, General Canby, since Fort Craig was out of danger, prepared to send Major Donaldson northward. He was to remove all government supplies from the path of the Confederates.

Several days later, Major Donaldson arrived in Albuquerque and ordered all government property that could not be

General E.R.S. Canby, Commander of Fort Craig and the Union forces in New Mexico in 1862.

that perhaps Canby, in an effort to prevent the crossing, might be lured out to fight.

Seeing this maneuver, General Canby sent out his best regulars to defend the position. The remaining forces in the fort were mostly volunteers who proved difficult to handle. A great battle, known as the Battle of Valverde, took place about 7 miles (11 km.) north of Fort Craig. The forces of Carson and St. Vrain performed very well in their attempts to halt the advance of the Confederates. Nevertheless they were badly beaten.

The Union forces retreated to Fort Craig, leaving Valverde crossing open to the Confederates. The Confederates first decided they should advance on

General H. H. Sibley, Commander of the Confederate forces in New Mexico during the Civil War.

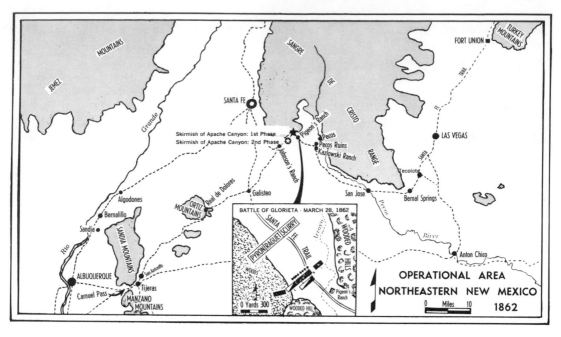

Northeastern New Mexico showing where Battle of Glorieta took place.

carried away to be destroyed. He and his command left the city and continued their march to Santa Fe. They arrived at the capital a few days later.

Meanwhile, the small detachment of Union troops, aided by local citizens, gathered all the supplies they could find and loaded them into several wagons. The provisions that were left behind were burned along with the supply depots. With the supply wagons loaded, Major Donaldson and his unit from Fort Craig began the long trip to Fort Union.

By this time, the Confederates had arrived in Albuquerque and found the city nearly deserted. Supply houses were abandoned or burned. Only a small quantity of provisions was obtained by the Southern Army.

After gathering the scattered supplies, General Sibley and his command head-ed north and arrived in Santa Fe. Upon arriving there they found a similar condition to that in Albuquerque. Disregarding the situation in Santa Fe, General Sibley established his headquarters at the capital city. The flag of the Confederacy then was raised over the Palace of the Governors. Search parties were sent from Confederate headquarters to gather supplies from nearby villages to support the garrison at Santa Fe. When Albuquerque and Santa Fe were permanently secured for the Confederacy, General Sibley made plans to attack Fort Union. He planned to capture the stronghold and to gain the entire Southwest for the Confederate States of America.

Before the Confederates arrived in Albuquerque and Santa Fe, however, the volunteers at these two cities had retreated to Fort Union. There they

▼▼▼▼▼▼▼▼▼▼▼▼▼▼▼▼▼▼▼▼

were reinforced by a small detachment of the First Colorado Volunteers consisting of 418 officers and men under the command of Major John M. Chivington. They were sent in advance of a total body of 1,342 men with eight field guns commanded by Colonel John P. Slough, a Denver lawyer. They arrived at Fort Union after an unbelieveable, forced march from their camp near Denver. Crossing the cold, windy, snow-covered Raton Pass, they had in one instance marched 92 miles (147 km.) in 36 hours.

Colonel Slough had ordered Major Chivington to secure a place to defend the Santa Fe Trail. He also was to at-tempt to halt the Confederate invasion force that would come eventually from Santa Fe. If Chivington did not encounter any resistance along the trail, then he and his command were to advance to Santa Fe to prepare to attack the city. Colonel Slough was to follow the advanced patrol to reinforce Major Chivington's command at the capital.

The Confederate commander concentrated his entire force at Santa Fe to proceed with his plans to attack Fort Union. He was soon bound for disappointment. Sibley's plan was to send a

Soldiers Quarters. Fort Craig 1865-1868. General Sibley by-passed the fort and headed for Santa Fe.

Site of the Battle of Glorieta Pass on the west side of the pass, looking east.

unit of cavalry over the Santa Fe Trail. It was an advanced detachment of the main army which was to follow a few days later. Confederate troops that began their march from Santa Fe were commanded by Major Charles L. Pyron of the Second Texas Cavalry. This cavalry unit, which consisted of about 600 men and two small field guns, was the vangard of a Confederate force numbering about 1,800 men with fifteen pieces of artillery.

Early on the morning of March 26, 1862, Major Chivington's detachment of "Pike's Peakers" left their camp just south of the old Pecos mission ruins. They hoped to make a surprise attack on the Confederates in Santa Fe. As the command was rounding a curve about a mile (1.6 km.) up Glorieta Pass, they came upon the advanced scouting party of Texans heading for Fort Union. A fierce battle then took place.

The Union troops moved forward to the entrance of Apache Canyon at the western end of Glorieta Pass the afternoon of March 26. Here the main body of the Texans, commanded by Major

Pyron, was encountered. The Battle of Glorieta Pass was about to begin. The Texans commanded the roadway with two guns and opened fire on the advancing Union Army. Realizing his situation, Major Chivington sent several men to the left of the road. He advanced one company to higher ground on the right. Firing was exchanged on all sides. Chivington's mounted force was sent to the rear to be held for a charge when the enemy began a retreat.

Firing continued, but soon the Texans fell back to a new position across a sixteen-foot bridge spanning an arroyo. They destroyed the bridge and spread out along the side of the canyon. Chivington continued his advance. His men again climbed the steep sides of the pass and drove the Texans from their roadblock with rifle fire. Both sides continued their fire for about an hour before the Texans were forced to retreat from their positions.

The mounted cavalry, under Captain Samuel H. Cook, charged according to plan. They ran the Texans down under their horses' feet. Private Ovando

Hollister, a member of Chivington's command, and later a noted journalist, describes the scene in his report as follows: "Captain Cook and his troopers went galloping down the road, low in the saddle, like a pack of howling Comanches, and with a long, wild yell leaped across the yawning chasm (the arroyo) at the bridge. Confederate

Site of Glorieta battlefield east of Santa Fe.

cannon proved 'too fleet-footed' to be captured, but in the midst of bullets which whistled and whined about their heads, Cook and his men rode back and forth through disordered ranks of the Texans, trampling them down, scattering them in every direction and taking 70 of them prisoners."

A member of the Confederacy describes it from the viewpoint of one who saw it coming: "Up came a company of cavalry at full charge with swords and revolvers drawn, looking like so many flying devils. On they came to what I supposed was destruction; but nothing like lead or iron seemed to stop them, for we were pouring it into them from every side like hail in a storm. We shot as fast as we could; and after fighting hand to hand with them, and our comrades being shot and cut down every moment we were obliged to surrender. Such a sight I never want to see again."

By the evening of the 26th, Colonel John P. Slough, commander of the army from Colorado, had arrived. A truce was arranged to take care of the wounded and to bury the dead. The Texans fell back to their camp at Johnson's Ranch at Cañoncito near the entrance to Apache Canyon. The Union Force returned to their campsite near Pecos. The next day, the 27th, both sides regrouped forces.

Early on the morning of March 28, Colonel Slough divided his command. He ordered Major Chivington to take 350 men and, by a round-about route, to attack the enemy's supply depot at Cañoncito. Colonel Slough marched forward then for a surprise attack upon the Texans at Pigeon's Ranch. However, during the night, the Confederates were reinforced by the Fourth Texas Cavalry, commanded by Lieutenant Colonel W. R. Scurry. The Union Army consisted of seven hundred men, artillery, and one hundred supply wagons. The Texans numbered about 1,100 and three pieces of artillery.

During the battle, the Union troops were forced to fall back three-quarters of a mile (1 km.) east of the ranch. At this point, Colonel Scurry and his cavalry made repeated attacks upon the Colorado column. These assaults caused the Union troops to fight on the defensive throughout the engagement. Charges were made five times by the Texas cavalry. This was similar to the desperate charge of Pickett's Brigade at Gettysburg. Each time the Texans were driven back by the determined fighters from Colorado and New Mexico.

After several hours of fighting and of suffering heavy losses by both sides, the Union troops returned to their camp near the old Pecos mission. Meanwhile, unknown to Colonel Scurry, Major Chivington's command, led by Lieutenant Colonel Manuel Chavez, approached the Texan's supply center near Johnson's Ranch. In a surprise attack on the Confederate camp, the Colorado Volunteers drove off the guards. Then they burned seventy wagons, along with supplies and provisions, and destroyed the ammunition center. All the horses and mules were killed and the campsite burned. This single act brought defeat to the Confederates and saved New Mexico and the Southwest for the Union.

That evening, both sides returned to the area to care for their comrades lost in battle. More than five hundred

"Glorieta Battlefield Chivington's Rock." The bridge at Apache Canyon which was destroyed by the Confederates during the battle at Glorieta Pass.

Confederate and Union soldiers lay dead or wounded upon the battlefield.

Colonel Scurry, the Confederate cavalry commander, reported that every inch of ground was bitterly fought for. On several occasions Confederate and Union soldiers engaged in hand-to-hand combat along the rocky slopes of Glorieta Pass. He said he had never seen more gallant fighting men in his lifetime.

When the Texans realized their situation, they quickly made plans to retreat to El Paso. Meanwhile, General Canby marched north with 1,200 men from Fort Craig to head off Sibley's retreat. Colonel Kit Carson remained at Fort Craig in command of the garrison. A small battle took place at Peralta, located south of Albuquerque. Here General Canby felt that additional fighting was unnecessary and permitted the Confederates to escape to Texas.

Cerán St. Vrain, one of the commanders of the New Mexico Volunteers during the Civil War in New Mexico.

In August 1862, the California Column arrived with 2,350 men, commanded by General James H. Carleton. This army greatly increased the military force in New Mexico. With New Mexico so well defended, the Confederates never again attempted an invasion of the territory. Later, General Carleton succeeded General Canby as department commander of the Territory of New Mexico.

This stone marker, a few miles east of Santa Fe, New Mexico, marks the Battle of Glorieta Pass, March 1862. Here Union forces defeated Confederate forces in a decisive Civil War battle.

159

During the war, the north boundary line of New Mexico was established in 1861 when Colorado was organized as a territory. Arizona was admitted as a territory in 1863, creating the west boundary line. Shortly after the Civil War, an agreement was reached on the boundary line between New Mexico and Texas.

Indian Campaigns

The invasion of New Mexico by General Sibley caused all of the regular troops from forts in the Indian country to withdraw. Settlers were left unprotected from the Apaches and the Navajos. Many New Mexicans left their

The Union Army made a surprise attack upon the Texans at Pigeon's Ranch near Glorieta. This single act brought defeat for the Confederates in New Mexico.

The Jicarilla Apache and Ute Indians proved helpful during the war years as guides and soldiers. The Pueblo Indians demonstrated their loyalty also during this time. For their help, President Lincoln presented a silver cane to each of the 20 chiefs of the pueblos. Further aid was extended by Isleta Pueblo. They provided $18,000 in gold to pay the salaries of Union troops. Later, President Grant repaid the loan made by the pueblo. The Jicarilla, Ute, and Pueblo were the only "Union Indians" during the war.

General James H. Carleton, commander of the California Column, provided additional forces for the Union in New Mexico. Later, General Carleton became the Department Commander of the Territory of New Mexico.

Fort Sumner: Navajos under guard after their capture in 1864. The commander at Bosque Redondo was Col. J. Francisco Chavez, who had assisted Kit Carson in capturing and moving the Navajo there.

homes and jobs to volunteer for active service against the Confederates. When the war finally came to an end in the territory the volunteer army was released. The men returned to their homes to find much destroyed either by the Confederates or the Indians. In the south, near Fort Stanton, the ranches were completely abandoned. Many people were killed. Their homes were destroyed, and the cattle were driven off by the Apaches.

In 1862, General James H. Carleton, commander of the New Mexico territory, ordered the capture of all the Indians who were raiding the settlements. They were to be placed on reservations. There they were to be taught how to farm and how to make a living.

The first efforts in New Mexico to halt Indian-Anglo warfare were with the Mescalero Apaches. Colonel Kit Carson and five companies of New

Mexico volunteers captured a band of Mescaleros and transferred them to the Bosque Redondo Reservation on the Pecos River near Fort Sumner. By the spring of 1863, about 400 Apaches were living on the reservation. The next campaign was against the Navajo in 1864. Kit Carson was again called upon, and he and his men surrounded the Indians at Canyon de Chelly where the Navajos surrendered. By the end of the year, over 7,000 Navajos occupied part of the Bosque Redondo.

The program for the Indians at the Bosque Redondo Reservation was a complete failure. The Navajo, used to herding, was unprepared for the farming he was made to do on the reservation. Because of disease and their lack of skill, farming failed. Also, the reservation was continuously attacked by the Comanches and other Indian tribes of the plains. Each time, large numbers of cattle and sheep were

First fort at Fort Sumner built in the winter of 1862-1863, southwest of the later fort.

stolen. The military and the Mescalero often quarreled. The Mescaleros left the reservation in 1866, and throughout the territory the Apache raids continued.

Problems for the Navajo continued, and many died from disease and starvation. A peace treaty was signed in 1868, and the Navajo returned to their homeland. More than 7,500 Navajos then walked for thirty-five days to their present reservation. This journey is known as the "Long Walk" or the "Navajo Trail."

When the Civil War finally ended in 1865, thousands of people who had lost all they had during the war moved west. They sought new land and wanted to forget the terrible events of the past. New towns and cities were started in the Midwest and west of the Mississippi River. Grazing areas for cattle gave way to the dirt farmer, and the cattlemen moved farther west. The Indians moved toward the mountains. But there they met further difficulties since mining was developing rapidly. Copper, zinc, lead, and some gold were found. Each brought in more settlers.

The buffalo, which had provided food and clothing for the Indians for centuries, was slaughtered by the thousands by buffalo hunters to make way for the white man. Now that the white man had taken the Indian land and was destroying their only means of survival, there was nothing left for the Indian to do but to fight. It is not too difficult then to understand why the Indian fought so hard against the white man.

Kit Carson's Cave, in western New Mexico, near Gallup, was carved out of soft sandstone by natural erosion processes. Kit Carson camped in this cave during his campaign against the Navajo Indians in 1864.

Indians killed as many white settlers as they could and burned their buildings in an effort to drive them away. The white man felt he had a stake in this country, too. He fought hard to win the land, for he had invested fortunes and his life to develop it. Now the white man was willing to die to protect the land he now claimed as his alone.

In 1868, when the reservation at Bosque Redondo was abandoned, the Chiricahua Apaches were removed to Ojo Caliente Reservation in Grant County, New Mexico. These Indians remained there with one of the greatest Apache chiefs, Victorio. In 1877, the Apaches were transferred to Arizona

and placed on the San Carlos Reservation. John P. Clum was the Indian agent for the reservation. The idea behind the placing of Indians on reservations was to set up a training camp to teach them how to farm and how to govern themselves like the white man wanted. Neither one of these programs really benefited the Apache.

Under Clum, though, the goals of the reservation program were partially successful. But the poor living conditions and the false promises of the reservation officials were more than the Apache could bear.

Even though Clum managed to bring part of Victorio's warriors to the reservation, they did not remain there long. Geronimo was already planning his escape. Shortly after arriving at San Carlos, Geronimo and some of his warriors left the reservation. Clum and forty of his Apache policemen found Geronimo camped near Ojo Caliente. They returned him and his warriors to San Carlos without firing a shot. When Clum retired, the reservation became poorly managed, and once again the Apache became troublesome.

Chief Victorio was determined not to stay on the reservation at San Carlos. In April 1879, Victorio revolted and left the reservation. He began a war that lasted ten years.

Victorio had a force of no more than 300 warriors and two sub-chiefs, Loco and Nana. With his warriors, he attacked wagon trains, ranches, mining camps, and American and Mexican troops. He outwitted generals of both the United States and Mexico. In one campaign alone, he captured over five hundred horses from Mexico.

For more than six years, Victorio successfully eluded the armies of the United States and those of Mexico. He

Part of the ruins of old Fort Cummings in southwestern New Mexico. This fort was established in 1863 to protect stagecoaches traveling through Cooks Canyon, where Apache warriors often waited in ambush. Fort Cummings was abandoned in 1891.

and his warriors killed over 200 New Mexicans, more than 100 soldiers, and 200 citizens along the border of Mexico. At one time, the combined armies of Mexico and the United States surrounded Victorio's camp in order to capture him. Still he managed his escape. In 1883, Victorio and his men were surrounded by the Mexican army near the mountains in Chihuahua. Victorio was killed, and his warriors, having run out of ammunition, surrendered. Victorio and his warriors had fought a brave, long, and hard battle.

During the ten years of warfare in the Southwest, the Ninth and Tenth Cavalries fought bravely against the Indians. These two cavalry units were considered by many as the best troops in the Southwest. They were made up largely of well-trained Black soldiers. Lieutenant Henry O. Flipper, first Black to graduate from West Point and the first Black officer assigned to the Tenth Cavalry, led his unit on several combat missions against the Indians. The Indians referred to them as the "Buffalo Soldiers." On another occasion Clinton Graves, a Black soldier serving with the Ninth Cavalry, was cited for bravery during the campaigns against the Indians in the Florida Mountains in

▼▼▼▼▼▼▼▼▼▼▼▼▼▼▼▼▼▼▼▼

In 1879, Victorio, one of the greatest Apache chiefs, left the reservation at San Carlos, Arizona, and began a war that lasted for 10 years.

Luna County, New Mexico. Graves was the first Black to receive this nation's highest award for outstanding courage, the Medal of Honor. Lt. Flipper, after leaving the Army, was an engineer on important road and water projects in southern New Mexico.

In March 1883, another chief, Chato, revolted and left the reservation in Arizona. He began raiding, burning, and killing throughout Grant and Luna Counties. General George Crook and a cavalry unit engaged the Apaches in May of that year. Chief Chato and his warriors were forced to surrender. A peace treaty was then agreed upon, and the Apaches went back to Arizona.

The last Indian chief to surrender was Gokliya, known in history as Geronimo. He was the most feared of all the famed Apaches and a skillful leader.

On May 17, 1885, two years after Victorio's death, Geronimo, Natchez, and Mangas, son of the famous Apache Chief Mangas Coloradas, left the reservation with less than fifty warriors. They began raiding throughout southern New Mexico. They burned ranches and killed settlers throughout the territory and in Mexico.

In 1886, General Nelson A. Miles became the military commander of New Mexico. He continued operations against Geronimo. Later that year, General Miles forced Geronimo deep into Mexico to the Yaqui country, 200 miles (320 km.) south of the New Mexico boundary. General Miles sent Lieutenant Charles B. Gatewood to Geronimo's camp to demand his surrender. Lieutenant Gatewood, with a small detachment from the Sixth Cavalry, overtook Geronimo, forced him to surrender, and brought the proud Apache chief to the military camp. He was placed in prison along with other Apache chiefs who had all surrendered to the military.

Later, Geronimo and his followers were released from prison and placed on various reservations in New Mexico and Oklahoma. Geronimo was sent to Fort Sill, Oklahoma, where he died in 1909. His wife died in 1950, and his son, Robert, chief of the tribe, died in 1967 on the Mescalero Reservation in New Mexico.

The capture of Geronimo ended the war with the Indians. Peace once again

Geronimo and his warriors left the reservation in Arizona and began raiding settlements throughout the territory.

was restored to the people of New Mexico and Arizona.

Lawlessness in New Mexico

During the 25 years following the Civil War, New Mexico experienced one of the worst crime waves in the history of the United States. It was a time when killing, stealing, and lynching were the common practices of the day. It was said that at one of the many taverns in northern New Mexico, eleven men were killed in a single month. Every community had many gambling houses and taverns to encourage conditions outside the law. Other areas of the United States had methods to enforce the law. But in New Mexico Territory, little law existed to enforce and few men were willing to enforce it.

During the years that New Mexico was a territory, there was much political trouble. This was true when education was lacking and most of the citizens could neither read nor write. They had to depend on what others told them. Crooked politicians took advantage of the people, arranging for their own election by having someone "stuff the ballot box" and cheat during the counting of votes. Some politicians acquired land and property through shady deals. During much of the territorial period, "The Santa Fe Ring" controlled New Mexico. These were ambitious politicians who helped lawyers, businessmen, large ranchers, and land promoters to gain what they wanted to further their own interests.

New Mexico, a frontier community, attracted men from all walks of life. Here, men came to establish "reputations," to make their marks in the world. Many did not care too much how it was done.

As new towns developed on the frontier, they became well known for their lawlessness. Soon these same communities were made the hideout for all types of criminals. The men who came were generally misfits in their

Geronimo, born a Chiricahua Indian, was the most feared of all Apaches. In his later years, he was a successful farmer at Fort Sill, Oklahoma.

own cities or towns. They drifted to New Mexico looking for new opportunities where they could be free from any law except their own. As law and order came to the surrounding states, more of these lawless individuals found their way into New Mexico. The territory was the catch-all for all sorts of shady characters.

New Mexico was also the place for the "lawless breed" to come and stay until their criminal activities elsewhere had quieted down. Doc Holiday operated a dental office in Las Vegas, New Mexico, when he was not conducting a stage robbery or a murder. Jesse James visited New Mexico to hide from the law. During his brief stay he worked for the railroad. In 1882, Wyatt Earp operated a gambling hall in the Old Town of Albuquerque. He was soon forced to leave.

New Mexico was only a stop-over for these individuals until they could resume their activities elsewhere in the West. However, justice was swift in the frontier communities. Often the people were willing to take matters into their own hands. Law and order was slowly coming to the territory when Judge Roy Bean, who once lived in Mesilla, became "The Law" west of the Pecos.

Frontier life was cheap, and killing was not considered a terrible crime. It was easily accepted if done to protect oneself, his family, or his property. Too, the six-shooter hanging from the hip was the emblem of safety and security for most of the people. To others it represented authority and a challenge to determine who was "faster on the draw." Personal quarrels usually ended with a gun fight. Groups of men would end their differences in a gun battle which might last for hours. Still others would continue their differences for months on end.

Ranch hands and owners kept a good supply of weapons to protect their lands and cattle from homesteaders and rustlers. Quarrels, which often involved whole communities, also took place between owners and employees of different ranches. When barbed wire was introduced to the territory, it added more fuel to the smoldering fire.

By 1877, the smouldering fires broke out in a feud among Lincoln County cattlemen. The bloody conflict that ensued is known as the Lincoln County War. This fight lasted for more than three years. Lincoln County in the 1870s was all of southeastern New Mexico. It was the largest county in the United States with some seventeen million acres.

The range war bitterly divided the area. John H. Chisum, the cattle king

McSween Store in Lincoln, New Mexico, during the Lincoln County War.

of New Mexico, declared that Lawrence G. Murphy, who controlled all the business in Lincoln County, was stealing his stock. By September of 1877, the feud between Chisum and Murphy spread throughout the territory. During the months that followed, Lincoln County started drawing outlaws from other sections of New Mexico, Texas, and Mexico. Both sides brought in their own gunmen. Fights and shoot-outs between hired hands for both Chisum and Murphy became commonplace. While neither man was ever directly involved in these incidents, they did nothing to restrain their hands.

One of the outlaws who came to Lincoln was William H. Bonney, better known as Billy the Kid. He used two other names during his brief life: Henry McCarty and Billy Antrim.

Billy, born in New York City on November 23, 1859, was named Henry McCarty.

Shortly after the Civil War, Billy's father died leaving the family almost destitute. Then, in 1870, the family mov-

ed to Augusta, Sedgwick County, Kansas. While in Kansas, Billy worked for William H. Antrim. Later, both families moved to Santa Fe, New Mexico where Billy's mother, Catherine McCarty, married William H. Antrim on March 1, 1873. After the marriage, Antrim decided to try his hand at mining and moved his new family to Silver City, New Mexico. There Billy attended school for a short period of time. Several months later, Billy went to work as a waiter at Mrs. Sarah A. Brown's boarding house after his mother died in 1874.

When Billy was about seventeen years old, he was confined in the Silver City jail for stealing. He escaped from jail and headed for the Arizona Territory. Soon after arriving, Billy shot and killed Frank P. Cahill near Camp Grant, Arizona. He was jailed the following day. Once again, Billy escaped from jail. His career in robbery and murder had begun.

Billy moved around finally heading for New Mexico staying with his brother Joe in Georgetown located about eighteen miles north of Silver City. In September 1877, Billy left Georgetown and arrived in Mesilla, New Mexico when the range wars were well underway. While there, he became involved in cattle rustling and horse stealing.

In October 1877, Billy came to Lincoln, changed his name to William H. Bonney, and worked a short time for William Brady. Then he went to work at various "cow camps" owned by Lawrence G. Murphy. Within a few weeks, Billy left Murphy's employ. Later, John Chisum hired Billy as a cowboy on the

William Bonney, known as "Billy the Kid," began his career of violence at the age of 17. Four years later, he was shot and killed by sheriff Pat Garrett.

South Spring Ranch near Roswell, New Mexico. By January 1878, Billy was working on the Tunstall Ranch near the Rio Feliz.

In 1876, John Henry Tunstall, a wealthy Englishman, arrived in Lincoln. He became associated with John Chisum. Tunstall was also closely allied in various business ventures with Alexander McSween. He was a lawyer who had recently arrived in Lincoln County from Kansas.

The Murphy-side was based on a partnership between Murphy and two fellow Irishmen, James J. Dolan and John P. Riley. Murphy had also had another partner, Emil Fritz. Fritz's death touched off a bitter dispute between the two factions.

Before the outbreak of the range was in Lincoln County, the partnership of Murphy-Dolan-Riley-Fritz operated a general store and gambling house in Lincoln. The partnership had a life insurance policy attached. It provided a $10,000 policy for each member of the L. G. Murphy Company. Emil Fritz, one of the partners, died without leaving a will to determine who should receive his estate.

After several months of searching for the will of Emil Fritz, Murphy and Dolan prepared to establish a claim for the insurance money. Florencio Gonzales, Probate Judge of Lincoln County, appointed William Brady as administrator of Emil Fritz's estate. Murphy became ill and sold the company to his partner, James J. Dolan. Murphy then left Lincoln and settled on his ranch in Carrizozo, New Mexico. Brady was a candidate for the office of sheriff. Because of a conflict of interest, Brady

Lincoln County Courthouse before restoration. "Billy the Kid" was held in the Courthouse, but within a few hours he made his escape after killing two guards.

resigned as administrator of the Fritz estate. Charles Fritz and Emilie (Fritz) Scholand, brother and sister of Emil Fritz, were named to succeed him. They furnished a $10,000 surety bond as protection for the insurance money. The bondsmen were James J. Dolan and Alexander McSween. The attorney was authorized by the court to handle the legal matters of the estate. Through manipulations and double dealings, Mc-Sween received the insurance money. Charles Fritz, Emilie Scholand and James Dolan, unaware of the deal, were left out of the inheritance.

Shortly after receiving the money, McSween and Tunstall made plans to open a general store. They intended to control the business activities including land and cattle in Lincoln County. Tunstall also received several thousand dollars from his father, John P. Tunstall, merchant, living in England. But the Tunstall - McSween store was nothing more than a front for the new entrepreneurs to carry on their land schemes. The mercantile store though began at-

tracting the cowboys who usually did their buying at the Dolan store. The small ranch owners began buying at the Tunstall-McSween store and were required to sign promisory notes for the goods. If they could not pay their debts Tunstall, with McSween's help, intended to take court action against them. Soon Dolan and Riley were being hurt by the new store.

At this time, the range wars in Lincoln County were underway. The conflicts attracted gunmen who had been wanted criminals in other areas of the country. Some of them became associated with either the Dolan-Riley group or the Tunstall-McSween forces.

Since McSween had not returned the insurance money to the administrators, Charles Fritz and Emilie Scholand went to court and filed criminal charges and a civil suit against McSween. The frightened attorney escaped f r o m Lincoln to a hideout near Roswell furnished by the Cattle King, John Chisum. Immediately, the court issued warrants for the arrest of McSween and to attach

170

▼▼▼▼▼▼▼▼▼▼▼▼▼▼▼▼▼▼▼▼

his property in town and elsewhere in Lincoln County. Some of his property was located at the Tunstall Ranch on the Rio Feliz. Sheriff William Brady was ordered by the court to prepare the necessary attachment papers for t h e Tunstall - McSween property. Then he and his deputies began an inventory of the gambling hall and store.

After swearing in several deputies, Sheriff Brady sent his men toward the Tunstall ranch to serve the attachment papers on his property. Some distance from Lincoln, the sheriff's posse met Tunstall and some of his men. A gun fight broke out. During the gun fight, Tunstall was shot and killed by the sheriff's deputies. With the Tunstall men was William Bonney alias Billy the Kid, who managed to escape the sheriff's posse. Shortly after McSween was notified of Tunstall's death, he quickly made plans to protect himself. McSween knew that Brady had the attachment papers and the warrant for his arrest. The attorney hired Billy the Kid and his gang and offered them $500 to assassinate the sheriff.

On April 1, 1878, a party of five men led by Billy the Kid hid in a corral behind the Tunstall-McSween store. When Sheriff Brady appeared, t h e gunmen shot and killed him. Shortly after the killing of the Lincoln County sheriff, Billy and the others fled to Fort Sumner.

On July 17, 1878, a sheriff's posse trailed Billy to McSween's house. There a three-day battle took place. During the battle McSween was killed, but Billy the Kid made his escape.

The territorial governor, Samuel B. Axtell, was unable to cope with the existing conditions in New Mexico. He had very little experience with the law-

Lincoln County Courthouse as it appears today.

General Lew. Wallace, Territorial Governor of New Mexico during the Lincoln County War, and author of *Ben Hur.*

lessness that had virtually taken over the territory. Therefore, he hesitated many times to find measures to halt the serious problems affecting areas such as Lincoln County.

In the face of the governor's failure to keep order, the President of the United States was urged to remove Governor Axtell from office. These complaints by New Mexicans, coupled with other reports of Axtell's poor handling of business in New Mexico, prompted the president to remove Axtell. Appointed as territorial governor was General Lew. Wallace. (Lew. Wallace wrote the story *Ben Hur* during his term of office.)

Governor Wallace acted quickly and asked for government troops to put down the range wars. He offered full pardon to those who were involved

with the affair. Soon after, Billy surrendered to the sheriff and was placed in jail. Before the trial began, Billy, feeling he would not be treated fairly, escaped from jail. He then formed a gang of outlaws. Pat Garrett, who was elected sheriff, went after Billy. The outlaws were captured, tried, and sentenced to be hanged. After shooting the two guards at the jail, once again Billy escaped and headed for Pete Maxwell's home at Fort Sumner. On July 14, 1881, Billy the Kid was shot by Sheriff Pat Garrett, after Garrett had trailed the Kid to the Maxwell Ranch.

Lincoln County was not the only area of lawlessness in New Mexico. During this time, various groups in Colfax County were involved in the age-old problem of land ownership. Colfax County at that time was most of northern New Mexico. At times the dispute in the north seemed minor compared to the Lincoln County incidents in the south. Yet the issue over which the Colfax County War was fought were far more reasonable and sound. The controversy was over the legality of the Maxwell Land Grant. Lucien Maxwell was the apparent owner of the area in question. As long as he retained possession farmers, ranchers, and miners who paid some form of tax to Maxwell were permitted to use the land.

Shortly after 1870, the grant was sold to an English-Dutch combine. This group was interested in a profit venture and sent eviction notices to the unsuspecting tenants. The foreign owners had little difficulty in removing the squatters by law. But carrying out the eviction notices was a difficult procedure. Those who settled on or near the grant believed that the area was free land. However, the grant had greatly increased in size through clever manipulations of the previous owners. Thus, the people who had settled outside the grant became involved in the scandal. People in the area split into two groups: the pro-grant and the anti-grant factions.

In 1875 the land grant issue was seriously affected when a Methodist preacher, the Reverend F. J. Tolby, was murdered. Another clergyman, the Reverend Oscar P. McMains, became the leader of the anti-grant faction and he accused the foreign company of the crime. However, no legal action was ever brought against the combine.

For the next several years, frequent feuds took place between the two factions. Bloodshed sometimes resulted.

The real flare-up occurred in 1885 influenced by the shift in national politics. Republicans had always favored big business controlling the grant. But the owners began to worry that the newly elected Democratic officials might render decisions favorable to the settlers.

Early in 1885 the owners acted to avoid the possibility of further legal suits. The land grant leaders had convinced Governor Sheldon that they would need help to enforce the decision of the court. The pro-grant leaders organized a militia composed of thirty-five men under the leadership of a notorious gunman, James H. Masterson. Most of the men were professional

One of the earliest schools in New Mexico was located in Mora.

Loretto Academy in Santa Fe during the nineteenth and early twentieth centuries.

gunmen and killers who were eager for a fight. Realizing their situation the settlers made a formal protest to the governor and the band of hired killers was relieved of its duty. Later, several men were killed in a gunfight in Springer between the settlers and the land grant faction. By 1893, the settlers realized that they had to accept the dictates of the court.

This was not the end to lawlessness in New Mexico Territory. Several murders occurred, and gang wars continued for many years after the Colfax County incident. A group known as the "White Caps" caused considerable unrest in and around Las Vegas, New Mexico. Some of the ranchers, having finally received clear titles to the lands they had

claimed, began driving off the other settlers who were on their lands. These settlers, mostly of Spanish descent, put on white hoods and began a series of cattle rustlings and killings. By 1897, the citizens banned together and broke up the gang.

Another incident was the murder of a newspaper man and politician, Albert J. Fountain, and his son in 1896. Sheriff Pat Garrett, assigned to the case, set out to get the killer. Oliver Lee, a well-known rancher was arrested and brought to trial. During the trial, many of the leading politicians sided with Lee; however, some were against him. When the trial was over, Lee was acquitted. Still another strange case was the murder of Sheriff Pat Garrett,

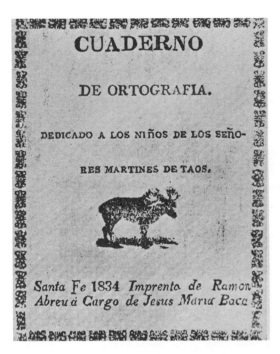

CUADERNO

DE ORTOGRAFIA.

DEDICADO A LOS NIÑOS DE LOS SEÑO-

RES MARTINES DE TAOS.

Santa Fe 1834 Imprenta de Ramon Abreu á Cargo de Jesus Maria Baca

Title page, *Cuaderno de Ortografia,* first book printed in New Mexico in 1834. The author, Padre Antonio José Martinez, posed for the first photograph taken in New Mexico in 1847.

who was traveling on a lonely mountain road when he was killed by an unknown assassin.

Much work needed to be done by the law-abiding citizens of New Mexico Territory. Many hearty and courageous men became sheriffs. With the assistance from the townspeople, they were able to bring some of the outlaws to justice. Criminals convicted by a court of law were sent to the territorial prison built in 1885. By 1905, the territorial government had organized a police troop to assist local sheriffs in their fight against crime. Laws were enforced, and men were no longer allowed to wear guns. New Mexico was on its way toward law and order.

Education

Another means to bring law and order to New Mexico was to educate the youngsters. In schools children learned to be good citizens. The first schools in New Mexico were directed

St. Michaels Academy, Santa Fe.

Donnelly Library . . . One of the newest buildings on the Highlands University campus in Las Vegas, Donnelly Library houses over 100,000 volumes. The University was established in 1893.

The picturesque Administration Building at Eastern New Mexico University, Portales. The college was founded in 1934.

View of the modern campus at the University of New Mexico founded in 1889 in Albuquerque.

Western New Mexico University in Silver City was founded in the 1890s as a normal school for training teachers. Today it is a campus of modern buildings and facilities.

New Mexico State University was established in 1899 at University Park, Las Cruces. This view of Corbett Center is an example of the modern buildings erected on the campus.

The once bustling city of White Oaks stands as a ghost town today in central New Mexico. Billy the Kid frequented the saloons and dance halls of White Oaks during its heydays as a gold mining town and trade center of the Lincoln County cattle country.

by the Catholic Church under the leadership of the Franciscan friars. The friars introduced the Indians to Spanish customs at the nearby missions. Music was one of the first methods used to make peace with the Indians. The first European music teacher in the United States was a Franciscan priest named Percival de Quinanes. He came to the territory between 1598 and 1604. Quinanes brought an organ with him and soon taught the Indians to sing at church services. Bells, violins, and guitars were also used as part of the worship service. This method impressed the Indians, and some finally became

members of the local church. But for over two hundred years, there was no formal education for the people in New Mexico.

In 1834, a small spelling book entitled *Cuaderno de Ortografía* (Notebook of Spelling) was printed at Santa Fe. The spelling book, the first book printed in New Mexico, was written by Padre Antonio José Martínez. It was published by Ramón Abreu who owned the press at the time, and was printed by Jesús Maria Baca. The same press used in 1834 to print the spelling book was also used in 1846 to print the first laws in New Mexico. This document was the Kearny Code.

By 1852, the Sisters of Loretto had started an academy in Santa Fe. In it they taught reading, writing, arithmetic, and good conduct.

The first college in the territory was organized by the Christian Brothers in 1859. They also started schools in Mora, Taos, and Bernalillo. Later, the Jesuits built a college in Las Vegas after 1878 and opened a school for girls in Albuquerque in 1881.

Several Protestant schools were built during this period. The Presbyterians established schools in Las Vegas and Santa Fe between 1866 and 1869. The Methodists opened a school in Albuquerque in 1887. Between 1878 and 1880, the Congregationalists built schools in Santa Fe and Albuquerque and established a college in Santa Fe

Mogollon, a once-prosperous mining town, lies in the heart of the giant Gila National Forest in southwestern New Mexico.

in 1881. By an act of the territorial legislature in 1889, a university was founded in Albuquerque, a school of mines at Socorro, and an agricultural school in Las Cruces.

In 1891, Governor Bradford Prince urged the legislature of New Mexico to pass a law providing for a public school system in the territory. The territorial legislature created a board of education and required the governor to appoint the superintendent of public instruction. The first superintendent was Amado Chavez. Schools were to be supported by a tax levied on property and business. In 1898, the United States gave millions of acres of government land to New Mexico. This land was to be leased to private individuals to provide additional income for the schools.

Since 1891, New Mexico has made great strides in the field of education. Efforts are continuing to provide even better programs in education to meet the needs of everyone, regardless of race, creed, color, or sex. Besides the lessons of the classroom, "book" learning was available outside schools during the territorial period. A lending library system was set up, and the first librarian in the territory was a woman, Julia Asplund.

Mining

The economy of New Mexico during the late nineteenth century centered on mining, stock raising, farming, and the railroad. In 1828, gold was discovered in the Ortiz Mountains between Albuquerque and Santa Fe. In what may be the oldest gold mining district in the United States, more than $80,000 worth was taken out by 1835.

The Ladrón Mountains rise above the plains of central New Mexico, a few miles west of Socorro. Ladrón is Spanish for "thief," and regional folklore tells of thieves and stagecoach robbers hiding out in these forbidding mountains.

When the Americans arrived, the mines were producing gold valued at more than three million dollars.

After the Civil War, several areas in New Mexico produced gold. Some were located near Taos and Elizabethtown on the Maxwell Ranch, and in White Oaks near Lincoln. When a gold strike was made, new towns sprang up. Many became ghost towns soon after.

Blacks also contributed to mining in New Mexico. In 1881 a Black named Bowman found traces of silver at the northern end of Burro Mountain. Later, John Black and his associate Sloan discovered the source as the Blue Bell Mine, later known as the Alhambra.

In 1863, Magdalena and Socorro were the centers of silver mining in New Mexico. But it was Silver City that was to become the leader in silver production. By 1916, the value of the ore had climbed to more than one million dollars per year. But it declined

to less than two hundred thousand dollars in 1958.

Most of the early copper mining was at Santa Rita in the southwestern part of the state. Although there were other copper mines in New Mexico, 90 percent of the total production was in Grant County.

Farming and Stock Raising

For centuries, wherever people settled in New Mexico, farming and stock raising were the main industries. The Indian, for example, depended on crops that were growing wild in the fertile river valleys and on the plains. Some attempts were made by the Indian to irrigate these crop lands in northern Arizona and New Mexico. In most cases, though, they were unsuccessful.

One interesting early agricultural activity of both the Indians and Spaniards was the gathering of piñon nuts. The tiny piñon nuts, gathered from nearby hills and sold at the local

Early settlers in New Mexico constructed flumes out of logs to carry irrigation water for their fields. The crude type of flume is still in use in many isolated mountain areas. This picture was taken near the village of Las Trampas, in northern New Mexico.

markets, were roasted at home. They were also sold to local traders who shipped them, particularly to the New York area. Although never profitable, the piñon industry has continued to the present time.

For many years, New Mexico has depended to a large extent on the raising of sheep and cattle and on farming. Sheep and cattle were first introduced to this area by the Spanish in 1541. As the Spanish developed settlements in the territory, sheep raising became a major industry. Sometimes, as many as 250,000 sheep were owned by one family. Sheep were able to graze in most parts of the territory. Shortly after the Civil War, thousands of sheep were being raised in almost every part of New Mexico. The Navajo raised

Miners and gamblers rushed into the Red River country of northern New Mexico in great numbers after gold was discovered in 1866. The settlement of Elizabethtown sprang up almost overnight. Within 10 years the settlers had begun to drift away, and "E-town" is numbered today among the ghost towns of New Mexico

Cotton field near Conchas Dam in northeastern New Mexico. Conchas Dam provides water for irrigating 45,000 acres of land in the vicinity of Tucumcari.

many sheep, and even today this industry is very profitable for the Indians. By 1880, wool shipments exceeded four million tons. Today sheep are still raised in the state, but the day of the big sheep ranch has long since passed.

Cattle ranches, on the other hand, developed later. The Texans brought the great herds into New Mexico and established the cattle industry. In 1866, Charles Goodnight and Oliver Loving combined their herds and began a cattle drive to New Mexico. They not only sold many of their cattle but also found a suitable place to raise beef in the territory. Profitable cattle ranches later sprang up in various parts of New Mexico. As the sheep industry declined, cattle raising increased to become a major industry in the state. The ranches

formed an association called the New Mexico Cattle Growers' Association. This group still has much influence in New Mexico.

During the period of the Westward Movement, many Blacks came with the wagon trains over the Great Plains. Others drove cattle to the railheads for eastern delivery. Black cowboys such as Bose Ikard, Jim Fowler, and Sam Woods were part of the team that drove some of the first herds up the Goodnight-Loving Trail.

A large number and variety of crops are grown in New Mexico today. During the early period of the territory, however, the land was not suited for many crops. As irrigation facilities increased, the land became suitable enough to produce excellent crops and greater yields. Cotton was first grown in New Mexico by the Indians, and today it is an important crop in the state.

Corn was also grown by the Indians centuries before the Europeans came to this land. Today more than 1.5 million bushels are harvested each year.

Railroads

The coming of the railroads between 1879 and 1882 opened a new period of prosperity for the people of New Mexico. Rail lines linked the people in the industrial centers in the East with those living on the western frontier. Trains furnished transportation not only for people but also for eastern manufactured goods. Eastern products could be sent directly to major cities and towns in the West. Railroads also offered a better way to ship western cattle, sheep, and wool to eastern markets and to California.

Before the Civil War, there were only a few scattered railroad lines in Texas and California. Wagon trails and stage-coach lines were the only direct routes to New Mexico and the far West. A move to improve westward travel began when government surveyors were sent

Cowboys rounding up cattle for branding. Most cowboys were law-abiding and only a very few were outlaws. One of every five cowboys was Black, and many others were Hispanic.

First train and first engineer that ran into Santa Fe, New Mexico, in 1887.

out to locate the best railroad route to California. Building the railroad would cost a great deal of money; therefore, the people asked Congress to help. Congress responded by passing the Railroad Act in 1864. This bill provided for the Union Pacific to build a railroad line west and the Central Pacific to build their line east to meet the Union Pacific in Utah.

The federal government made loans to the companies and gave them land to be sold to raise money for the construction of the railroad. On May 10, 1869, the two railroad companies met at Promontory Point near Ogden, Utah. The first railroad line connecting the East with the West had been completed.

A rail line to Kansas was begun by the Atchison, Topeka, and Santa Fe. The railroad was built west to Colorado and entered New Mexico through the Raton Pass in Colfax County on February 13, 1879. In 1880, the main line was completed to Albuquerque,

and a spur track was laid from Lamy to Santa Fe. By 1881, the Santa Fe track had been extended to Deming, where they joined with Southern Pacific from Texas. During that year, the Denver and Rio Grande built a narrow-gauge line in northern New Mexico. Today this line runs between Chama and Antonito, Colorado, as a scenic railway.

Within five years, these major railroad companies had constructed 1,255 miles (2,008 km.) of track in New Mexico. By the early 1900s, over 3,000 miles (4,800 km.) of track serviced New Mexico. The railroad brought in a variety of tools and machines for the farmer and ranch owner. Mining increased because mining equipment could be shipped more economically by rail. The railroad changed forever New Mexico. In the north, it aided the mining boom. In the southeastern part of New Mexico, the railroad helped bring settlers to homestead the land and to found towns. Charles B. Eddy and James J. Hagerman arranged for a railroad to Carlsbad and Roswell in the early 1890s. Eddy then extended the railroad to Alamogordo and Carrizozo by 1902. This line and others opened the land for homesteading. Immigrants from points east flocked to the southeast part of New Mexico. Towns followed the route of the railroad, and along the lines the virgin prairie soil was planted by farmers.

Movements for Statehood

Shortly after the signing of the Guadalupe Hidalgo Treaty, several groups in New Mexico began working on a constitution. This constitution, requesting permission to become a state, was sent to Washington. Because of disputes over the slavery question, the land dispute with Texas, and many other disagreements in Congress, New Mexico lost its bid for statehood. The Congress, through the Compromise Bill of 1850, admitted New Mexico as a

Train gang laying track, preparing to drive the last spike on Santa Fe Central Railway. There are 3,250 ties per mile of track, all cut and laid by hand.

Theodore Roosevelt at the first Rough Riders Reunion at Las Vegas, New Mexico, 1899, in front of the Castañeda Hotel, Las Vegas. One-third of the Rough Riders were from New Mexico.

territory. Further attempts were made soon after, but without successful results. After the Civil War, the territorial governor and members of the New Mexico legislature made feeble attempts to gain statehood for the territory. In Washington, the Congress had made attempts to organize the territory of New Mexico into the state of Lincoln in honor of the assassinated and beloved President. This measure also failed.

In 1872, the legislature prepared another constitution to be submitted to the people of the territory for vote.

Charges of election corruption, fraud, and general mismanagement surrounded the election before the people cast their ballots. Less than one-third of all the eligible voters went to the polls on election day. Since there were not enough votes cast at the polls, all efforts to present Congress with a workable constitution had failed.

The next year, Governor Marsh Giddings again attempted to encourage New Mexicans to consider the statehood question. Agreement was finally reached on a state constitution, and the New Mexico delegate to Congress,

Stephen Elkins, was on his way to Washington.

In Congress, Elkins introduced an enabling act for the territory of New Mexico. The Colorado territorial delegate also introduced plans for statehood. Both plans received favorable recommendations from both the Senate and House of Representatives. The hopes for statehood were dashed when one day Elkins walked into the House chamber just as a northern congressman was concluding a fiery speech in which he had viciously attacked the South. Elkins was impressed by this eloquent oratory and rushed up to the congressman, shook his hand, and congratulated him on his effort. When the statehood roll call was taken, the southern congressmen voted against the bill. Elkins' handshake lost for New Mexico the opportunity for statehood for many years. Colorado, on the other hand, was proclaimed a state on August 1, 1876, by President Grant.

In 1891, another constitution was sent to the people of New Mexico for their approval. Because of the political, religious, and cultural issues involved, the citizens rejected the constitution by a vote of 16,180 to 7,493.

Several other bills were introduced in Congress regarding statehood for New Mexico. One bill, proposing that New Mexico territory be admitted under the name of Montezuma, was defeated.

Spanish-American War

One of the main events of importance to the territory during the administration of Governor Miguel A. Otero was the organization of New Mexico volunteers to fight in the war with Spain. The War Department from Washington requested that New Mexico send 340 men for combat duty in Cuba. The governor offered an additional

Governor Miguel A. Otero, who worked hard to get statehood for New Mexico.

William J. Mills, last territorial governor of New Mexico.

number of cavalry and a battalion of riflemen.

For three years, the Cubans had been fighting for their independence from Spain. As the revolution went on, many Americans became sympathetic toward the people of Cuba in their struggle for freedom. During the third year of the revolt, President William McKinley sent the battleship *Maine* on a trip to Cuba. Shortly after arriving, the battleship was blown up and sunk, and in April 1898, the United States declared war on Spain. "Remember the Maine" became the battle cry as the Americans prepared for war.

The major part of the regiment that fought at San Juan Hill in Cuba was made up of men from Arizona, New Mexico, Oklahoma, and the Indian Territory. It was commanded by Col-

onel Theodore Roosevelt. More than 30 percent of Roosevelt's "Rough Riders" came from New Mexico. Among the men were clerks, mechanics, college men, miners, ranchers, printers, railroad workers, and many others who responded to the president of the nation in time of need. It made no difference to the men who hurried to Santa Fe to enlist in this great regiment what kind of work they had done; they became soldiers. They performed their duties well. By their actions under fire, they commanded the admiration of the world.

In a war that lasted about one hundred days, more men died from disease than from battle. The war was over by September, and the Americans came home. The Rough Riders met in Las Vegas the following year for a reunion. During a speech, Roosevelt promised to help New Mexico to become a state. Two years later, he became President of the United States. He kept his promise to work for statehood for New Mexico. But he was unable to accomplish it during the years he was President. At any rate, New Mexicans had a friend in Washington who was doing all he could for them. This brightened the hopes for statehood in the near future.

Final Action for Statehood

In 1901, Governor Otero called a new constitutional convention into session. The opinion of the people in the territory was still divided on the question of statehood. Those who were opposed felt that state government would require higher taxes. They further stated that many of the citizens of Spanish ancestry were not ready to take part in their own government. Some of the problems were resolved at the convention. However, the Congress passed an act in 1905 which would enable New Mexico and Arizona to become one large state. The "Jointure Act" (joint statehood act) provided for the citizens of the two territories to vote for or against the proposal. In Arizona, the voters rejected the act with an overwhelming vote of more than eight to one. In New Mexico, for various reasons, the election was reversed, with 26,195 voting for the act, and 14,735 voting against joining the two territories. Even though New Mexico had not achieved success in attaining its goal at this time, it was evident that the majority of the voters wanted statehood. They were so anxious for statehood they were prepared to lose the historic name of New Mexico.

In 1909, William H. Andrews, the last New Mexico territorial delegate in Congress, requested action on statehood for New Mexico. After many hours of debate, Andrews finally persuaded the Congress to consider his proposals.

On March 1, 1910, William J. Mills, the last territorial governor, took the oath of office in front of the capitol in the presence of a large crowd. The chief justice of the territorial supreme court administered the oath.

During the next few months, Congress prepared an enabling act which was signed by President Taft on June 20, 1910. Soon after the act was signed, a constitutional convention met at Santa Fe to draft New Mexico's State Constitution. The convention was dominated by the Republican party delegates, and many of the proposals made by the Democrats were omitted. Despite objections by the party, many of the Democrats voted for the proposed constitution. It was then submitted to the people for final action. New Mexico voters adopted the constitution by a vote of 32,742 to 13,399. There were only twenty-six counties in New Mexico at this time. Only four — Lincoln, Roosevelt, San Juan, and Sierra — voted against adoption of the constitution.

The constitution was sent to Washington for approval by the Congress. A resolution was prepared admitting New Mexico as a state by the House and Senate, and President Taft signed the resolution on August 21, 1911. There were some changes made, and a constitutional amendment was accepted by the people to make the constitution more easily amended. In December, Congress approved the bill for statehood, and on January 6, 1912, President Taft signed the proclamation admitting New Mexico as the 47th state in the Union. On January 15, 1912, William C. McDonald became the first governor of the state of New Mexico. The population of the new state was approximately 327,396. In April of the same year, Arizona was admitted to the Union.

REVIEW ACTIVITIES

1. Imagine you lived in Santa Fe at the time of Kearny's arrival.
   Write a story about it.
2. From outside reading, make out a report of General Sibley's march to Santa Fe.
   Map the Civil War campaigns in New Mexico.
3. Prepare a time line of the events leading to statehood, from 1898 to 1912.
4. Compare the Lincoln County War with the Colfax County War.
   Identify the similarities. What were the differences?
5. Imagine you are a congressman in 1850. Debate the slavery issue as it relates to admitting New Mexico as a state.
6. Explain the Kearny Code and tell why it was rejected.
7. Why was New Mexico denied statehood in 1850?
8. What did New Mexico gain from the Gadsden Purchase?
9. Explain the importance of Fort Union to New Mexico and to the Santa Fe Trail.
10. Describe the attitude of the people in New Mexico during the Civil War.
11. Why was New Mexico valuable to the Union?
12. What important action did the Indians of New Mexico take during the Civil War?
13. Who was Lieutenant Henry O. Flipper? For what is he noted in New Mexico history?
14. Who was Clinton Graves? For what is he noted in New Mexico history?
15. Describe the action taken against the Navajos and the Apaches in the 1860's.
16. List the causes of lawlessness in New Mexico during the late 1800's. Name some of the "shady" characters who made New Mexico their hideout.
17. Who were the "White Caps"? Why did this group cause unrest in New Mexico?
18. Describe early day education in New Mexico.
19. Where is the oldest gold mining district in the United States? When was gold discovered in this area?
20. Explain how the railroad aided the economy of New Mexico in the early days.
21. Explain Stephen B. Elkins' fatal handshake.
23. What influence did Theodore Roosevelt have on New Mexico statehood?
24. Describe the final action of New Mexico's fight for statehood.

▼▼▼▼▼▼▼▼▼▼▼▼▼▼▼▼▼▼▼▼▼

RECOGNIZE AND UNDERSTAND

James Calhoun

Compromise of 1850

James Gadsden

David Meriwether

June 2, 1851

Butterfield-Overland Mail Route

General Sibley

Colonel John Baylor

Battle of Valverde

Kit Carson

Battle of Glorieta Pass

Cerán St. Vrain

Battle of Peralta

California Column

General James Carleton

Bosque Redondo Reservation

Navajo Trail

John Clum

Victorio

Buffalo Soldiers

Geronimo

Lincoln County War

Colfax County War

Penitente

John Chisum

Alexander McSween

John Tunstall

Billy the Kid

Murphy-Dolan

Sheriff Brady

General Lew Wallace

Samuel Axtell

Pat Garrett

Maxwell Land Grant

Albert J. Fountain

Oliver Lee

Cuaderno de Ortografía

Amado Chávez

Charles Goodnight

Oliver Loving

Atchison, Topeka, and Santa Fe

Stephen B. Elkins

Rough Riders

Jointure Act

January 6, 1912

William C. McDonald

William H. Taft

CHAPTER X

New Mexico in the Twentieth Century

The end of the nineteenth century saw rapid development in New Mexico's economy and life. The quality of beef improved and gradually replaced the wild longhorns. Thousands were shipped by railroad, and the long cattle drives were no longer necessary. During this period, the once hated sheep of early territorial days became a part of the great cattle ranches throughout New Mexico. Because of new methods and better machinery, agriculture made great strides toward building the economy of the state. New mining facilities aided in the prospects for further development in that area.

In 1881, the first telephones were used in Santa Fe. The first electric lights were turned on in Albuquerque during the 1890s.

Brighter days were ahead for New Mexico as the twentieth century brought even more changes. New colleges began. The first oil well drilled in New Mexico was in Eddy County in 1909. By 1922, the oil industry had begun to boom with additional discoveries in Artesia and San Juan Counties. By 1954, eight out of New Mexico's thirty-two counties had started producing oil. The discovery of uranium and the development of the atomic bomb at the Los Alamos Laboratories ushered in the Atomic Age in New Mexico by 1945. Since that time New Mexico has continued to grow and to prosper. Many New Mexicans helped with the Surveyor Moon Program and contributed to the success of the first lunar landing. These are only a few of the contributions New Mexicans have made to make our nation great.

Porfirio Díaz, and Francisco Madero became president. Soon after he assumed his duties, he was assassinated. Mexico was left in utter confusion. Many different parties sprang up, each wanting to control the government.

For years, American citizens had owned property in Mexico, but the revolutionaries caused great damage to their homes and business places. One of these revolutionary groups was led by Pancho Villa. He was supposed to have raided towns along the border of the United States in January of 1916.

William C. McDonald, first governor of the State of New Mexico in 1912.

Early Years

Soon after New Mexico was admitted to the Union, the people began the difficult task of strenthening and improving their state government. New tax laws were passed, and a state budget was adopted to operate the government. Other laws were designed to regulate court procedure and elections. The state legislature also elected the first two senators, Thomas B. Catron and Albert B. Fall: to Washington. George Curry and Harvey B. Fergusson were both elected as representatives to Congress and served one year respectively in 1912 and 1913.

Shortly after statehood, New Mexico became involved with an international problem. In 1911, a revolutionary group overthrew the dictator of Mexico, Don

Pancho Villa, the Mexican revolutionary, raided the border towns between the United States and Mexico.

Villa Hill, Columbus, New Mexico. On this hill Villa directed his troops in the raid on Columbus.

He was accused of attacking and killing a number of people at Columbus, New Mexico two months later. No one actually saw Pancho Villa during the raid on Columbus. Yet it is certain that several Mexican outlaws did cause widespread damage in the town.

President Wilson sent General John J. Pershing and a detachment of regular army troops to protect the border at Columbus. The New Mexico National Guard provided 800 troops to support the mission into Mexico. They did not capture Villa but instead almost caused an international crisis by sending American troops into Mexico. Shortly after the expedition into Mexico, the troops were ordered back to the United States.

The army spent almost one year at the border, and during that time, the troops constructed a military airbase and motor pool. The first military use of airplanes and land motor vehicles by the United States was in support of Pershing's campaigns into Mexico.

At this time, a major war was well under way in Europe. In August 1914, Russia, France, and England declared war on Germany, Austria, and Turkey. In 1917, Germany sent submarines into the North Atlantic to sink supply ships, including those of the United States. In March 1917, it was learned that Germany offered Mexico a chance to recover lost territory in New Mexico, Texas, and Arizona. Mexico was urged to join Germany in declaring war on the United States. Because of the offer to Mexico and the attacks on neutral shipping, President Wilson on April 2, 1917, asked Congress to declare war on Germany. Soon after the declaration of war, New Mexico's National Guard was called to active duty to be sent overseas. Many men enlisted, and others were drafted. More than 17,000 New Mexicans served in the armed forces during the First World War. New Mexicans at home did their part during the war. Some of the people volunteered for civilian work. Others offered their services to the farmers and ranchers to provide additional supplies of food for the military forces in Europe. Production in mining was increased considerably during this time.

When the war ended in November 1918, the need for these goods suddenly dropped. Income dropped, and producers everywhere had to cut back in labor and in volume of production. During this time, service men were returning to civilian life in search of jobs. But not enough jobs existed for them. Many people suffered greatly from unemployment after the war. Businessmen who had borrowed large sums of money to expand their businesses during the war found it difficult to pay their debts. Some went bankrupt; others sold their property for whatever they could get to pay their debts. Besides these problems, a severe drought caused additional hardship for many years.

By the middle of the 1920s, business had begun to improve. The automobile industry offered some relief. The industry developed during the war, and in 1923, the assembly line provided many more automobiles than ever before. New highways became necessary and helped to encourage prosperity throughout the nation.

Large sums of money were poured into these and many other industries by private investors. These people bought part ownership in companies through purchase of stocks, or shares. Many people did this and quickly sold the shares when prices rose. This kind of investing only hurt business in the long run.

Soon stocks became worthless as prices for them were not based on the ability of the company to earn a profit. Indeed, businesses were overextended and many were unable to pay back their loans. The stock market collapsed in 1929. Businesses were wrecked, and many investors were ruined. Banks were closed, and the entire nation faced the most serious depression in history.

Depression and War

The depression caused great hardship to New Mexicans. Many of the people in the state depended on farming to make a living. But aid to farmers did not come until the 1930s when a broad-based relief program was introduced by

General John J. Pershing, Commander of the American troops sent to Columbus, New Mexico. In 1917, he became the Commander of the American Expeditionary Force sent to France.

the federal government in 1932.

Franklin D. Roosevelt was the new president and his program was called the "New Deal." For the hard pressed farmer the program meant various kinds of aid. The Agricultural Adjustment Act set prices for goods so that farmers earned more. The Farm Credit Administration provided federal loans to the farmer to buy seed, fertilizer, and farm equipment. He was also able to pay off his mortgage and put his farm on a paying basis. Both agencies were set up in 1933. The New Mexico congressional representatives were active in creating the laws behind them.

Other programs were started that helped to relieve unemployment. The Federal Emergency Relief Administration (FERA), begun in 1933, provided food and clothing to those who were out of work. One of the most beneficial programs was the WPA (Works Progress Administration) begun in 1935. This effort provided many jobs in the construction of highways, bridges, college facilities, and municipal buildings. Two outstanding examples of WPA contributions in Albuquerque are the old terminal building of the Albuquerque Airport and the main library on the University of New Mexico campus. Another program was the homeowner's loan corporation to help thousands of homeowners to borrow money to keep up their mortgage payments. Later, the Federal Housing Administration (FHA) was organized for purchasing and improving homes. The Civilian Conservation Corps (CCC) provided jobs for young men out of work. Special camps were constructed near their jobs where workers built roads, dams, and picnic areas. Other CCC men planted thousands of trees on state and federal lands under the reforestation program. In

New Mexico, Governor Clyde Tingley (1935-38) was especially committed to the New Deal policies for recovery.

There were other New Deal programs which had long-range objectives. Congress passed a law designed to protect depositors against losing their money if a bank failed. The Federal Deposit Insurance Corporation (FDIC) provided for the insurance of bank deposits. Today, each bank deposit is insured up to $100,000. Perhaps the most important legislation of this period is the Social Security Act, passed by Congress in 1935. This act provides federal support for disability insurance, old-age pensions, public health services, and care for the blind and for needy children. A recent addition to Social Security is the Medicare program for the aged.

By the middle of the 1930's, the depression had begun to ease. Then, in 1939, the Second World War broke out in Europe. Almost overnight, demand increased for American products. Factories opened up all over the United States, providing jobs for millions of Americans. On December 7, 1941, Japan made a surprise attack on the naval base at Pearl Harbor, Hawaii. The next day the United States declared war on Japan and the other members of the Axis Powers — Germany and Italy. Plans were immediately made by the United States government to establish training bases for the Army Air Corps. Army camps were set up in various places throughout the states. Colleges accepted government sponsored Reserve Officers Training Corps (ROTC) programs with their regular courses of study. Atomic projects were set up later at Los Alamos and Holloman Air Force Base. New industries were established. Farmers in the state of New Mexico were called upon to produce food for

SPAIN

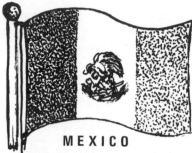

MEXICO

CONFEDERATE
STATES OF AMERICA

UNITED STATES
OF AMERICA

a war-time economy. A site near Roswell was also selected as a prisoner of war camp for Germans captured in North Africa. Many of these fought under General Erwin Rommel, the "Desert Fox."

Many New Mexicans were called to active duty in the armed forces of the United States. The Two-Hundredth Coast Artillery, composed largely of men from New Mexico and stationed in the Philippines, fought bravely during their heroic stand against overwhelming Japanese forces on Bataan peninsula and Corregidor. Bataan fell on April 9, 1942, and the American forces at these outposts surrendered to the Japanese. Those who survived became prisoners of war. During their march to prison and during the three years of confinement, the soldiers suffered terrible hardships. Many from New Mexico died from beatings, disease, and starvation. The war in the Pacific was very harsh, but New Mexicans of Native American heritage defended their country with great courage. One was a Marine who helped raise the American flag during the bitter fight on the island of Iwo Jima in 1945. Many others distinguished themselves in military communications. The Indian languages were used to pass messages, and the Japanese were unable to understand them. In August 1945, the first atomic bombs ever used in warfare were dropped on Hiroshima and Nagasaki. On August 10, 1945, Japan surrendered to the United States. During the war, more than 60,000 New Mexicans served in the armed forces, and some 1,500 gave their lives in the service of their country in Asia, in

The present Capitol Building located between Don Gaspar and College avenues, Santa Fe, New Mexico.

Africa, and in Europe. One of those killed in the final months of the war in the Pacific was New Mexico-born Ernie Pyle. As a newspaperman, Pyle was famous for the firsthand reports he made on battles.

Hundreds of New Mexicans were in service during the Korean War (1950-53), and many more served their country overseas in Vietnam (1965-73).

Santa Fe — The Capital City

New Mexico, the fifth largest state in the United States, has an area of 121,666 square miles. It is bounded on the north by Colorado, on the east by Oklahoma and Texas, on the south by Texas and Mexico, and on the west by Arizona.

Santa Fe, the capital city of New Mexico, has both the newest and oldest capitol buildings in the United States. The oldest is the Palace of the Governors, built in 1610 on the north side of the tree-lined Plaza in mid-town Santa Fe. The newest is the cluster of "territorial" style statehouse buildings, facing the Santa Fe River over broad

landscaped lawns. The new Legislative-Executive Building was completed in 1966. It was ready for use during the regular session of the legislature in 1967. It is located between Don Gaspar and College avenues, with Paseo de Peralta on the south. The State Library Building is on the corner of Don Gaspar Avenue and De Vargas Streets, and a Supreme Court building annex adjoins the original structure to the north.

The old Palace, now the Museum of New Mexico, was, for almost three centuries, the seat of government: Spanish, Mexican, and American. For twelve years it was headquarters for a loose federation of Indians during the Pueblo Revolt, which lasted from 1680 to 1692. For a few days in 1862, the old Palace housed the command of a Confederate army which captured and held Santa Fe briefly in March of that year.

When the Palace was erected in 1610, it was the first major building in the new city of La Villa Real de la Santa Fé. The large one-story structure was surrounded by an adobe wall. Inside

198

Zozobra (Old Man Gloom) towering over Santa Fe, New Mexico, heralds the start of La Fiesta de Santa Fe, held each year in early September. The Fiesta commemorates the reconquest of New Mexico and Santa Fe by Don Diego de Vargas in 1692-1693.

were quarters for soldiers, several government buildings, and stables for the soldiers' horses. At one end of the long portal was the storeroom for gun powder; at the other, a chapel. After the United States forces took possession of New Mexico in 1846, they established themselves in the same Palace.

In 1886, a new territorial capitol was built on the south side of the Santa Fe River, near the site of the present statehouse. Six years later, a mysterious fire burned it to the ground. Territorial officials were given approval to build a new capitol after the fire, but the treasury was short of funds. Not until three years later was a definite start made.

A second new capitol was completed on June 4, 1900. Its dedication saw a great parade move through the streets of Santa Fe. The dedication was by Chief Justice William J. Mills, who twelve years later was to be the last territorial governor to occupy the capitol.

The Territorial Legislative Assembly in 1907 authorized the construction of what was to be the first of several annexes to the capitol, as well as a Governor's Mansion on the same tree-shaded grounds. In 1922, a new wing was added to the building facing Don Gaspar Avenue. In 1936-37, a new State Supreme Court Building was built. In 1936, the National Guard Armory was constructed on the outskirts of Santa Fe on the Las Vegas Highway. A new building was completed south of the capital city on the Cerrillos Highway in 1963.

In 1955, the executive residence for the governor was completed on the northern edge of Santa Fe. The State Highway Department Building, located on Cerrillos Road, was completed in 1956. A new Land Office building was erected on College Avenue in 1960. Santa Fe combines the ancient cultural traditions with those of modern society.

The Santa Fe Fiesta commemorates the bloodless reconquest of New Mexico by de Vargas in 1692. On the first day of Fiesta, a de Vargas Mass, in honor of the hero of reconquest, is held in Saint Francis Cathedral. The festivities start with the burning of Zozobra (Old Man Gloom), a papier-mache monster. It makes hideous noises and signifies that all the bad spirits and gloom have been driven away from happy events to come. Fiesta in Santa Fe is the time for costumes, which range from early Spanish period clothes to modern style, western outfits. The Conquistadores

STATE FLAG
(Zia Sign)

STATE SONG
"O Fair New Mexico"
by Elizabeth Garrett

"Así es Nuevo Méjico"
by Amadeo Lucero

STATE MAMMAL
Bear

STATE BIRD
Roadrunner

Ball is a gala event with brilliant and colorful costuming. The Fiesta, which begins on Friday, ends with the Baile de la Gente (People's Dance), a picturesque street dance.

The Santa Fe Opera Company first performed on July 3, 1957, in a new outdoor theater north of Santa Fe. The founder and general manager of the company is John O. Crosby. In the first ten years of its life, the Santa Fe Opera Company had more than two hundred performances, plus special events for youth. On July 27, 1967, the opera stage was destroyed by fire a few hours after one of the performances. However, despite the fire, the Santa Fe Opera did not miss a single performance. The remainder of the opera session was continued in Sweeney Gym in Santa Fe. Immediately after the fire, a nationwide campaign was launched to raise one million dollars to rebuild the opera theater Construction was completed in time for the 1968 season.

The opera theater is located on a hilltop about 5 miles (8 km.) north of' Santa Fe, on U.S. Highway 64-84. There are 27 performances annually on Wednesday, Friday, and Saturday nights, starting in June and ending in late August. The theater has grown from 480 seats in 1957 to more than 2,800 in 1969.

State Seal. The "Great Seal" was designed for New Mexico when it became a territory in 1851. The original seal has long since disappeared, and since that time several other designs have been used by different territorial secretaries. W. G. Ritch, Secretary of the Territory from 1873-1884, however, used the great territorial seal often, and in 1882, added several features to the design. The present design was established by law in 1915. The seal is

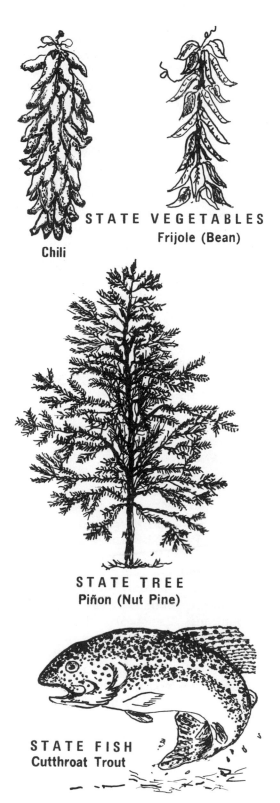

Unit 4

STATE VEGETABLES
Frijole (Bean)
Chili

STATE TREE
Piñon (Nut Pine)

STATE FISH
Cutthroat Trout

circular with the words "Great Seal of the State of New Mexico" written around the edge of the circle. Below is the date, 1912, when New Mexico became a state. Above the date are the words "Crescit Eundo" (It grows as it goes). The larger of the two eagles on the seal represents the American bald eagle with extended wings, grasping three arrows in its claws and shielding the small Mexican eagle (harpy eagle). The small eagle is holding a snake in its beak and cactus in its claws.

State Flag. The present state flag is a combination of the Zia sun symbol in red on a golden yellow background. The symbol of the Indians of Zia Pueblo represents perfect friendship. The colors, red and yellow, are those of Queen Isabella of Castile. They were carried by the first Spanish *conquistadores* (conquerors) to enter New Mexico.

The major share of the credit for the flag belongs to the New Mexico Chapter of the Daughters of the American Revolution. In 1923, they offered a prize for the best design submitted for a state flag. Doctor Harry Mera, an outstanding Santa Fe physician and archeologist, won the prize. In March 1925, Governor A. T. Hannett signed House Bill 164, making the flag produced by Dr. and Mrs. Mera the official state flag. Mrs. Mera made the first flag and stitched the first red Zia symbol on a field of yellow.

The official salute to the state flag is: "I salute the flag of the State of New Mexico, the Zia symbol of perfect friendship among united cultures."

State Song. "O, Fair New Mexico" was written in 1914 by Miss Elizabeth Garrett, blind daughter of Sheriff Pat

Garrett, the territorial lawman who shot Billy the Kid. The 1917 state legislation adopted it as the official state song. The Spanish adaptation, Así es Nuevo Méjico written by Amadeo Lucero; was approved by the State Legislature in 1971.

State Flower. There are seven varieties of yucca that grow in New Mexico. On March 14, 1927, the New Mexico legislature passed a bill making the *Yucca elata* the official state flower. In early summer when the yucca is in bloom it produces many cuplike blossoms flowering from the tips of stalks. These stalks sometimes grow to a height of 10 feet (3 m.) out of a cluster of sharp pointed leaves, which are sometimes called Spanish bayonets. During pioneer days, the women used the roots of the yucca, called "amole," as a source of soap. The Indians for centuries have used it as a shampoo.

State Tree. The familiar, useful piñon, or Rocky Mountain nut pine *(Pinus edulis)*, grows on the high mesas and foothills of the state. The trees vary in height from 10 to 30 feet (3 m. to 10 m.). The tiny pine nuts were discovered as tasty food by the prehistoric Indians and by the Spanish when they came to New Mexico more than four hundred years ago. Today they are sold as roasted nuts or in candy. The wood is used in construction. When it is burned, it gives off a pleasing fragrance making it a favorite fireplace fuel. The legislature officially adopted the piñon as the state tree in 1948.

State Bird. The roadrunner *(Geococcyx californianus)*, also called paisano, chaparral, ground cuckoo, and snake killer, is found throughout the state except in the mountains of northern New Mexico. The state bird, approximately two feet (.6 m.) in length

including the tail, has a long bill and crested head. His coloring is mostly brown and white, but in the sunlight the feathers attain a glossy green, camouflaging it among the yucca, mesquite, and cedar. The nests are about one foot (.3 m.) in diameter and are usually found in the cactus bushes or low trees. With his long, slender legs, the roadrunner attains speeds up to 15 and 20 miles (24 km. to 32 km.) per hour. The state bird earned the name "roadrunner" because it kept to the middle of the wagon ruts a few yards ahead of the pioneers' Conestoga wagons. The legislature officially adopted the roadrunner as the state bird on March 16, 1949.

State Fish. The native cutthroat trout *(Salmo Clarki)* became the official state fish by the act of the New Mexico legislature in 1955. It gets its name from the streaks under the throat. The fish is dark olive and has scattered black spots. The cutthroat trout is found in the cold mountain streams and lakes of northern New Mexico, and it averages from 6 to 8 inches (15.24 cm. to 20.32 cm.) in length. Some of the larger ones are 14 to 15 inches (35 cm. to 37.5 cm.) and weigh more than one pound (.5 kg.) They are excellent game fish and good fighters.

State Mammal. The black bear *(Ursus americanus)* is found throughout New Mexico in wooded areas and in the mountains. The bear, which may be brown, cinnamon, or black, was chosen as the state's official mammal by the 26th state legislature. Smokey, the most famous bear and a living symbol of fire prevention, was born in the Lincoln Forest near Capitan. He was found after a forest fire had destroyed his home and killed his mother. After his death he was returned to the Lincoln Forest.

For his diet, the bear will eat grass, berries, and fruit, as well as smaller wild game and occasionally livestock. The bear, which may be hunted by a licensed hunter during the proper season, usually weighs between 250 and 300 pounds (109 kg. to 135 kg.).

State Vegetables. The chili and fríjol were adopted by the legislature in 1965 as the official state vegetables. In the adobe villages of New Mexico, long strings of red chilies may be seen suspended from the roofs to dry in the sunshine. There is a great demand for chili from outside markets. It has become one of the principal exports of the state.

The fríjol or pinto bean, another principal product of New Mexico, is either a dark reddish color or a light tan with dark brown spots. In the early stages of New Mexico's history, the colonization and rapid growth of the state could not have been possible without this quick growing, high protein plant.

State Gem. In 1967, the state legislature adopted turquoise as the state gem of New Mexico. The Southwestern Indians have used turquoise in jewelry making for centuries. The bluish-green gem stones are mined in several parts of the state, but high quality stones are becoming scarce. Today, Indian craftsmen make outstanding turquoise jewelry which sells for several hundred dollars.

State Fossil, Insect, and Cookie. In 1981, the state legislature adopted the *Coelophysis* dinosaur (pronounced see-LA-fisis) as the state fossil. Skeletal remains were uncovered near Ghost Ranch north of Santa Fe in 1947. Later, the 39th legislature adopted the Tarantula Hawk Wasp (*Pepsis formosa*) as the insect and at the same time, the biscochito (*bizcochito*) officially became the state cookie.

Cotton, alfalfa, corn, and grain sorghams are raised in abundance in the Mesilla Valley near Las Cruces in southern New Mexico. Water is provided by the Elephant Butte Reservoir.

Newly-baled hay lies in a fertile field along the Rio Grande, near Albuquerque, New Mexico. Waters of the Rio Grande are used extensively for irrigation. The rugged Sandia Mountains are in the background.

Modern Farming and Ranching

Modern farming began when thousands of people from the East invaded New Mexico shortly after the coming of the railroads between 1879 and 1882. As fast as the rail lines were built into the territory, the nesters and homesteaders followed them. By 1900, more than five million acres had been cultivated. Today there are more than 47 million acres under cultivation.

Among the early farming towns established in New Mexico during the late territorial period was an all-black community known as Blackdom. The town site was located approximately 18 miles (29 km.) south of Roswell and 8 miles (13 km.) west of Dexter in Chaves County, New Mexico. This was an attempt by Black settlers to homestead the land and establish their own culture. By 1929 they had erected two churches and one school. There was

also a general store and post office located in the center of the town surrounded by more than 50,000 acres of homestead land. Within the next few years, all of the people had moved away from the community and Blackdom became a ghost town.

In the beginning, the established cattlemen tried to keep out the farmer by fencing in the water and using force, when necessary, to frighten off the homesteader. However, the federal government provided 160 acres of land in the West to anyone who would cultivate the land and continue to produce crops. The farmer was soon to find that the same amount of land suitable for farming in the East for one family would not do in the semi-arid areas of New Mexico. Many farmers moved away. Some stayed, mastered the techniques of dry-land farming, and raised crops suited to the arid condi-

tions. Crops such as millet, grain sorghum, and corn were introduced. The dry-land farmer also began raising cattle as an additional income when rainfall was scarce.

In some areas where a great deal of surface water was available, farming was carried on extensively. When the water was gone, the farmer had to find new methods for raising crops. The Bureau of Reclamation, originally known as the Reclamation Service, was established in June 1902, for the purpose of constructing irrigation works for land in the West which was not suited to farming. Over the years, as needs have developed, the Bureau's program has been extended. It has been able to supply water to industries and towns, to generate electric power, to provide water for recreation, and to provide service for many other uses. By 1905, 485 water wells had been drilled in the southeastern part of New Mexico. In the years that followed the

Milo-maize growing near Tucumcari, New Mexico. The Conchas Dam in northeastern New Mexico provides water for thousands of people and for irrigating 45,000 acres of neighboring land.

Livestock — Tucumcari Project — New Mexico. One of the major industries on the Tucumcari Project is cattle. Shown here is a small portion of the cattle at the Weisbert Feed Lot approximately 4 miles (6 km.) northeast of Tucumcari.

establishment of the Reclamation Act, several dams and reservoirs were constructed throughout the state.

Reservoirs such as Sumner, Caballo, Cochiti, Conchas, Elephant Butte, El Vado, and the Navajo Dam and Reservoir (located in San Juan County) were constructed for redistribution of water. Besides furnishing water for irrigation, these dams provide recreational facilities for tourists and citizens of New Mexico. Besides the numerous dams and reservoirs, water wells provide additional water for irrigation and household purposes throughout the state. New Mexico presently diverts more than three million acre-feet of water annually for irrigation of about one million acres of land. Of this amount, some 1,662,000-acre-feet is diverted as surface water, and the remaining 1,415,000 acre-feet is pumped from wells.

In 1960, there were more than one hundred flowing wells and at least 4,000 pumping wells in the state. Dams were built to provide additional water for farms. Scientific farming has developed also through crop rotation, modern fertilizing methods, and better seed.

The Rural Electrification Administration (REA) was created in 1935 by the federal government to provide loans to privately owned power companies to enable them to bring electric power to farms and ranches all over the country. Today almost every farm and ranch in the state of New Mexico has electricity.

Canals, dikes, contour farming, and cover crops have improved farming conditions greatly throughout the state. Weather conditions still play a major role in growing and harvesting crops in New Mexico. But since the introduction of modern farming methods, the value of farm crops has steadily increased from $10 million in 1900 to $200 million in 1974. The state's leading farm crops are cotton, hay, grain sorghums, corn, fruits, and peanuts.

Hay and sorghums are grown primarily for use in feeding livestock, especially through the period of bad range conditions.

More than 125,000 acres of land are planted with wheat each year. New Mexico produces the spring and winter varieties, valued at more than $5 million.

There are many areas in New Mexico which grow oats, rye, barley, broom-corn, and potatoes; peaches, apples, peanuts, and truck crops have added to the exanding economy of the state.

Through the years, the ranching industry has changed from the raising of sheep and cattle on the open range to the raising of high grade stock on fenced ranches. In 1974, cattle on New Mexico farms and ranches totaled 1,553,000 head. The "feed lot" industry makes possible the increase in cattle raising.

The value of all cattle in New Mexico in 1974 was more than $208 million. As cattle increased in number and value over the years, the number of sheep has decreased sharply. In 1974, the total number of sheep on farms and ranches totaled 529,305. Sheep numbers have declined each year since estimates were started in 1881, and this is the

The pecan orchard at the Stahmann Farms near Las Cruces, New Mexico, stretches over 4,000 acres and is said to be the largest in the world. Pecans are an important crop in the Mesilla Valley of southern New Mexico.

lowest number on record. Farming and ranching since territorial days have changed to meet the needs of a modern society.

Modern Mining

During the early period of mining in New Mexico, gold and silver production was fairly strong. Soon, though, many mines were worked out and abandoned. Other mine fields were left because it became too expensive to mine the ore. Modern facilities have increased gold and silver mining, and the combined value of the ores in 1978 amounted to nearly $3 million.

Coal mining developed rapidly before 1900. Estimated production was more than one million tons. During the next several decades, coal mining became a major industry in New Mexico. Because of the increased production and use of natural gas after World War II, the need for coal decreased sharply. For several decades very little coal was being shipped from the state. By 1983, coal will be in major production again with both surface (strip) and sub-surface mining. Since 1972, the Coal Surface Mining Commission (Reclamation Commission) has been issuing permits and monitoring the coal producing areas of New Mexico.

Copper mining has continued to increase over the years, except for those years that the various companies were involved in a labor strike. At Santa Rita, the Kennecott Copper Company uses machines to take the ore out of an open pit. The company also built a

This smokestack at Hurley, New Mexico, can be seen for many miles around. The town of Hurley is located 10 miles (16 km.) south of the Santa Rita copper mine and serves as a treating point for copper ore. The concentrate is then shipped to smelters and refineries.

▼▼▼▼▼▼▼▼▼▼▼▼▼▼▼▼▼▼▼▼▼

Above — Buffalo once roamed the plains of southeastern New Mexico where oil derricks rise today. These wells are in an oil field northeast of Lovington, New Mexico.

Right — Since its discovery by the Spanish in 1800, the large open pit mine at Santa Rita, New Mexico has produced many thousands of tons of copper annually. When the mine came under American management in 1873, mass development was begun. Santa Rita is said to be the largest open pit copper mine in the world.

refinery at Hurley to separate the copper from the ore. When present operations began more than 50 years ago, one of the first buildings erected was a power plant at Hurley to generate electricity for the operations of the mine and the refinery. In 1969, the value of copper produced in New Mexico was more than $116 million. New Mexico ranks fifth in the nation for copper production. In the near future, copper will be extremely valuable in the production of solar energy.

The Phelps-Dodge Corporation's new open-pit copper mine at Tyrone, located southwest of Silver City, added to the growing copper industry in New Mexico. Near Fierro, in Grant County, the construction of the new Continental copper mine and mill project of the United States Smelting, Refining and Mining Company has been completed. Underground mining is carried on at the site, but recent investigations show that sufficient ore has been found near

Here is a scene in the "downtown" section of Tyrone, New Mexico, once called the only deluxe ghost town in America. Because of a new mining operation begun in the 1970s, Tyrone was destroyed.

the surface to justify an open-pit operation. Mining operations are underway at this site. Additional drilling programs are underway near Lordsburg, in Hidalgo County, to develop additional reserves.

Lead and zinc, found in the same area as copper, add to the economy of New Mexico. The production was valued at more than $26 million in 1976. Other minerals that have helped in the growth of the state are manganese, molybdenum, and vanadium.

New Mexico ranks first in the nation in the production of potash. More than 85 percent of the potash produced in the United States comes from the Carlsbad area. In 1931, a rich potash deposit was found near Carlsbad. Recently, geologists have indicated that potash deposits may be found as far south as the Pecos Valley in Texas. In 1977, production was valued at more than $178 million.

Potash, used mainly for fertilizer, has some use in the chemical industry and in silk manufacturing. It is also used in making gun powder.

Since the development of the atomic age, the demand for uranium has greatly increased. In 1950, the ore was discovered by Paddy Martínez, a Navajo, on the reservation. In less than ten years, it has become one of the nation's most valuable minerals. So far in New Mexico, uranium has been mined in the area around Grants and Gallup, and some mining is being carried on in San Juan County and Sandoval County. More than 70 percent of uranium ore in the United States is centered near Grants, New Mexico, the "uranium capital" of the world.

The mining process of uranium is very expensive, and the true value of the industry has not been determined. Uranium is a radioactive metal used in

Giant Domes in the Hall of Giants in Carlsbad Caverns National Park in southern New Mexico. Although 37 miles (59 km.) of the Caverns have been explored, no one knows how far they extend under the Guadalupe Mts. Tours are made daily over 7 miles, (11 km.) of the lighted corridors 750 feet (225 m.) underground.

the development of atomic energy. By the later 1970s, New Mexico led the nation in production with over fifteen million tons. At the present rate of excavation, it is expected that there will be six new mines producing uranium in the Grants area by 1983. Meanwhile, the search for uranium is continuing near Pietown in Catron County.

The first discovery of oil in New Mexico was in 1882 on the Navajo reservation in San Juan County. In 1909, the first oil was drilled near Artesia, in Eddy County. In 1922, both oil and gas were discovered in large quantities in northwestern New Mexico. Oil wells were dug in 1924 in the Artesia district, and by 1930 the Hobbs pool was established.

Following World War II, deep

discoveries in south Lea County and later in north Lea County caused southeast New Mexico to become one of the most active areas in the country and added greatly to the state's oil and gas reserves. During the 1950s, continued activity in the southeast counties was supplemented by the discoveries of additional reserves of both oil and gas in San Juan and Rio Arriba counties in the northwest. During the "boom" years of the 1950s, oil rigs were seen throughout the counties of Eddy and Lea, as well as the counties in northwestern New Mexico. Oil pumps have replaced the rigs. Since the boom years, the number of drilling rigs has decreased sharply. However, Lea County is still one of the nation's top oil producers.

In the Hobbs area, some drilling is being carried on. In 1969, an automatic drilling machine, first of its kind to be used in New Mexico, was set up by the Bandera Drilling Company of Dallas, Texas, for the Continental Oil Company lease on the western edge of Hobbs. The new drilling machine has additional safety features, and it can be operated by one man. The automatic drilling machine has provided a new method in drilling for oil. The total value of all minerals produced in New Mexico in 1977 was more than $2.5 billion. Oil and gas production made up more than 50 percent of this figure.

New Mexico is leading the nation in the search for new energy sources. Sandia Corporation is involved in solar research that promises to be a future source of energy for home and for industrial use. Solar research is also being conducted at New Mexico State University in Las Cruces. Solar energy

Roswell's Nancy Lopez Knight, champion golfer.

could supply about a quarter of the nation's energy needs by the year 2000.

At the present time, geothermal excavations are being conducted near Lordsburg in Hidalgo County and near the town of Socorro in Socorro County. The only geothermal producing area in New Mexico at the present time is located at Jemez in Sandoval County.

Even the wind is being harnessed as an energy source, particularly in southern and northeastern New Mexico.

The need to find new sources of energy is urgent. Oil and gas now supply most of our energy needs. But they are being used up rapidly. The search for alternative energy sources — such as solar—has become a major concern for both the state and the nation as well.

Recreation

Improved transportation and highways have brought millions of tourists to New Mexico. There are more than

12,000 miles (19,200 km.) of paved roads in the state. These join all the cities and towns, and most of the roads lead to the historical sites and recreational areas. Recreation and tourist trade have grown rapidly since World War II. Together they have become a big business in New Mexico. The federal and state governments have set aside vast areas of forest land for picnic areas and overnight camping. Many historic places have been designated as state and national monuments to provide additional sites for tourists from outside of New Mexico and for the people of the state.

New Mexico is famous for its many ghost towns scattered over the state. These towns were at one time thriving frontier towns, stage stops, railroad stations, and mining camps. Some of the most colorful boomtowns were the mining camps in Mogollon, located in Catron County, and in the Cerrillos Hills south of Santa Fe.

There are more than 50 state and national parks and monuments in New Mexico. The National Park Service was established in 1916, and the State Service in 1936. Refer to the appendix, page 274, for a list of the various parks and monuments found in New Mexico.

Wildlife is protected in New Mexico. During the hunting season, if one has a license, certain animals may be hunted throughout the state. Fish hatcheries were built by the State Game and Fish Department. Many lakes and mountain streams have been stocked for citizens of the state and tourists. Everyone 14 years of age or older must have a license to fish in the state of New Mexico.

Besides state and national parks, many towns and cities in New Mexico have established local recreational attractions for the townspeople and visitors. There are museums, parks, and swimming areas within the towns. Many communities enjoy the local rodeos during the season.

In the winter, skiing occurs in many parts of the state. The areas around Cloudcroft and Ruidoso in southern New Mexico are being enjoyed by more and more skiers every year. In northern New Mexico, Sandia Peak, Taos Ski Valley, Raton, Santa Fe, and many other ski areas have contributed to the winter wonderland of the state.

There are five areas in the state that promote horse-racing: La Mesa Park in Raton, New Mexico State Fair in Albuquerque, Ruidoso Downs in Ruidoso, the Downs at Santa Fe, south of Santa Fe, and Sunland Park, south of Las Cruces. Each year hundreds of the finest thoroughbreds and quarter horses in the country delight local sportsmen as well as out-of-state fans with their running ability. New Mexico is internationally known for the Futurity Race at Ruidoso Downs every Labor Day. It is the richest horse race in the world. The fine abilities of a New Mexico thoroughbred were seen in 1968 when Iron Card, trained under the expert guidance of G. W. McClanahan, became the second horse to win three out of four feature races since racing began in New Mexico in 1938.

Golf is enjoyed year around in many parts of New Mexico, and the sport has been given a real boost by Roswell's Nancy Lopez Knight. In 1978, her first season as a professional, she was named best lady golfer of the year after winning an unprecedented nine tournaments and earning nearly $190,000 in prize money. An achievement such as this must be mentioned because it has brought worldwide fame to an outstanding New Mexico athlete.

Atomic Age and Space Age in New Mexico

The Atomic Age in New Mexico had its beginning during World War II. The military picture at that time was very grim in Europe, as well as in the South Pacific. It became necessary to find a means to end the war as quickly as possible. Germany had experimented with a rocket called the V-2 rocket that was capable of destroying cities, towns, and military areas many miles from its launching site. In addition to the V-2 rocket, German scientists were working toward an atomic bomb. No one in America knew for sure just how much they had accomplished in their research. Besides these events in Europe, the American forces in the South Pacific had not yet recovered from the terrible disaster that was suffered at Pearl Harbor. Also, the Japanese Kamikaze (Divine Wind) planes were causing severe damage to warships, resulting in the loss of hundreds of American troops and many ships in the South Pacific.

Because of the dangerous situation at that time, the American government in 1942 decided that an atomic bomb must be made. It would be used as a means for bringing World War II to an end.

Very little information had been gathered, however, in connection with an atom bomb. One important event happened in 1942 that led to the development of the bomb. A Chicago group, under the direction of Enrico Fermi, had succeeded in bringing about the world's first man-made nuclear chain reaction. But no technological information had been gathered as far

▼▼▼▼▼▼▼▼▼▼▼▼▼▼▼▼▼▼▼▼▼

as bombs were concerned. At any rate, the next year the decision had been made, and a site was selected for research and development of an atomic bomb at the Los Alamos Boys Ranch in northern New Mexico.

As rapidly as possible, the Boys Ranch was converted into the Los Alamos Laboratory, or "Project Y" as it was called. The work there was the most closely guarded secret of the century. The group of scientists to develop and construct the bomb was under the direction of J. Robert Oppenheimer. Some of the members of this outstanding group of scientists who came from laboratories all over the country and world included Enrico Fermi, Emelio Segre, I. I. Rabi, Neils Bohr, Bruno Rossi, and Hans Bethe, together with Rolf Landshoft, Edward Teller, Otto Frisch, John van Neumann, Joseph Kennedy, George Kistiakowsky, Edwin McMillan, and Richard Feynman. All of them came to Los Alamos, some for just a short time and some as permanent members of the staff. The University of California was selected to operate the new laboratory. A formal non-profit contract was soon drawn with the Manhattan Engineer District of the Army. By early spring of 1943, the best scientific minds that could be found in the world had begun the work of developing the atomic bomb.

During the months that followed, security and secrecy of the project became a way of life. Members of the research team and their families were not allowed to contact relatives or friends outside the heavily guarded and fenced area at Los Alamos. Nor were

they permitted to travel more than one hundred miles (161 km.) from the project. Famous names and occupations of the scientists were not mentioned. Everyone was an engineer, and the word "physicist" was forbidden. Names of the scientists were changed; for example, Enrico Fermi became "Henry Farmer." Besides these changes, drivers' licenses, automobile registrations, bank accounts, income tax returns, ration cards, and insurance policies were issued as numbers instead of names.

The first atomic explosion on the Alamogordo Bombing Range in the Jornada del Muerto.

Marker on the sight of the world's first atomic explosion.

White Sands National Monument in southern New Mexico. The dunes are composed of pure white gypsum crystals, and cover 176,000 acres in the Tularosa Basin. Part of the area is used for testing missiles.

When the project began, there were less than three hundred people at the laboratory. By July 1945, the number had increased to 2,500 army and civilian personnel.

The first formal arrangements for the bomb test were made in 1944. A place needed to be selected to explode the bomb. Also some sort of container needed to be designed to house scientific instruments to record the blast. The choice was made to explode the bomb on a part of the Alamogordo Bombing Range in the Jornada del Muerto. The code name was "Trinity Site." A huge oblong container weighing two hundred tons, called "Jumbo," was finally constructed and set in place on a tower eight hundred feet (200 m.) above the blast area. On July 16, 1945, the first nuclear bomb was exploded with a thunderous roar that "shook the world" and ushered in the Atomic Age. One month later World War II was over, and in 1947, Congress established the Atomic Energy Commission. This agency put atomic energy under civilian control. Since that time, the University of California has operated the Los Alamos Scientific Laboratory (LASL).

During the years that followed the war, the Los Alamos Scientific Laboratory has built the famous electronic brain, MANIAC, to handle complex calculations. In 1952, the world's first thermonuclear device, called "Mike," was built by the laboratory at Los Alamos and exploded on the island of Eniwetok in the Pacific. The Los Alamos laboratory has, in the last ten years, built computers, a medical research center, nuclear reactors to determine how the atom works, and several other projects to aid the world in its progress towards peace.

One project that the Los Alamos Scientific Laboratory is currently working on is called "Project Sherwood." This program was set up to seek a method to control the speed of energy released by the atom. Another program, called "Project Rover," is being studied to develop a nuclear-driven rocket. In the near future man will be sent into space by means of nuclear rockets. There are numerous other projects going on at the laboratories in Los Alamos which will contribute to the future of mankind.

During the early years of World War II construction began on Holloman Air Force Base, then Alamogordo Army Air Field. The base was used as a training base for heavy bombers.

After the war, Holloman Air Force Base became a part of the nation's missile test program in 1947. Missile testing in New Mexico had begun on December 30, 1930, with a rocket launched by Dr. Robert Goddard from a site near Roswell. The basic design of his rockets were the models for those flown today. Near White Sands, Holloman was an ideal base for testing and developing the guided missile program. In July 1947, the Holloman Air Force Base launched its first ground-to-air pilotless aircraft to open the space age in New Mexico. One year later a jet bomb, similar to the German V-2 rocket, was launched at Holloman. Since that time, thousands of missiles have been fired. Some of the missiles tested include the *Snake, Matador,*

Air Force Missile Development Center, Holloman AFB, N.M. Appearing to be a flying bedstead, this weird looking contraption tested the highly successful surveyor spacecraft landing system during descent and drop tests at the Air Force Missile Development Center prior to the surveyor's lunar landing.

Rascal, Hound Dog, and *Bullpup,* which later contributed greatly in the achievements of guided missiles.

In 1954, Colonel John P. Stapp, in a rocket-sled at Holloman, attained the speed of 632 miles (1011 km.) per hour, a record at that time. Another great achievement came in 1960 when Captain J. W. Kittinger bailed out of an open balloon and parachuted to safety from a height of 102,800 feet (30,840 m.).

The Holloman Air Force Missile Development Center is one of five research and development centers under the Air Force Systems Command. Many different kinds of work are connected with the center, such as testing, evaluating, operating, and developing a variety of guidance systems. The largest rocket fired by a Holloman crew on the White Sands Missile Range was the Honest John-Mike-Nike. This project was part of a program to test the re-entry parachute on the Apollo spacecraft for the National Aeronautics and Space Administration (NASA). Many guidance systems for space flights have been tested at Holloman Air Force Base for additional Apollo and Voyager missions for the future.

A branch of the Cambridge Research Laboratories is located at Holloman Air Force Center. The Cambridge Research Laboratories are located in Bedford, Massachusetts. They were established soon after the war in 1945. The Cambridge Laboratory at Holloman sends large balloons into the atmosphere for scientific research. In September 1968, Holloman supported the launch of the largest balloon in history that reached a record height of 158,300 feet (47,490 m.).

Many programs are presently going on at Holloman that will continue to assist the various space missions that are planned for the future. Holloman Air Force Development, as well as many other research agencies, aided in the success of the first man on the moon. Many New Mexicans working at the Houston Space Center and the Cape Canaveral launch area are part of the team that made space travel possible.

In July 1969, one of the greatest projects in history, *Apollo XI,* was launched from Cape Canaveral with a crew of three astronauts—Neil A. Armstrong, Edwin E. Aldrin, and Michael Collins. Their mission was to land the spacecraft *Eagle* on the moon. Everyone in the world was to share in an outstanding achievement of mankind. On July 20, 1969, Neil Armstrong became the first man to set foot on the moon at Tranquility Base. Moments later, Edwin E. Aldrin became the second man to walk on the lunar surface. The words that Neil Armstrong spoke as he stepped onto the moon seem to sum up the efforts of everyone in the past, present, and future, whether he works directly with the space program or not. "That's one small step for a man, one giant leap for mankind."

About ten years later another historic flight was accomplished by three Albuquerque men — Ben Abruzzo, Maxie Anderson, and Larry Newman. In August 1978, the Double Eagle II balloon with these three crewmen left Presque Isle, Maine. Six days later they set the craft down in a wheat field 60 miles (96 km.) west of Paris near Evreux, France. The 3,200 mile (5120 km.) journey by the three New Mexicans was the first successful flight to cross the Atlantic in a balloon. The feat set a world record for both distance and endurance; the three Albuquerque balloonists succeeded where 17 previous missions had failed.

REVIEW ACTIVITIES

1. Make a time line showing when the cattle trails, stagecoach lines, railroads, and modern highways appeared in New Mexico.
2. From outside study, write an essay on the energy problems facing New Mexico. What can you do to help solve the growing shortage of crude oil and natural gas? Explain what is meant by the term "alternative energy source."
3. Make a scaled line chart showing New Mexico's major products, with some pictorial comparison of each product's annual contribution to the state's income.
4. On a map of the state, locate the important tourist areas in New Mexico. See how many you can find in your own area.
5. When was the first telephone used in New Mexico? What effect did this form of communication have on the citizenry?
6. When was electricity first used in New Mexico? How did this new energy source aid the various industries in the state?
7. What part did New Mexico play in the Atomic Age?
8. Name the first senators and representative from New Mexico.
9. What problem did the citizens of New Mexico have with the revolutionaries of Mexico?
10. Name several ways that the people of New Mexico contributed to the war effort during World Wars I and II.
11. List causes of recession in New Mexico after World War I.
12. How did the automobile aid the economy of New Mexico during the middle 1920s?
13. Why is the year 1929 remembered in United States and New Mexico history?
14. Who wrote "O, Fair New Mexico"?
15. Describe the state seal and state flag.
16. What is the name of the state flower, state tree, state bird, state fish, state mammal, state vegetable, and state gem?
17. How was the ranching industry changed in New Mexico?
18. How does New Mexico rank in the production of potash, oil, gas, and uranium?
19. List several reasons for New Mexico's high tourist trade.
20. Name some recent contributions Los Alamos Laboratory has made for the space program.
21. What are some of the achievements made by Holloman Air Force Development Center in recent years?

RECOGNIZE AND UNDERSTAND

Francisco Madero
Pancho Villa
John J. Pershing
The New Deal
CCC
WPA
Two-Hundredth Coast Artillery
REA
Kennecott Copper Company
Dr. Robert Goddard
Nancy Lopez Knight

Phelps-Dodge Corporation
Project Y
J. Robert Oppenheimer
Trinity Site
MANIAC
Holloman Air Force Base
Tranquility Base
Neil A. Armstrong
Paddy Martínez
Double Eagle II

CHAPTER XI

The Counties of New Mexico

Natural and Man-Made Boundaries

Boundaries have always been present in the settlements of mankind. The earliest boundaries were made by nature — mountains, rivers, and deserts. Where early man lived in the Southwest was determined by where he could find land and water to support himself. Over the centuries, though, these natural boundaries have given way to man-made ones. These are drawn according to political and cultural control of an area. But these later divisions often are influenced by the settlement patterns set by nature. The counties of New Mexico, for example, owe much to both natural and political factors.

Early Years

Centuries before the Europeans came to the Southwest, the early Pueblo Indians built their homes near rivers and streams. Since they were primarily engaged in farming, the Indians built simple diversion dams for irrigation. When the Spanish arrived, they followed the pattern established by the Indians. The Europeans limited their homesites to the same areas, where land and water were available for farming and where hostile Indians were less likely to attack. Not until the early eighteenth century did the Spanish settlers expand their area of settlement to any extent. By the early nineteenth century, Spanish settlements extended to California. Trade was opened throughout the Southwest, and with it came many new people to New Mexico.

Farming and ranching were the major industries during the early days of the territory. However, in addition to agriculture, mining played a key role in the history and development of New Mex-

220

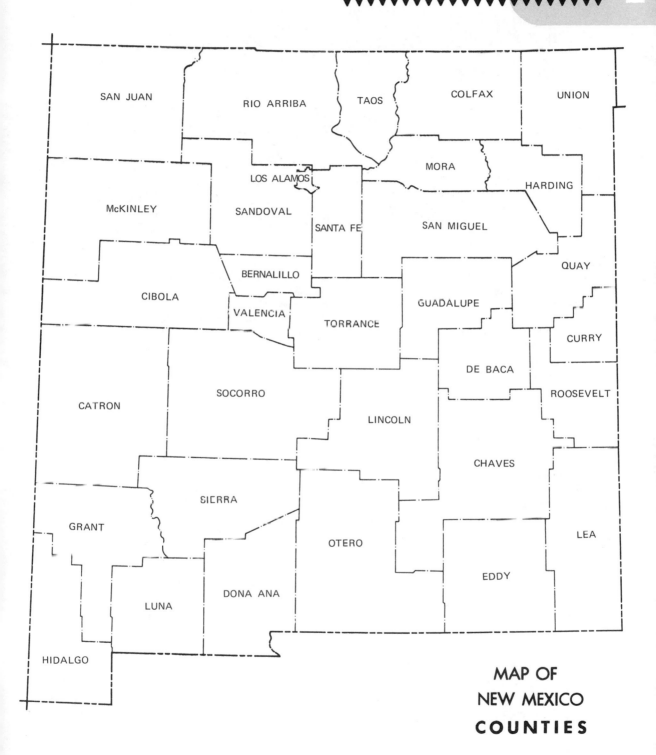

MAP OF
NEW MEXICO
COUNTIES

Navajo Dam — Navajo Indian Irrigation Project — New Mexico. Aerial view looking north of the Bureau of Reclamation's Navajo Dam and a portion of Navajo Lake. Navajo Dam is located on the San Juan River approximately 40 miles (64 km.) northeast of Farmington, New Mexico. By controlling water, man can live in more places because the land is irrigated and crops can be grown.

ico. All of these activities created numerous new settlements.

Because of settlements throughout the territory, roads were constructed to provide easy access to villages and towns. The trail along the Rio Grande, known as the El Camino Real, continued to link the villages, missions, and forts with the centers of authority in Mexico. Other trails were established to Arizona and to California. During the final years of Spanish occupation of the Southwest, the Santa Fe Trail offered a route for trade goods from the East.

By 1821, Mexico had gained independence from Spain. There were few changes, if any, from the established way of life. However, eastern traders provided a new avenue for trade with the New Mexicans. Trade goods from the East were less expensive compared to the products sent from Mexico. Thus,

the people of New Mexico welcomed the traders and their goods from the East and rejected goods sent from the south.

By 1836, Texas rebelled against Mexico, and in 1846, the United States and Mexico engaged in a war that lasted for two years. The war was over in 1848, and the United States gained control of the Southwest.

Before the United States occupied the territory, New Mexico in 1844 was divided into three districts or departments under Mexican rule. Each district was governed by a magistrate (governor or judge) who was directly responsible to the governor of the territory. The departments of the territory were identified as Northern, Central, and Southeastern. The boundaries, though, were not too well defined. The magistrates were usually located in the larger towns that divided the territory, and included Taos in the Northern

District, Santa Fe in the Central District, and Albuquerque, which at that time managed all the territory east of the Colorado River in Arizona.

Later Years

The different shapes of the counties established when New Mexico became a territory of the United States in 1850 were not the same as the Mexican departments. The new United States territory did keep the same names as originally assigned by the Mexican government.

James Calhoun, the first territorial governor, drew a map to identify the first seven counties. He used names of towns, an Indian village, a particular place, the capital city, and names of outstanding **Spanish** families. **The** boundary lines of these counties were not definitely known except for Gov-

ernor Calhoun's map. The names of the first counties were Taos, Rio Arriba, Santa Ana, Santa Fe, San Miguel, Bernalillo, and Valencia. Between 1852 and 1855, the shape of the original counties changed. Some of the counties were extended to reach the boundary line of California at the Colorado River. In 1852, the counties began to organize. During this period of changing county boundaries, the government surveyors came to the territory in 1854. Some attempts were made to survey the land and identify the counties. The Gadsden Purchase in 1853 made further changes in the boundary lines. All of the new land purchased from Mexico became part of the new county, Doña Ana. The

Site of the Abiquiu Dam on the Chama River of northern New Mexico. A popular fishing stream, the Chama rises in southern Colorado and flows southward into the Rio Grande.

Elephant Butte Dam, as seen looking from the side. The reservoir formed by this dam is about 40 miles (64 km.) long, covering approximately 40,000 acres. The dam's capacity is 2,500,000 acre feet.

first nine counties, organized between 1850 and 1860, were situated near the main river beds along the Rio Chama and Rio Grande. In 1861, Colorado was made a territory. This established the northern boundary of New Mexico. By 1863, Arizona had been made a territory, and a boundary line was established separating New Mexico from Arizona. After the Civil War, Texas agreed to the east boundary line of New Mexico. Because of the new territorial boundaries, the county lines were relocated once more, this time inside the present state boundaries. After the Civil War, additional counties were established by the territorial legislature. Lincoln, Colfax, and Grant counties were located near river beds that provided the needed water. In 1876, Santa Ana County was joined with Bernalillo County and became the only original county to disappear from the map of New Mexico.

During the next several years, there were additional changes made on county boundary lines. In all, the territorial legislature a u t h o r i z e d twenty-six counties. But in 1912, under the State Constitution, the legislature was not allowed to make laws affecting county boundaries, except when creating new counties. Under this new law, no changes were made to alter county boundaries until 1947. At that time, the legislature passed a law permitting a part of one county to be joined with another county. Because of this law, some of the boundary lines in Sierra, Harding, and Quay counties were changed. In 1949, Los Alamos became the last county to be organized as a result of conditions which took place during World War II and because of the 1947 law allowing for redrawing some county boundaries. Cibola County was organized in 1981 and become the thirty-third county in the state.

Cultural Boundaries

Traditionally, New Mexico is thought of as a tricultural society — Indian, Spanish, and Anglo. Certainly each group is an important part of the heritage of the state. However, many other cultural groups have expressed their ideals, shared their ideas, and given of themselves during the past century. Therefore, in January 1979, Governor Bruce King signed a proclamation recognizing New Mexico as a multicultural society.

The many waves of different people and cultures coming to New Mexico make this state one of the most culturally diverse in the United States. Our state is truly a Land of Enchantment because of the rich heritage around us. New Mexico today is home to many traditions, customs, and languages — in Albuquerque alone in 1978 more than thirty different languages were spoken in the homes.

The cultural diversity at times gives rise to dramatic contrasts in the daily lives of people. For example, Los Alamos — a city identified with atomic research — is reached from the east by driving past the Indian pueblos of San Ildefonso and Santa Clara. Many members of these pueblos work at the Los Alamos Scientific Laboratories. Their daily drive to work takes them from a centuries-old village to jobs where they help shape the future.

An interesting record of the varied cultures of New Mexico is the architecture throughout the state. Buildings are an expression of what a culture finds interesting and worthwhile. In all parts of New Mexico, a rich blend of styles of construction is found. The materials and layout of buildings and towns reflect many influences. Adobe of the Pueblo Indians, the courtyard and plaza of the Spanish, the wooden

Conchas Dam — Tucumcari Project — New Mexico. Conchas Dam is a Corps of Engineers structure on the Canadian River 31 miles (49 km.) northwest of Tucumcari, New Mexico.

Sumner Lake, 17 miles (27 km.) north of Fort Sumner in eastern New Mexico. Alamogordo Dam was built by the Reconstruction Finance Corporation to impound waters of the Pecos River and provide irrigation to 6,000 acres. Sumner Lake is one of the most popular recreational spots in east-central New Mexico, and until 1974 it was known as Alamogordo Lake.

frame houses of the migrants, and the pitched roof and brick of the Southwest ranch house are all popular today.

The diversity in architecture is a result of the newcomers to the state wanting to keep some of what was here but also to bring in styles and materials they were used to seeing. The new arrivals to New Mexico beginning in 1846 —and continuing to the present-day— included the Irish, the Germans, the Scotch, the Greeks, the Italians, the French, the Jews, the Chinese, the Vietnamese, the Blacks — and the list goes on. Today, all of the groups play key roles in the economic, social, cultural, and political affairs of our state. Individuals from all the ethnic and racial groups found in New Mexico are well-known throughout the state and the nation for their outstanding accomplishments.

One particular group of people that have made New Mexico their home are important because of the talent they have for painting and writing about the state. These artists who have adopted New Mexico continue the tradition of fine art which dates back centuries. The pueblos had been making pottery and doing weaving and basketry before the Spaniards arrived. After 1598 and the introduction of sheep, the Navajos began weaving the rugs for which they are world renowned. Both the Indians and the Spanish had a very rich tradition of stories. Today, the crafts and literature of these earliest New Mexicans are major parts of the life and culture of the state. Potters like Maria Martinez of San Ildefonso Pueblo, painters like the Navajo R. C. Gorman, Indian writers like N. Scott Momaday or the Hispanic author Rudolfo Anaya are present-day representatives of a deep artistic spirit in New Mexico.

Many people have come to New Mexico just to be in the midst of the creative activity in the state. Beginning in the early 1880s, artists began to discover in New Mexico a setting and a culture unique in the United States. In 1898, two artists from the East—Ernest Blumenschein and Bert Phillips—were on a sketching tour in the West. In northern New Mexico, they became fascinated with the landscape, the Indians, and the chance to add new scope to their work. They settled in Taos and began painting. This was the beginning of the famous Taos art colony. Other artists soon arrived, including Oscar Berninghaus and E. Irving Couse. By 1914 Taos was a major center for artists, and the Taos Society of Artists was formed that year. A decade later, Santa Fe began to rival Taos as the art center of New Mexico. Other parts of the state have inspired famous artists as well. The painter Peter Hurd, whose work superbly captivated the overwhelming approval of the art ctitics throughout the world, has made famous the landscape and lore of the southeastern part of the state. Sculptors also work in New Mexico, including the well-known Black Oliver La Grone. Many writers also have found in New Mexico a setting and experiences that have enriched the literature of the twentieth century. A few of the titles about New Mexico or by New Mexicans are found in the Bibliography.

Women in New Mexico

History is a *selective* account of past events. We do not have records for everything that has happened. Also, we cannot possibly discuss all that we have accounts about. History books, then, present only the most important events of the past. The writing of history by professional historians began in the late nineteenth century. So much that has been preserved has been put down by these people, most of whom were men. Men historians selected and decided what was most important about the past, and all too often they overlooked the role of women in history.

Women, though, have made major contributions to the development of New Mexico. But it is not just famous women that have made their mark on the state. It is all those who toiled daily in the colonial and territorial period to feed and cloth families, to care for the ill, and to raise the young. In the twentieth century, women have gradually entered into areas once not open to them. New Mexico women now have careers in medicine, law, business, engineering, politics — and of course many of these same women are homemakers as well.

Culture in New Mexico has been particularly enriched by women. The first conductor of the Albuquerque Symphony was Grace Thompson Edmister, who also was the first woman to conduct a civic symphony orchestra in the United States. Georgia O'Keeffe is considered one of the most important painters of this century. From her home in Abiquiu, she influences artists the world over. Equally influential, but in the area of pottery, is Maria Martinez of San Ildefonso Pueblo. The revival of excellent pottery-making owes much to her work. An outstanding photographer is Laura Gilpin. These are only a few of the female artists of New Mexico who have enriched our lives with their work.

Women writers in New Mexico are numerous as well. The Indian poet and novelist Leslie Silka is regarded as one of the major writers to emerge in the 1970s. Fabiola Cabeza de Baca is considered one of the best regional writers in America. Erna Fergusson is perhaps the best known woman writer in the state.

Without a doubt New Mexico is changing rapidly. No longer is the state isolated either from the East or from the West. Some of the old ideas have given way to some new ideas. Indifference has given way to reason. Basic needs have taken on a new importance for everyone who is concerned about our state. The contributions of all our citizens make New Mexico what it is.

TABLE OF COUNTIES OF NEW MEXICO

CO.	CO. SEAT	AREA SQ. MI.	INDUSTRIES	RECREATIONAL AREAS	HISTORIC AREAS
Berna-lillo	Albu-querque	1,169	Electronics, Manufacturing, Farming, Military Bases, Mining	Sandia Ski Area, Aerial Tramway (longest in world)	Isleta Pueblo, Old Town, Albuquerque
Catron	Reserve	6,898	Lumbering, Mining, Ranching	Gila Wilderness, Apache National Forest, Gila National Forest	Gila Cliff Dwellings, Cerro Colorado Site (archeological site), many Ghost Towns
Chaves	Roswell	6,095	Farming, Petroleum	Bottomless Lakes, Bitter Lake National Wildlife Refuge, Fishing, and Hunting	Site of first rocket launched by Dr. Robert Goddard, December 30, 1930, Blackdom
Cibola	Grants	4,420	Farming, Ranching and Mining	Cibola National Forest, Ice Caves, Hunting and Fishing, Blue Water Lake	Pueblo Indian Reservations such as Laguna, Acoma and Zuni; El Moro (Inscription Rock) National Monument, Acoma Pueblo, El Malpais National Monument
Colfax	Raton	3,771	Ranching, Coal Mining, Lumbering	Horse-racing, Philmont Scout Ranch, Eagle Nest Lake, Ski area	Folsom Site, Raton Pass (northern route of Santa Fe Trail), Ghost Towns
Curry	Clovis	1,404	Ranching, Shipping Center for Stock, Military Base	KOA	
DeBaca	Fort Sumner	2,366	Ranching	Sumner Lake State Park	Fort Sumner State Monument, site for beginning of "The Long Walk" for Navajos site of Billy the Kid's grave
Doña Ana	Las Cruces	3,804	Ranching, Farming	Leasburg Dam State Park	Mesilla, Butterfield Trail Stop, Forts Filmore and Thorn, Fort Seldon State Monument, Jornada del Muerto, Cliff Dwellings
Eddy	Carls-bad	4,180	Potash Mining, Petroleum, Farming, Ranching	Carlsbad Caverns, Red Bluff Reservoir (lowest point in NM) McMillan Lake, Lincoln Nat. Forest, Sitting Bull Falls, Living Desert State Park	Carlsbad Caverns National Park (only National Park in New Mexico)
Grant	Silver City	3,970	Mining, Farming, Ranching	City of Rocks State Park, Gila National Wilderness, Fishing and Hunting	Fort Bayard, Cameron Creek Ruins (archeological site), Ghost Towns
Guada-lupe	Santa Rosa	2,999	Ranching, Farming	Spring Fed Lakes, Alamogordo Reservoir	Puerto de Luna
Hard-ing	Mos-quero	2,138	Natural Carbon Dioxide, Ranching	Fishing, Chicosa Lake State Park	Kiowa National Grasslands
Hidalgo	Lords-burg	3,447	Ranching, Farming, Mining	Hunting, Fishing, Coronado National Forest	Banner Mine, Ghost Towns, Butterfield Trail Stop
Lea	Loving-ton	4,394	Petroleum, Farming, Ranching	Green Meadow Lake, Chaparral Park, Harry McAdam's State Park	Knowles (Ghost Town) Western Heritage Center
Lincoln	Carri-zozo	4,859	Ranching, Farming	Hunting, Fishing, Horse-racing, Lincoln National Forest, Valley of Fires State Park, Sierra Blanca Ski Area	Lincoln County Court House State Monument, Torreon (a three story adobe tower, used for a fortress against the Indians), Fort Stanton, Ghost Towns, Pictograph writings, Capitan Mountains

228

TABLE OF COUNTIES OF NEW MEXICO (Continued)

CO.	CO. SEAT	AREA SQ. MI.	INDUSTRIES	RECREATIONAL AREAS	HISTORIC AREAS
Los Alamos	Los Alamos	111	Nuclear Weapons Laboratory		La Pajarito Plateau (Little Bird Plateau), Cliff Dwellings
Luna	Deming	2,957	Farming, Ranching, Mining	Rock Hound State Park, Pancho Villa State Park	Old Butterfield Trail Route, Ft. Cummings, Camp Furlong, headquarters for Gen. John J. Pershing's expedition in 1916.
Mc-Kinley	Gallup	5,461	Farming, Ranching, Lumbering, Mining, Indian products	Kit Carson's Cave, Blue Water Lake State Park, Cibola National Forest, Hunting and Fishing	Chaco Canyon National Monument, Indian Capital of the Southwest, Zūni Pueblo, Fort Wingate
Mora	Mora	1,944	Farming, Ranching, Lumbering	Hunting, Fishing, Mora River Valley, Santa Fe National Forest	Fort Union, Camp Davis, Santa Fe Trail
Otero	Alamo-gordo	6,638	Ranching, Farming, Flower and Fruit Growing, Lumbering, Mining, White Sands Proving Ground	Lincoln National Forest, Hunting, Fishing, and Ski Area, Sacramento Peak Observatory, White Sands National Monument	Mescalero Apache Indian Reservation, Dog Canyon
Quay	Tucum-cari	2,883	Farming, Ranching	Ute Lake State Park, Hunting and Fishing	Tucumcari Historical Institute Museum
Rio Arriba	Tierra Amarilla	5,861	Farming, Ranching, Lumbering	Kit Carson National Forest, Hunting and Fishing, Santa Fe National Forest, El Vado Lake State Park, Navajo Lake	Ruins of First Capitol of New Mexico, San Gabriel, Pūye Cliff Dwellings, Ghost Towns, Ghost Ranch Museum, Abiquiu, Jicarilla Apache Reservation
Roose-velt	Portales	2,457	Farming, Ranching, Dairy Products, Processing plants	Oasis State Park	Blackwater Draw (archeological site)
Sandoval	Berna-lillo	3,714	Farming, Ranching, Lumbering, Mining, Fruit Growing	Tent Rock Canyon, Jemez State Monument, Battleship Rock, Fenton Lake, Holy Ghost Spring, Santa Fe National Forest, Cochiti Lake	Bandelier National Monument, many Pueblos such as Jemez, Zia, Cochiti, Santa Ana, Santo Domingo, and San Felipe; Valle Grande (one of the largest extinct volcanic craters in the world), Coronado State Monument
San Juan	Aztec	5,516	Farming, Ranching, Fruits of many different varieties, Petroleum	Navajo Lake State Park	Aztec Ruins National Monument, Fossil beds near Nageesi, Chaco Culture National Historical Park, Navajo Reserv. Ute Mountain Reservation, Shiprock
San Miguel	Las Vegas	4,767	Farming, Ranching, Lumbering	Storrie Lake State Park, Villanueva State Park, Fishing and Hunting, Santa Fe National Forest, Pecos National Park, Conchas Lake State Park	Fort Bascom, Indian Pictographs, Cliff Dwellings in Gallinas Canyon, Pecos National Monument

TABLE OF COUNTIES OF NEW MEXICO (Continued)

CO.	CO. SEAT	AREA SQ. MI.	INDUSTRIES	RECREATIONAL AREAS	HISTORIC AREAS	
Santa Fe	Santa Fe	1,931	Farming, Ranching, Lumbering, Mining	Santa Fe River State Park, Hyde Park Memorial State Park, Santa Fe Ski Basin, Santa Fe Opera	Santa Fe Fiesta, Palace of the Governors, Mission of San Miguel, Cristo Rey Church, Pueblos such as Nambe, and Tesuque; Santa Fe, the oldest capital city in the United States	
Sierra	Truth or Consequences	4,231	Farming, Ranching, and Mining	Cibola National Forest, Elephant Butte Lake State Park, Caballo Lake State Park	El Camino Real, Jornada del Muerto	
Socorro	Socorro	6,634	Farming, Ranching, and Mining	Cibola National Forest, Hunting and Fishing	Fort Craig, world's first atomic bomb explosion, July 16, 1945, Gran Quivira National Monument, El Camino Real, Valverde, and Gallinas Canyon Ruins	
Taos	Taos	2,257	Farming, principally grain, Lumbering and Mining	Kit Carson Memorial State Park, Rio Grande Gorge State Park, Kit Carson National Forest, Mount Wheeler (highest point in New Mexico), Sipapu Ski Area, Red River Ski Area, and Taos Ski Valley, Hunting and Fishing	Taos Pueblo, Mission of Saint Francis, Taos, third white settlement in the United States	
Torrance	Estancia	3,355	Farming and Ranching	Cibola National Forest, Hunting	Salinas National Monument (Abo, Gran Quivira, and Quarai); Pueblo Blanco Ruins, Red Canyon, and Chilli State Park	
Union	Clayton	3,817	Farming and Ranching	Clayton Lake State Park	Old Santa Fe Trail, Goodnight-Loving Trail, Capulin Mountain National Monument	
Valencia	Los Lunas	1,218	Farming and Ranching	Cibola National Forest, Hunting	Pueblo Indian Reservations such as Laguna and Isleta; Historic towns such as Tome and Peralta	

(ORIGIN OF THE NAMES OF THE COUNTIES—SEE APPENDIX)

REVIEW ACTIVITIES

1. Make a list of the cultural groups and their contributions and accomplishments to the growth of New Mexico.
2. Write a paper on the architectural changes that have occurred in New Mexico since the time of Spanish occupation.
3. Why is New Mexico considered a multicultural society? Explain your answer.
4. What are some of the major contributions women have made to influence the growth of New Mexico?
5. Explain the county structure of New Mexico under Mexican rule.
6. List the first counties, and explain from what sources their names were chosen.
7. Who is given credit for naming the seven original counties?
8. Explain the different changes to county and state boundaries between 1852 and 1876.
9. What three counties border a foreign country? (Use a United States map.)
10. Which county is supported almost entirely by government funds?
11. In which county will you find the lowest point in the state? The highest point?
12. Name the counties and county seats of New Mexico. List the industries, recreational areas, and historical areas of each one.
13. Locate at least one special point of interest in each county.
14. In which county is natural carbon dioxide found?
15. What counties have the largest deposits of oil, natural gas, coal, potash and uranium?
16. Where are the most important farming, timber, and ranching areas in New Mexico?
17. Which of New Mexico's great dams is nearest you? What effect, if any, does it have on your community?
18. In what ways other than providing water for irrigation can the building of a dam benefit the state or a community?
19. What evidence can you find, in your locality, of too little water? Of too much water?

RECOGNIZE AND UNDERSTAND

Torreon

Jornada del Muerto

Taos Society of Artists

Grace Edmister

Pajarito Plateau

Valle Grande

Maria Martinez

231

CHAPTER XII

State and Local Government

The Need for Government

As far back as history is recorded, men built communities to live together in groups. Basically, man is a social creature and enjoys being with others. Besides this very fundamental reason, man has found mutual aid and protection in settled communities. In a settled society man could, through a united effort, build roadways and buildings and perform many acts of great skill which one man could never have accomplished. In addition to this, group living provides individuals with the opportunity to excel in special skills and apply them where they are most useful. Man's cultural development moved forward with great speed because of group living. Communities encouraged the free exchange of thoughts and ideas for better and more comfortable living.

As man began to build his social unit, rules were necessary to regulate the actions of the individuals of the group and the group itself. Rules became laws. These were needed to insure individuals and the group some measure of protection against those persons or groups that would cause harm or injury to others in society. In addition, laws were designed to promote the general welfare of those who live under them. In this way, certain activities which cannot be fulfilled as well by private persons are carried out.

When communities grew larger, more laws became necessary to meet the wishes of the group. Leaders were selected to make and enforce these laws. Thus, the idea of a social organization or government became the agency to rule or to have authority over a city, a district, a state, or a country. All over the world as communities grew larger and as they came in closer contact with each other, governments and populations increased. Today, each group has its own town, city, or county government, which are all controlled by the state.

Various forms of government have been tried throughout the world. Each one gained a certain amount of success, but many of these governments fell in ruin. The United States Constitution, since 1789 the basic document on government in the United States, guarantees a republican form of government. This means that each state enjoys the privilege of sending elected representatives to a central government to

The new State Supreme Court Building, part of the Capitol group in Santa Fe, New Mexico. It is built in a modified form of territorial style architecture, and decorated with the Zia Indian sun symbol.

make and enforce laws. This sharing of power between a central government and states is called federalism. Laws are made by the people and based upon the will of the majority. This is what is meant by democracy, where the will of the majority of the people is the will of the community. If the minority do not peaceably give consent to the decisions, the majority has the power and right under the Constitution to correct this problem. The principle of majority rule is a basic one in our political system. The United States is a federal republic with the Constitution as the most important document.

One of our famous statesman, Benjamin Franklin, once said soon after the Constitution was written, "This document was the greatest work conceived by man, and if the Constitution lasts for twenty years, it will last forever." The Constitution is now more than 200 years old. It remains the basic document of our government because it sets the broad framework within which each generation solves the specific problems of its time.

The Need to Study Government

Unfortunately, governments have not all been successful from the standpoint of the people. For many centuries, men and women lived under the absolute rule of kings, dictators, and oligarchies. They had no voice in matters of the state. Therefore, the people felt that there was little use to study or learn about their government. Under the system of absolute kings, usually the heir to the throne and his immediate aids were schooled in law and government. Their will was law. In much the same manner, this is also true when people live under a dictator. The one man who rules usually acquires his position as supreme ruler by force and

false promises. He keeps the group in line by the use of a strong army and a police force. An oligarchy is rule by a small group of men, such as the government in Russia. This form of government, which has been practiced for centuries in many countries, permits the citizens little or no voice in their governments.

Today, less than two percent of the world is ruled by kings, but the threat of world control by a small ruling class is ever present in our time. Fortunately, some countries are practicing a form of democracy, and many more are turning toward the principles of self-government. Throughout the world, people are being permitted to voice their opinions on law.

Still in many countries, the small ruling class of a Communist state performs all of the necessary acts related to government. There the people of the state perform only the act of accepting the laws of their government without the opportunity to disapprove them. Through the voice of a few, communism persuades people by the use of force and promises that will seldom be kept. These citizens live under a government where the will of the people is unimportant.

Therefore, we need to study our system of government to see how it works, to see what it offers us, and to see what part the individual plays in a democratic society. To keep a fair and impartial government, every citizen must know his rights and responsibilities. Everyone must take an interest in being involved with government if we are to continue to have a democratic society.

Over the past years in our country, everything has not gone altogether well because people have not taken their

▼▼▼▼▼▼▼▼▼▼▼▼▼▼▼▼▼▼▼▼▼▼

civic responsibilities seriously. It appears that as time goes by, fewer people feel a necessity to learn and to take interest in government. This is not good in a democracy because instead of many people voicing their opinion just a few speak out and they decide for us all. In a democracy, every voter is responsible for deciding who will represent them. If only a few people vote, then these few speak for everybody. A small minority then determines the will of the majority.

The Federal Constitution

The Constitution of the United States consists of the preamble, seven articles, and twenty-six amendments. The language is clear and easy to understand. It provides for a federal system of government with three branches, legislative, executive, and judicial. The power of government is divided among these three branches. This division of power is the basis for our system of checks and balances through which every government act must pass. This prevents any one branch of government from having more power than the other.

The Constitution gives certain specific powers to the federal government. It also delegates certain and specific powers to the states. It prohibits the use of certain powers and practices to both federal and state governments. Another important feature of the Constitution is a provision to amend it. By "amending" we mean changes or additions to the Constitution, when ratified by three-fourths of the state legislatures or by convention in three-fourths of the states. The first ten amendments are the "Bill of Rights," which provide for the people certain privileges, rights, and freedoms. Since ratification of the Bill of Rights in 1791, only sixteen amendments to the United States Constitution have been approved.

In our system of government, the Constitution is the "Supreme Law of the Land." This means that the Constitution sets the guidelines for all government. It gives to the Congress the authority to make laws that must be obeyed by everyone in the United States. In addition to the laws of the federal government, each state is guaranteed the right of self-government under the Constitution to make and enforce laws within its boundaries. Then, finally, each state permits local communities to make and to enforce laws in a county, city, town, or village to keep peace and order.

Constitution of New Mexico

"The State of New Mexico is an inseparable part of the Union, and the Constitution of the United States is the Supreme Law of the Land."
New Mexico Constitution: *Article II Section 1.*

This provision in the Constitution of New Mexico assures the citizen of the state that New Mexico cannot be separated from the Union of States, and that the laws of the United States Constitution are the fundamental principles under which we live.

"We, the people of New Mexico, grateful to Almighty God for the Blessings of liberty, in order to secure the advantages of a state government, do ordain and establish this Constitution."
New Mexico Constitution: *Preamble.*

The constitution of the state was written in 1910 and approved by the people the following year. (In January 1912, New Mexico was admitted to the Union.) It is similar to the United States

Constitution and has three main parts: a preamble, twenty - four articles, and twenty-three articles in the Bill of Rights. The constitution also provides for a separation of powers into three branches: the legislative, the executive, and the judicial.

Bill of Rights. Article II of the New Mexico Constitution contains the twenty-three articles in the Bill of Rights. Just as the federal Bill of Rights was placed in the United States Constitution as a restriction against the United States government, it is also true that the state Bill of Rights is placed in our constitution as a restriction against the state government. In this way, the rights and privileges of the people are protected against bad laws that would directly affect the freedom of the citizens. Review the New Mexico Bill of Rights and discover that through the entire twenty-three "rights" or "privileges" will be found the first ten amendments of the United States Constitution. It is easy to see that the federal government and the state of New Mexico work in a cooperative manner to protect the citizens of New Mexico.

Amending the Constitution. There are several other articles governing a wide range of activities, and from time to time these articles need to be revised or changed. There is a provision in the constitution outlining an orderly and peaceful way of making changes in the document. This is known as the amending clause (Article XIX, Section 1).

The amending process works in the following way. Any amendment to the constitution may be proposed in either house at any regular session of the state legislature, and if a majority of all members in both houses vote in favor, it is then sent to the secretary of state. It is then the duty of this officer to see that the amendment is published in both English and Spanish in at least one newspaper in every county in the state at least two weeks prior to election. If a majority of the people voting for the proposal ratify the amendment, it then becomes part of the constitution.

Revising the Constitution. The constitution may be completely changed when it is needed. The amending process serves very well to correct particular features of the constitution. But it is too slow in its working to provide a means of keeping all sections of the document in line with the times. According to the constitution (Article XIX, Section 2) the legislature, by two-thirds vote of both houses, may submit to the people the question of calling a convention to change the constitution. If a majority of the registered voters voting in the election are in favor of it, the legislature must, at the next session, provide by law for calling the convention. The convention members must consist of no more than the total number of senators and representatives in the New Mexico legislature. All other details concerning the organization and work on the convention are left to the legislature.

In 1969, a convention was called to revise the 1912 New Mexico Constitution. This was the first time since that date that an attempt had been made to write a new constitution for the registered voters of the state to approve. On December 9, 1969, the new document was sent to the people and was defeated by a small margin of 3,478 votes. The total votes cast (122,606) represented about one-third of the total

Voting Machine
Sample Ballot
GENERAL ELECTION

NOVEMBER 7, 1978   LEA COUNTY, NEW MEXICO

Boleta de Muestra
Para Maquina de Votar
ELECCIÓN GENERAL

7 DE NOVIEMBRE, 1978   CONDADO DE LEA, NUEVO MÉXICO

Representative District 63

QUESTIONS ➡
PREGUNTAS ➡
OFFICES ➡
OFICINAS ➡

INSTRUCTIONS TO VOTER

Move the RED HANDLE completely to the RIGHT. This closes the curtain and unlocks the machine.

Constitutional Amendments and Special Questions

To vote for an amendment or question, turn down the pointer over the word "for" under that amendment or question. To vote against an amendment or question, turn down the pointer over the word "against" under that amendment or question.

Turn down a voting pointer over each candidate's name you wish to vote for from this position.

Straight Ticket

To Vote a "Straight Ticket" Pull out the Party Lever of the Party of your choice. This will turn down the voting pointers over every candidate's name in this particular party and will give you a "straight" party vote.

IMPORTANT: You can make as many changes as you desire while the RED HANDLE is to the RIGHT. The machine is arranged so you cannot turn down more than the proper number of voting pointers for each office, so you cannot spoil your ballot by voting for too many candidates. To make a change simply push up the pointer back and make another selection.

Write-In Candidate: To vote for a write-in candidate, lift up the write-in slide cover bearing the name of the designated office and write-in the name of the person of your choice. Once a voter lifts a write-in slide, however, he cannot change his mind and use a candidate pointer in that office. This prevents over-voting.

Once you have made your selections, LEAVE THE POINTERS DOWN and move the RED HANDLE completely to the LEFT. This records your vote, clears the machine, and then opens the curtain. No one outside the machine can tell how you have voted.

Each voter in New Mexico is allowed a maximum of three and one-half (3½) minutes in which to vote. Vote promptly and leave the machine so the voter following you may have his turn.

INSTRUCCIONES PARA VOTAR

Mueva la PALANCA ROJA completamente a la DERECHA. Esto cierra la cortina y abre la máquina para votar.

Enmiendas Constitucionales y Preguntas Especiales

Para votar por la enmienda o la pregunta mueva el indicador sobre la palabra "por" baja esto, etc., enmienda o pregunta. Para votar en contra la enmienda o la pregunta mueva el indicador sobre la palabra "en contra" bajo eso enmienda o pregunta.

Baje el indicador de votar sobre cada nombre de candidato por el cual usted desea votar de esta posición.

Ticket de Partido

Para votar por un "Ticket de Partido" mueva la Palanca del Partido de su preferencia.

Esto moverá para abajo los indicadores sobre cada nombre de candidato, en este partido particular y le dará un voto a todos los candidatos en ese partido.

IMPORTANTE: Usted puede hacer tantos cambios como usted desen mientras que la PALANCA ROJA esta a la derecha. La máquina está arreglado para que usted no puede bajar la palanca por mas que el propio número de indicadores de votar, por cada puesto, para que así usted no puede echar a perder su boleta al votar por demasiados candidatos. Para hacer un cambio simplemente empuje el indicador otra vez para arriba y haga otro selección.

Candidato Write-in (no en la lista): Para escribir en nombre de un candidato write-in (no en la lista) levante la lámina de write-in (no en la lista) que tiene el número correspondiente al puesto designado y escribe el nombre del candidato write-in en la lista. Una vez que el votante levante la lámina de write-in (no en la lista), no obstante, el no puede combiar de opinión y usar un indicador de candidato en ese puesto. Esto lo previene votar otro vez.

Una vez que usted haga sus selecciones, DEJE LOS INDICADORES ABAJADOS, y mueva la PALANCA ROJO completamente a la IZQUIERDA. Esto registra su voto, limpio la maquina, y entonces abre las cortinas. Nadie fuera de la máquina se da cuenta como usted voto.

A cada votante en Nuevo México se le permite un máximo de tres y medio (3½) minutos para votar. Vote prontamente y deje la máquina para que así el votante que le sigue pueda tener su turno.

A sample of the ballot used in elections throughout New Mexico.

Notice that the ballot is in both English and Spanish.

number of registered voters in t h e state. Only seven of New Mexico's thirty-two counties gave a majority vote approval to the proposed new constitution. The counties voting in favor were Bernalillo, Chaves, Doña Ana, Eddy, Los Alamos, McKinley, and Valencia.

Voting. Since there are no residency requirements, a man or woman who is a citizen of the united States, who is over eighteen years of age, and who has registered in his or her county of residence at least 28 days prior to the election is entitled to vote in all state and federal elections. The twenty-sixth amendment to the U.S. Constitution and the 1972 Federal Voting Rights Act have restricted states in the setting of voting requirements. The only persons denied the right to vote in New Mexico are insane persons and persons convicted of a serious crime who have not had their rights restored. Persons who have been convicted of felonies and have served terms in the state penitentiary may have their political rights restored by special action of the governor.

The first, if not the most important, business of every citizen of New Mexico is to vote in all elections in which he is entitled to take part. It is not only a

VOTING IN NEW MEXICO...........A SIMPLE PROCEDURE

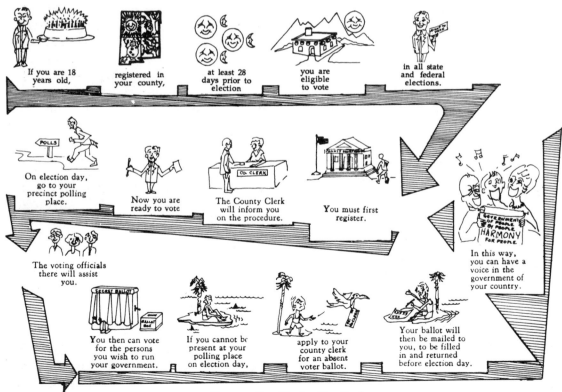

Courtesy New Mexico Blue Book

right but a responsibility, a duty to the citizen himself and to the people who are running for office. It is in this way that citizens express themselves on issues that may become laws. No one can consider himself a good citizen unless he takes his civic responsibilities seriously enough to vote. Many consider themselves too busy to vote; others are too indifferent to want to vote; neither are being good citizens.

It should be kept in mind that the government of New Mexico is run by the voting citizens of the state for their interests. The state government is just what the people make it. If it fails to serve them efficiently and honestly, the people need only to wait for the next election. Then, by their vote, they can change government at the next election. Therefore, it is important that citizens not only understand their government, but try to improve it. This can best be done by voting intelligently for candidates whose policies will most likely promote the best interests of the state.

To promote more citizen involvement, the legislature in the late 1960s authorized a convention - primary system. But in 1985, the New Mexico legislature reversed its earlier decision and approved a bill to eliminate the preprimary convention. On February 22, 1985, Governor Toney Anaya signed into law the controversial legislation abolishing the convention system. All candidates must be selected by the voters in their party in a primary election in June before they can run for office in November.

Checks and Balances. The system of checks and balances is provided for in the New Mexico Constitution. All state laws must be passed by the legislature. The governor then either approves or rejects the laws. Then, if anyone challenges the law, the judiciary decides if the law is constitutional. This feature of the constitution prohibits one branch of government (legislative, executive, or judiciary) from having more power than the other. A safeguard such as this assures the citizens of New Mexico fair and just laws for all.

Referendum. Article IV, Section I of the New Mexico Constitution provides another guarantee to the people of the state. This provision is called referendum. This means that when the people of New Mexico dislike a law that has been made by the legislature, they have the constitutional "right" to do away with it. However, a definite process must be followed.

A petition signed by 10 percent of the qualified voters of three-fourths of the counties and not less than ten percent of the qualified voters of the state must be filed with the secretary of state at least four months before the next general election. At that time, the law is submitted to the people for their approval or rejection by a majority vote, provided that majority is not less than 40 percent of the votes cast for the governor or some other state officer in that election. This is an involved process, but it does provide another protective feature for the people of New Mexico.

Some laws are excluded from the process of referendum. They are general appropriation laws (laws dealing with money to support state government), or laws providing for the preservation of the public peace, health, or safety, or laws providing for the payment of public debts, or laws providing for the

The House of Representatives' chamber in the new Capitol Building at Santa Fe.

maintenance of public schools or other state institutions.

The Legislative Branch

"The Legislative Power shall be vested in a Senate and House of Representatives which shall be designated the Legislature of the State of New Mexico, and shall hold its sessions at the seat of government."

New Mexico Constitution: *Article IV Section 1.*

The legislature or law-making body of the state is bicameral. That means it has both a Senate and House of Representatives. It consists of 42 senators and 70 representatives elected by the people of New Mexico. It is the duty of the legislature to provide for the "general welfare" of the state.

Neither the Senate nor the House of Representatives acting alone can pass a law. Instead, both houses must act on all laws. The legislature is the only branch of government that has the constitutional right to enact a law for all the people who live in New Mexico. For this reason, the members of the legislature, who are entrusted with making laws, have a great responsibility to the citizens of our state. To be elected to the legislature is an honor and a great opportunity for service.

The House of Representatives. The state constitution provides that each member of the House of Representatives shall be elected for the term of two years. The 70 members of the House are chosen by the qualified voters of each county they represent. In some cases, one legislator will represent more than one county since after the House Reapportionment Act of 1965, the basis for selection of a representative is determined by population. Each member of the House may be reelected to office indefinitely.

To qualify for election to the House of Representatives, a person must be:

(1)   twenty-one years of age at the time of his election; and

(2)   a resident of the county from which he is elected.

The House of Representatives chooses its own officers. The presiding officer is called the "speaker." The speaker of the house is all-powerful. He appoints everyone on the various committees, controls all printing and supplies, and hires all extra help. He is the last one to vote on every bill. His name is called at the end of the voting roster.

The other officers include the majority leader, minority l e a d e r, majority whip, minority whip, chief clerk, sergeant-at-arms, parliamentarian, and chaplain.

The political party in the House which has a majority of the members selects the speaker and the majority leader. The other major party selects the minority leader. As at the national level, the two political parties in the legislature are the Democrats and the Republicans.

The whips are assistants to the party leaders. They find out how members of their party and others are going to vote and see that they are present for roll calls when their votes are needed.

Senate. The Senate consists of 42 members selected, following the Senate Reapportionment Act of 1966, on the basis of population.

Senators are elected for a term of four years, and they are elected by the qualified voters from the county or counties that they represent in the legislature. Senators may be re-elected as long as the people want them in office. One-half of the senators are elected every two years. In that way the remaining one-half always have a minimum of two years experience, except as new members are appointed to fill unexpired terms.

To qualify for election to the Senate, a person must be:

(1)   twenty-five years of age at the time of his election; and

(2)   a resident of the county from which he is elected.

The lieutenant-governor of the state serves as president of the Senate. Before 1957, the lieutenant-governor had the same power as the Speaker of the House. However, the Senate voted to change the rules in regard to the president of the Senate. The new rules have taken the authority and power away from the lieutenant-governor within the Senate, except what he can accomplish through personal friendship and persuasion. He is not allowed to vote, except to break a tie in the Senate.

When the lieutenant-governor, for any reason, cannot preside over the Senate, the Senate majority party elects a temporary president called the *president pro tempore.* He is considered the presiding officer of the Senate until the lieutenant-governor is able to resume his duties.

Other officers of the Senate are similar to those of the House of

Representatives: the majority a n d minority floor leaders, party whips, a secretary, a chaplain, and a sergeant-at-arms. The first woman majority whip of a state senate in the United States was Concha Ortiz y Pino de Kleven, formerly of Santa Fe, now of Albuquerque.

Vacancies in the Legislature. If a vacancy occurs in the office of a senator or member of the House of Representatives for any reason, the county commissioners of that county where the vacancy occurred are to appoint someone to fill that vacancy. If the vacancy occurs in a legislative district (more than one county represented by a senator or representative), the county commissioners of each county are to submit one name to the governor who, in turn, is to appoint the senator or representative from the names submitted by the commissioners. All such appointments will permit the newly appointed representative to continue in office until December 31 after the general election.

Legislative Sessions. Each regular session of the legislature begins at twelve noon on the third Tuesday of January following the general election, unless otherwise prescribed by law. The regular session convenes during the odd-numbered years (1979, 1981, 1983, etc.) and stays in session no longer than sixty days. Special sessions of the legislature assemble in January during the even numbered years (1980, 1982, 1984, etc.) and stay in session no longer than thirty days. The thirty-day session only considers bills sent by the governor, while in the sixty-day meeting any representative or senator may propose a bill.

Other special sessions of the legislature may be called by the governor, but no business is to be conducted except what is stated in the governor's proclamation. The legislature may call a special session when three-fifths of the members of both houses decide that an emergency exists in the state. When the governor receives certification of an emergency from the Senate and the House of Representatives, he must, within five days, call the legislature into session.

All sessions of the legislature are public. This means that anyone may visit the legislature when in session and listen to the proceedings.

Legislator's Pay. Each member of the legislature receives $75 per day during each session, and 25 cents per mile going to and from the legislature once each session.

In addition to the legislator's pay, each house determines the salaries for all extra personnel needed to carry out the business of law making.

The legislature is the only branch in our state government that has a salary set by the constitution. It will be necessary to have a constitutional amendment before legislators receive an increase in pay.

Impeachment. In the New Mexico state legislature, the House of Representatives may bring impeachment proceedings against the governor or any high official if the members feel he is not fulfilling the duties of his office properly. To impeach means to bring formal charges against an official of the state. This official charge does not necessarily mean the person is guilty. The Senate, which will have to hear the case, is the highest court in the state when trying a case of impeachment. If two-thirds of the Senate members present find the official guilty, he is removed from office.

Law Making

Law making is a complicated procedure and must be executed with careful consideration for every individual and group in the state. This is not an easy task for our state legislature. In most cases during the regular session, many hundreds of bills will be introduced in the legislature. However, only about 30 percent of these bills become law. In this way citizens of the state can be assured the best laws possible for carrying out the operations of government.

"No laws shall be passed except in the form of a bill" (Article IV, Section 15; New Mexico Constitution). Bills may be introduced in either the Senate or the House of Representatives; however, those bills to raise money through taxes or general appropriation must, by law, originate in the House of Representatives. The Senate may amend a part of the bill, but each amendment must be approved by the House before being sent to the governor for his signature.

Each house has "standing committees." These committees are determined by each house as provided by law and meet for the purpose of approving bills during a legislative session. For example, a standing committee would be an agricultural committee, a tax committee, an appropriations committee, or an educational finance committee. These committees work hard on all bills that are assigned to them for the best laws possible to improve the condition of our state.

By law, all bills must be introduced by a senator or representative in his respective house. Since there is no screening committee (a group to determine to which committee a bill should be referred) on bills in either house, a bill is assigned a number and referred to a committee for discussion and debate. (Additional information on a bill becoming law will be discussed later in this chapter.)

In many cases, the people take the first step in law making. Interested persons or groups will make it known to their senator or representative that they want a new law. This is often done by a "pressure group" which sends a "lobbyist" to the capital. A lobbyist is a paid member of a pressure group who tries to influence legislation.

A pressure group is a group of citizens such as business groups, a bankers association, an oil and gas association, an association of commerce and industry, labor organizations, teachers associations, and other citizen groups. They bring pressure on the legislature to make a new law. This is done by the lobbyist, who is paid by the interested organization to persuade the lawmakers to accept the views of the pressure group. However, lobbyists, sometimes referred to as the "third house," provide aid to legislators on their specialized areas. They serve a very useful purpose in supplying legislators with information regarding a particular bill. Lobbyists put together facts and figures on various areas under consideration by the legislature and assist the lawmakers during the process of drafting bills.

To help understand the process of lawmaking, let us trace a bill as it goes through the House of Representatives.

A bill is introduced by a member of the House and read by an individual called a "reading clerk." The bill is assigned a number by the clerk. The

PASSAGE OF A BILL....

1 *Introduction and Committee Referral.* A bill may be introduced in the House of Representatives or in the Senate. It is assigned a number, read twice by title, ordered printed and referred to the proper committee.

Committee Consideration. Committee meetings are usually open to the public. When there is sufficient interest, a public hearing is held. A bill may receive one of the following recommendations: Do Pass; Do Pass with amendments; Without Recommendation; or Do Not Pass. The committee can kill a bill by its failure to act upon it.

3 *Adoption of Committee Report.* Reports of committees are subject to adoption by the full House or Senate. When a favorable committee report is adopted, the bill is placed on the calendar, which is the list of bills ready for third reading and final passage.

Third Reading and Final Passage. This is the stage at which the fate of a bill is usually decided. Action may be to amend, to substitute a bill for another, to send it back to committee, refer it to another committee or kill the bill.

5 *Voting on Bill.* Following sometimes lengthy debate on a bill, a final and recorded vote is taken on whether the bill is to pass. Every bill requires at least a majority vote of the members present and voting.

What Happens Next? Sent to the other house, a bill follows much the same procedure. Both houses must agree on the final form a bill. If either house fails to concur with amendments, the differences must be reconciled by a conference committee representing the House and Senate. Compromises agreed upon by this committee are subject to approval by both houses.

7 *Enrolling and Engrossing.* After passage by both houses, a bill is carefully copied by the enrolling and engrossing staff of the house in which it originated, signed by the presiding officers of each house and sent to the Governor.

Governor's Action. The Governor may sign a bill, veto it or, if it carries an appropriation, partially veto it. It may be passed over his veto by a two-thirds vote of each house. If he does not sign a bill within three days or return it, it becomes a law unless the Legislature, by adjournment, prevents it return.

9 Following the adjournment of the Legislature, the Governor has twenty days to act upon any remaining bills. Bills carrying an emergency clause become effective immediately upon the Governor's signature. All other bills become effective ninety days following adjournment of the Legislature except those bills which carry a later effective date.

PREPARED BY:
New Mexico Legislative Council Service, 334 State Capitol, Santa Fe, New Mexico 1/71

first and second readings of the bill are by number and title only. The Speaker orders the bill printed and assigns it to a proper committee or committees. In the Senate, the sponsor of the bill will indicate to the president of the Senate to which committee he wants the bill assigned. However, the Senate, by a majority vote, can override the sponsor's proposal and the Senate can determine the committee for the bill.

On controversial bills, public hearings are conducted for interested parties. Interested groups may speak for or against the proposal. However, most bills do not have public hearings because they are only changes in established law. The bill is studied by the committee to determine its passage.

The committee may

(1) amend the bill;
(2) prepare a substitute for it;
(3) give it a "do pass" recommendation;
(4) give it a "do not pass" recommendation;
(5) report it out without recommendations;
(6) hold it in committee; or
(7) report it out with a recommendation that the bill be sent to a different committee.

When the bill comes out from the committee to the House, the committee report is read. If it is a "do not pass" report and the House refuses to accept the committee findings, then the bill goes on the calendar for debate. If the House accepts the "do not pass" report, the bill is dead. If the committee sends the bill out with a "do pass" report and the House accepts, the proposed bill will take its place on the calendar. However, if the House refuses to accept a "do pass" report, a motion to table the bill indefinitely will kill the bill. Ordinarily,

the bills with a "do pass" recommendation are not debated on committee report, but the bill is permitted to go on the calendar and is then debated in regular order. In all cases, a bill from a committee with their report must be approved by the majority of the members present in either the Senate or the House of Representatives.

Members of the House of Representatives may debate the bill and by simple majority pass or reject it. When the bill is debated it may be

(1) amended by floor amendment;
(2) changed with floor substitute bill; or
(3) sent back to committee.

If the bill is complicated and important, it may be referred to the "Committee of the Whole House" where anyone can speak for or against the bill. After debate on the bill, a vote is taken. If a majority votes for the proposal, it goes to the Senate. If a majority votes against it, the bill is dead.

Any bill that is held in committee or killed in the House may be revived. For example, a bill will stay in committee unless the sponsor or someone "blasts it out" of committee. A member can make a motion to have the bill removed from committee. A vote is taken by members of the Senate or House of Representatives to debate on the bill. By a simple majority vote, the bill will be placed on the calendar for further discussion.

A bill may be revived after being rejected by the Senate or House of Representatives. Someone who voted in the majority can, on the same day the bill was defeated or the next succeeding day, make a recommendation to reconsider the vote by which the bill failed. If there is a majority vote to reconsider the bill, then it is placed on the calendar for debate.

The "emergency clause" may be attached to any bill. This clause refers to the peace, health, and safety of the citizens of New Mexico. It takes a two-thirds vote in both houses to put the emergency clause on the bill. The bill becomes law immediately when the governor signs it.

If the bill passes the House, it is sent to the Senate where it goes through the same procedure. If the bill fails in the Senate, it is dead. If the Senate passes the bill in different form by amendment, then it is returned to the House for review and consideration. The House of Representatives may reject the Senate amendments and kill the bill. Suppose that the bill is a good one, but that it has several amendments attached to it. Each house must send certain members to a "conference committee" to approve or disapprove the bill. Either house may ask for a conference committee. If the conference committee agrees to the proposed amendments, they submit their recommendations to their respective houses. If both houses agree, then the bill passes. If either one of the houses disagrees, then the bill is dead.

When the bill passes both houses, it is typed in final form, signed by the speaker of the house, the president of the Senate, and the chief clerks of both houses. Then, the bill is sent to the governor. The governor must sign or veto the bill within three days during the session, or the bill will automatically become law. If the governor vetoes the bill, it is returned to the house in which it originated. If a bill is sent to the governor at the close of legislative session, he must sign or veto the bill

within twenty days. Or, he may refuse to take any action and set the bill aside. This is called a "pocket veto." If the governor vetoes a bill, the legislature may, by two-thirds of the members present and voting in both the House and the Senate, override his veto and make the bill law.

All bills signed by the governor become law ninety days after the legislature adjourns, unless they contain an emergency clause. The laws passed by the legislature and signed by the governor are called statutes, or the fundamental laws of the state.

Senators and Representatives in Congress

New Mexico has five representatives in the United States Congress: two senators and three representatives. According to the United States Constitution every state is allowed two senators, and they are to be elected by all the registered voters within the state. In this sense, then, both senators could be elected from the same areas of a state for a term of six years. However, only one-third of the senate is elected every two years, and the two senators from the state of New Mexico will never be elected at the same time.

Members of the United States House of Representatives must be elected from districts in each state for two years. In New Mexico prior to 1968, all congressmen were elected by the registered voters in the state, and at that time members of the House of Representatives could be elected from the same area in the state. Before the 1982 congressional election, the New Mexico legislature provided for three congressional districts (see p. 253 map on congressional districts) based on population required by the Congress of the United States. As time goes on and as the population grows, additional representatives will be added as required by law, and new districts will be established.

The Executive Branch

"The executive power of the state is vested in a Governor . . . , who shall, unless otherwise provided in the Constitution of New Mexico, be elected for the term of four years beginning on the first day of January next after election. The Governor and Lieutenant-Governor shall be elected jointly."
New Mexico Constitution: *Article V Section I.*

The executive branch of government is composed of a governor, lieutenant governor, secretary of state, state auditor, state treasurer, attorney general, and commissioner of public lands, who are all elected for four years. All officers of the executive department who have served two terms are not eligible to hold any state office for four years, except that the lieutenant-governor may be eligible to hold the office of governor.

To qualify for election to the executive department, a person:

(1) must be a citizen of the United States:

(2) must be thirty years of age before election time; and

(3) must have been a resident continuously in New Mexico for five years preceding his election.

The governor is inaugurated in January following his election. Other members take office the first day of January after their election.

The governor receives a salary which is determined by the legislature. His salary may be changed from time to time, but not during the governor's then existing term of office. A residence is provided for him in Santa Fe, and an automobile is furnished by the state for his use. He also has an expense account to hire various personnel to aid him in carrying out the duties of the executive department. The salaries of the other elected members of the executive department are also determined by law.

When the governor is unable to perform his duties for any reason, the lieutenant-governor acts in his place. Thereafter, the line of succession will be the secretary of state, president pro tempore of the senate, and Speaker of the House.

Governor's Powers and Duties. The governor has many powers which are similar to those of the president of the United States. He appoints people to various boards and commissions to aid him in performing the job as governor. Many of his appointments must be, according to law, approved by the Senate. He supervises many state administrative offices and is commander-in-chief of the state militia (National Guard and State Police.) He and his staff prepare the state budget, which he presents to the legislature for approval. The governor has the power to grant pardons and reprieves, except to those persons who have been convicted of treason. He meets with various legislative committeees to cooperate with them in planning the governmental programs of the state. In legislative matters he has the power to approve or disaprove, by veto, any laws that are passed by the lawmaking branch of government.

He has many duties in addition to his constitutional powers. The governor, first of all as head of his party, confers

U.S. 84 south of Cebolla in Navajo Canyon, Rio Arriba County. More than 50 percent of the funds provided for national roads are from tax dollars collected by the federal government.

with party members throughout the state and nation. He attends a variety of civic, social, and ceremonial activities throughout the state. He has so many requests that many times he cannot possibly fill all of them.

Other State Officials. The lieutenant-governor presides over the Senate during the regular and special sessions of the legislature. He acts as governor in the event of the governor's absence from the state or the governor's disability.

In addition to his specific duties, the full time lieutenant - governor is required to promote the cooperation between the people of New Mexico and the agencies of state government. By an act of the 1971 legislature, he is further directed to refer complaints from citizens to the proper agencies.

The secretary of state keeps both the legislative and executive records and publishes all the laws made by the legislature. Other duties are to make up the official register, to assist in the administration of state elections, and to attach the seal of the state to all official papers.

The state treasurer receives and

pays out state funds and keeps records of all money received and spent.

The duty of the state auditor is to check the records of many state agencies for accuracy.

The attorney general is the chief legal advisor to the governor and other state officials. He is chief representative for the state in all cases before the supreme court and prepares many legal documents required for state use.

The superintendent of public instruction is appointed by the state school board, which is composed of ten members elected by the registered voters of their area. As head of the public school system in New Mexico, he sees that the decisions made by the state school board are carried out by the local districts.

There are eighty-eight school districts in New Mexico, each with a locally elected board to oversee public instruction.

The commissioner of public lands is responsible for New Mexico's eleven million acres of land. Most of the state land was given to New Mexico by Congress for the support of education, welfare, and other institutions. This commission handles leases for oil companies, ranches, and lumber companies; the income from these leases is used to maintain state institutions.

The State Corporation Commission is composed of three elected members who issue charters for the regulation and control of corporations such as insurance companies, trucking companies, and bus lines. The Corporation Commission fixes rates charged by railroads, airlines, telephone companies, and other utilities operating within the state.

The State Highway Commission is made up of five members who are appointed by the governor with the approval of the Senate. The commission administers the law in regard to building highways throughout the state. The chief highway administrator, appointed by the commission with the governor's consent, carries out the commission's decisions on the location, building, and maintenance of highways.

There are, in addition to these offices, many other boards and commissions which deal with the administration of government in New Mexico.

Interstate 10 east of Deming, Luna County. More than 90 percent of the money to build the interstate comes from the U.S. government.

The Cabinet

In the early 1950s the "Little Hoover Committee" was established to study government. After several months of research, the committee made recommendations to the governor on reorganizing the executive branch. By 1967, after several years of studying the program, the state legislature created the Governor's Committee on Reorganization of State Government. Results of the study were clear that a cabinet system was needed. Finally on April 7, 1977 Governor Jerry Apodaca signed into law the Executive Reorganization Act and the bills creating the original departments. These cabinet offices were designed to make government work better for the citizens of the state in the area of particular needs. As a result of changing conditions in the state, reorganization has continued. In 1991, Governor Bruce King approved a bill to enlarge the executive branch creating five new departments, making a total of sixteen cabinet offices.

Fourteen of the 16 cabinet secretaries are appointed by the governor with the consent of the senate. The two cabinet secretaries who receive their appointments in different ways are the secretary of highways and the secretary of agriculture. Under reorganization, the secretary of the Department of Highways has the title of Chief Highway Administrator. Unlike the other secretaries, this official is appointed by the Highway Commission with the concurrence of the governor and consent of the senate. The Chief Highway Administrator serves on the Executive Cabinet as Secretary of Highways. The Director of the New Mexico Department of Agriculture serves as the secretary of agriculture on the cabinet. The di-

rector will continue to be appointed by and operate under the supervision of the Board of Regents of the New Mexico State University. (See chart on page 251).

The standard reorganized department was established by law for the administration of executive policy. The administrative powers for each department are granted to a single department head called a secretary. Under the secretary, the principal unit is a division under the leadership of a division director. The unit of a division is a bureau under the direction of a bureau chief. Under a bureau is a section headed by a section supervisor. The various boards, commissions, and other administrative offices are divided among the departments for better control. (See chart on page 252).

The main duties of each secretary are:

(1) to supervise, direct, organize, plan, administrate and execute the programs of the department;

(2) to develop and set policies for the department;

(3) to compile and submit reports for the entire office;

(4) to provide the governor with reports on departmental operations;

(5) to sit as a member of the cabinet to assist policy making;

(6) to establish rules for the efficient operation of the respective cabinet offices;

(7)) to provide for the organizational structure of the department;

(8) to review all laws involving the department to be certain they are consistent with the statutes of reorganization.

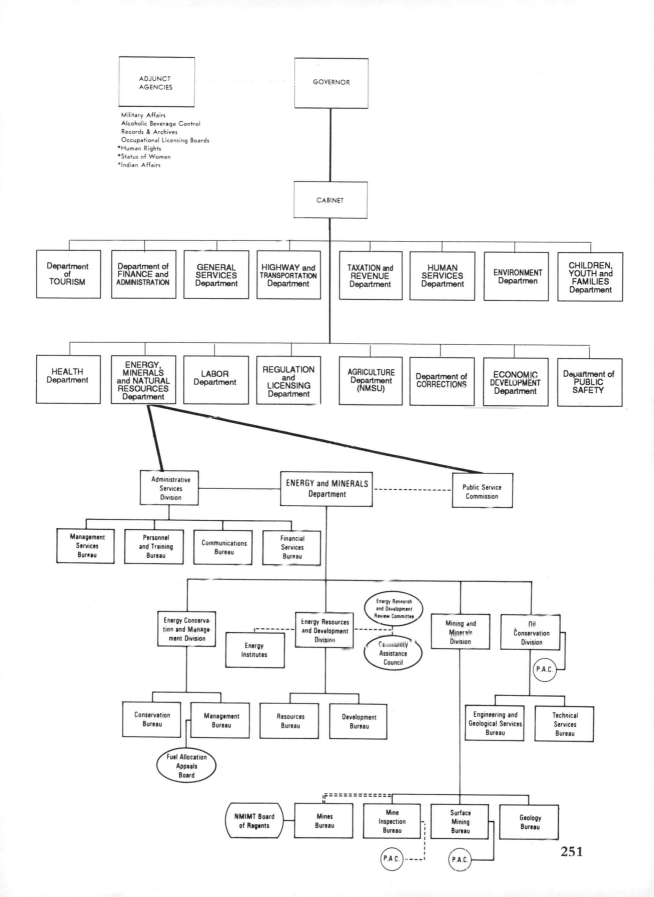

Standard Reorganized Department

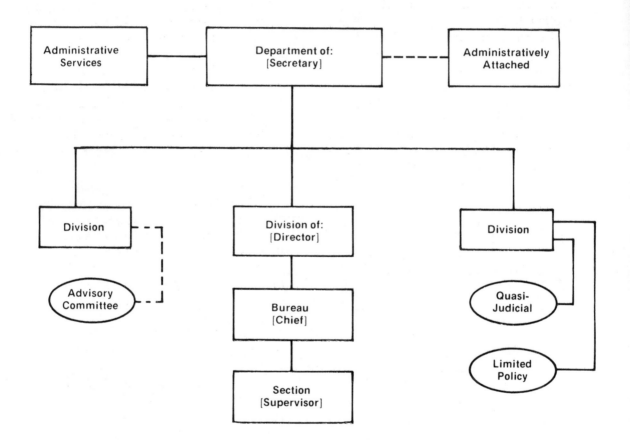

The Judicial Branch

"The Judicial Power of the state shall be vested in the Senate when sitting as a court of impeachment, a Supreme Court, a Court of Appeals, District Courts, Probate Courts, Magistrate Courts and such other courts inferior to the district courts as may be established by law from time to time in any district, county or municipality of the state."

New Mexico Constitution: *Article VI Section I.*

The Supreme Court of New Mexico is the highest court in the state regarding public and private cases. There are five justices of the supreme court who are elected for a term of eight years. They are eligible for reelection indefinitely. Each judge receives a salary, which is determined by law, and it may be changed from time to time by the legislature.

To qualify for election to the supreme court, a person must be:

(1) thirty years of age;
(2) learned in law; and
(3) in actual practice of law (lawyer), and resident in New Mexico for at least three years.

The supreme court has original jurisdiction (the court a case is first heard in) in certain cases, as well as jurisdiction over all cases, criminal and civil, brought to it on appeal from the lower courts. The decision of the court is final except in cases involving a federal question. The court does not hold a trial. All five judges hear a case, and each judge reaches his own decision. A majority must agree on any decision rendered.

Court of Appeals. In April 1966, the New Mexico state legislature establishing a court of appeals. This court consists of seven judges; one is selected as chief judge. The judges are elected for a term of eight years and receive a salary, which is determined by law. Their qualifications are the same as for members of the supreme court. Two women are now on the court of appeals.

The court of appeals was primarily designed to help the state supreme court because of additional cases on appeal. Sometimes there are so many cases before the supreme court that decisions will take months before they are rendered. This is why the legislature, according to law, provided for an additional court to handle additional appeals from the lower state courts.

The new appeals court has original jurisdiction on all cases on appeal from

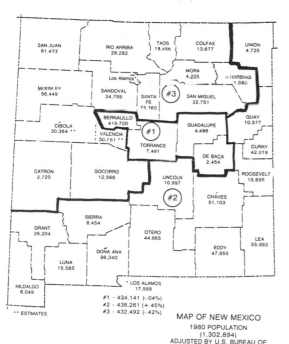

NEW MEXICO CONGRESSIONAL DISTRICTS
Average District - 434,298
Chap. 4, Laws 1982 (SS)

#1 - 434,141 (-.04%)
#2 - 436,261 (+.45%)
#3 - 432,492 (-.42%)

MAP OF NEW MEXICO
1980 POPULATION
(1,302,894)
ADJUSTED BY U.S. BUREAU OF
THE CENSUS (10-27-81)

district courts. Here the decisions are final, except in cases which are referred to the state supreme court. The court may review civil cases in which one or more of the parties seek damages from the other. In criminal action, it is the court of first appeal in all cases, except those in which a judgment of the district court imposes a sentence of death or life imprisonment. Those cases involving persons who have been given the maximum sentence required by law are reviewed by the supreme court only. The court of appeals may review cases for violation of municipal or county ordinances where fines or imprisonments are imposed.

Other cases that may be reviewed by the court of appeals include all actions under the Workmen's Compensation Act, the New Mexico Occupational Disease Disablement Law, and the Injury Act. The court renders decisions of those administrative agencies of the state where direct review by the court of appeals is provided by law.

District Courts. The New Mexico Constitution provides that the district courts shall have original jurisdiction in all matters and cases on trial, except those cases provided for by the constitution. The district court has jurisdiction over criminal and civil cases and proceedings directed to it by law. They also have appellate jurisdiction of all cases originating in the lower courts within their district. The court handles all juvenile cases when a trial is necessary within its jurisdiction. The district court may issue writs of habeas corpus (an order to appear before a court), injunction (a formal court order ordering some person or group to do, or refrain from doing, something), warrants, and any other writs as provided

by law.

New Mexico's thirty-three counties are divided into thirteen judicial districts (see map on page 255), presided over by forty-nine district judges. The judges of the district court are elected for a term of six years and receive a salary which is determined by the legislature. The qualifications of a district judge are the same as for the judges of the supreme court. The Second Judicial District has the only woman district judge.

The legislature may, from time to time, rearrange the judicial districts, increase the number of districts, or add additional judges. Each district court holds two regular sessions a year in each county in the district if there are enough cases to justify the sessions.

Each judicial district has a district attorney who is elected for a four year term. His salary varies in different districts. He receives an additional salary for acting as attorney for the juvenile court. His duties are to prosecute violations of criminal and civil laws in his district, to advise all county and state officials on points of law, to represent the county before the board of county commissioners, and to represent any county in his district in civil cases before the court of appeals or the supreme court.

Probate Court. Each county in each judicial district has a probate court. Its original jurisdiction is limited to determining ownership of property and money left to an heir of an estate.

The only qualifications necessary to hold the office is to be a qualified voter of the county from which elected. Probate judges are elected for a term of two years and may be reelected to serve as many terms as stipulated by law in the district. They receive a sal-

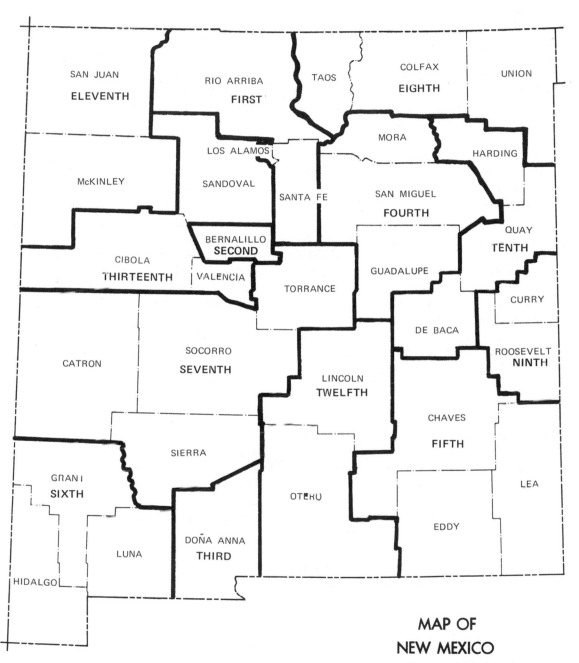

MAP OF
NEW MEXICO
JUDICIAL DISTRICTS

ary which is fixed by law.

The legislature may confer upon the probate court the duty to preside over civil cases involving not more than $3,000 and over cases of criminal misdemeanors involving less than $3,000. In the hearing of criminal cases, a six-man jury is used.

Small Claims Court. The small claims court, created by an act of the 1953 legislature, provides for a claims court to be established in a county having a population of 50,000 or more. Since that time, in 1963, the legislature changed this act to provide a claims court in a county having a population of 100,000 or more.

The court has civil jurisdiction within the county in matters not to exceed $2,000. The court tries no criminal cases, and no jury is required. The judges of the court are elected for a term of two years and must be practicing lawyers. The salary for the judges is fixed by law.

Magistrate Courts. The 1967 legislature provided for magistrate courts to replace the justice of the peace courts throughout the state. The number of magistrate courts is determined by law. Usually one magistrate court will be located in each city, town, or village, and additional courts will be established based on population.

To qualify for a magistrate judge, a person must be a qualified voter, learned in law, and reside in the district from which he is to be elected. Judges are elected for two years and may be re-elected indefinitely. They are paid a salary, which is determined by the legislature.

Magistrate judges have jurisdiction within their districts on civil cases involving not more than $200, or criminal cases involving fines and imprisonment of no more than $100 or six months, or both. If a trial is necessary, a six-man jury is provided to hear the case. Appeals from the magistrate courts may be taken to the district courts, where the case can be retried.

Metropolitan Court. The 1979 legislature passed a law, which was signed by the governor, to provide for a new court system in Bernalillo County. The act combines the magistrate, small claims, and municipal courts into a metropolitan court system with eleven judges. Qualifications and elections of the metropolitan judges are the same as those of the magistrate courts. The salaries of the judges are determined by the legislature.

The metropolitan courts will have the same jurisdiction provided for magistrate courts under state law. In addition, it will have extending jurisdiction over all offenses and complaints under the ordinances of Bernalillo County and of the city of Albuquerque.

Taxes

In New Mexico, as well as other states, a tax system has been established to provide the necessary funds to support state government and to provide services for the people of the state. Certain types of taxes are necessary if our state is to be self-supporting. Some money, for example, comes from outside the state in the form of federal grants to support education, welfare, and scientific research. Federal funds are provided for the state to build the interstate highways and other roads which form a giant network of highways throughout the United States. Tourists, who provide an additional source of revenue in sales tax and gasoline tax, help support state government. However, this is but a portion of the main source of income for our state. Every individual who lives in New Mexico must share in the responsibility of supporting his own state government. In order for this to be done, millions of dollars a year must be collected from us in the form of taxes.

There are many types of taxes which provide revenue for our state, and only a few of them will be mentioned in this chapter.

Every person earning money in the state of New Mexico is required to pay an income tax. This tax is in proportion to the amount earned. Tax rate schedules are available for each one to determine his wage bracket and the amount of tax he is to pay. Money collected from this tax is used for the support of education and other agencies of government.

Property tax is levied on all property in the state of New Mexico, except public lands. Values are fixed by assessors, and the tax is collected by the county treasurer, who sends the money to the Bureau of Revenue in Santa Fe. Part of the tax is returned to the districts to be used by the county for local support. The county distributes shares of the property tax to each city, town, and village in the county.

The sales tax is four percent throughout the state (four cents on each dollar spent). Part of the money received, of which one percent is returned to cities, goes for the support of public schools.

Cigarette taxes are collected to be used for the aid of the needy and aged.

Gasoline tax of eleven cents state and nine cents federal per gallon is used for the construction and maintenance of highways throughout the state. A New Mexican, Charles Springer, originated the idea of a gasoline tax in the early decades of this century. It quickly was accepted by the states.

Fees for license tags and drivers licenses are additional taxes which are collected for highways and for other governmental agencies.

These are only a few of the taxes levied by the state upon its people, but if New Mexico is to improve and provide all the services demanded by the people, then a tax structure is necessary. Changes in the tax structure are made when it is necessary for additional services or when the state general fund has been exhausted.

Services

There are many things that the people want state government to do for them. Health services and protective agencies are part of the services established by state government. Welfare programs and homes for the aged are necessary for those who cannot provide for themselves. The water we drink is constantly being tested by the state, and air pollution programs are being carried on to find a solution to the build-up of smog in New Mexico. Other services include employment agencies and unemployment insurance furnished by the state for those people who cannot find work. Additional services provided by the state are health and social services, industries for the blind, state hospitals, school for the visually handicapped, and vocational rehabilitation services.

According to the constitution, every child in New Mexico must attend school through the age of sixteeen. Everyone must share in this responsibility for the improvement of our state. It takes money to finance such an undertaking as education. Money for teachers' salaries, books, buses, new buildings, maintenance, and many other necessities is needed to provide the best education possible for the young people of New Mexico.

The state requires examinations for barbers, hairdressers, lawyers, and other professional groups. State government provides recreational areas for the people of New Mexico as well as tourists. This requires much money for maintenance and repair.

These are but a few of the many services which the state government, acting upon the will of the people, provides for each citizen of New Mexico.

Local Government

Every form of local government is provided for in the New Mexico Constitution. Before each local government can organize as a county, city, town, or village, the legislature may designate the type of government.

The Constitution of New Mexico provides for municipalities to govern themselves as the voters may decide by election, except where it is specifically prohibited by the legislature. Chartered municipalities may adopt, amend, or repeal a charter in the manner provided by law. In addition, communities are permitted to impose local taxes subject to the approval of the registered voters of the district. Thus, counties, cities, towns, and villages in New Mexico are afforded a certain degree of "home rule" within their respective localities.

Just as the states operate at a lower level of government and over a smaller area in our federal system, counties operate at a lower level and a smaller area under the state government. Each county is separate and independent from the others in New Mexico. Laws made by one county apply only to the people living in that county. In the same man-

ner, the state laws of New Mexico affect only the citizens of the state.

In New Mexico's thirty-two counties, only thirteen have county managers: Bernalillo, Chaves, Doña Ana, Lea, Lincoln, McKinley, Rio Arriba, Sandoval, San Juan, Santa Fe, Socorro, Taos, and Valencia counties. The remaining nineteen counties have either a purchasing agent or an administrator, who make out requisitions for the purchase of supplies for county use. They assist in the programs set forth by the county commissioners.

County Government.

Elected Officials:
  Three Commissioners
  Clerk
  Treasurer
  Assessor
  Sheriff
  District Judge
  District Attorney
Appointed by Commissioners:
  County Manager
  Purchasing Agent, or administrator
  Other necessary officials

Principal officers of the county are the three elected commissioners, who serve without pay. The commissioners meet a minimum of four times a year and provide for the "ordinances" (laws) of the county. They fix the tax rate and handle the county funds, provide for elections, and hire a manager. They also employ workers such as county health officers, coroner, county agricultural agent, and other county officials.

A manager is responsible for carrying out the ordinances set forth by the commissioners; he hires certain county workers such as highway personnel.

County clerks keep records of the commission meetings, land titles, sale of property, voter registration, and other legal papers; they also issue marriage licenses.

County treasurers collect county, city, and state taxes on property and pay the county bills.

The county assessor establishes property values and determines the amount of property tax each owner will have to pay. Once each year property owners must declare their property for tax purposes. Tax on property will include present land and buildings and additional improvements. Taxes are paid to the county treasurer.

The county sheriff is the police officer who has authority to enforce all laws throughout the county. He may employ deputies to assist him in enforcing the law. However, the sheriff cannot interfere with other police work, unless requested by a law enforcement agency for assistance. Usually all the law enforcement officers work together very well while performing their duty to enforce the law.

There is a county court located in each county seat which is presided over by the district judge. This court represents the court in the county. All civil and criminal cases are tried here. The district attorney is the lawyer for the county court (see Judicial Branch).

City Government. Whenever a local community grows to three thousand or more in population, it may be classed as a city. However, the responsibilities of a city are greater than those of a town or a village. More money is needed to provide for the necessary facilities which are part of a city.

Before a community can become a city, two hundred or more citizens must make a request to the board of county commissioners; they, in turn, put the question before the people in an election. If the voters approve the request, the change becomes official, and the

town becomes a city.

The most common form of city government is called the Mayor-Council Plan.

Elected Officials:
  Mayor
  City Council
  Judge
    (Magistrate or Metropolitan)
Appointed Officials:
  Police Chief
  Clerk
  City Attorney
  Treasurer
  Other deputy officials

The city is divided into wards and the voters in each ward elect "aldermen" for a term of four years. The mayor is elected for either two years or four years, and presides over the city council meetings. His duties vary, but like the governor, he is called upon frequently to make speeches, attend public meetings, and give support to the worthwhile programs of the people. He appoints many officials who are subject to approval by the council. The mayor-council system is favored by the larger cities, like Las Cruces, Albuquerque, and Santa Fe.

The council adopts ordinances, manages city funds and property, and provides for all city governmental functions such as street repair, health and sanitation, police and fire protection, water facilities, parks, and playgrounds.

Magistrate or metropolitan judges are elected for two years and handle cases in which the people are charged with violating a city ordinance.

Other members who may be appointed by the city council include the clerk, treasurer, attorney, police officers, and other officials.

Town Government. The Commission-Management Plan of government is widely used throughout New Mexico. Sometimes it is referred to as Council-Manager Plan. Regardless of what name is used, the main idea of this plan is to place responsibility on one man, and if he does not perform his job well, he is removed from office by the commissioners.

This form of government is restricted to municipalities having a population of three thousand or more persons. A community meeting these requirements may or may not adopt this form of government.

Elected Officials:
  Mayor
  Commissioners
  Clerk
  Judge (Magistrate)
Appointed Officials:
  Marshal
  Treasurer
  Other necessary officials

The commission is usually composed of five members who serve staggered terms and receive no salary. The municipality may be divided into five or more districts, and one commissioner is elected for each. Some city ordinances provide that a commissioner must reside in the district that he is to represent. However, in most cases, all commissioners are voted on at large.

Commissioners appoint a city manager who receives a salary. They hold him responsible for the proper and efficient administration of municipal government.

The city commission elects a chairperson from its membership. He presides as spokesman for the commission and signs all legal papers prepared by the commission.

The manager's basic duty is to supervise the actual operations of the city, while the commission sets policy. That is, the commission adopts ordinances, and the manager sees that the laws are carried out in accordance with the wishes of the commission. The manager also prepares the city's annual budget, makes recommendations to the commission on matters of municipal importance, and attends commission meetings. All appointments are made by the commissioners.

The other elected official in the Commission-Manager Plan of government is the judge. In New Mexico it has been established by the legislature to elect a magistrate judge by the voters of the town. He is elected for a term of two years and has jurisdiction over the local community when someone violates an ordinance (see Judicial Branch).

Other officials include the city clerk, the treasurer, the attorney, and additional department heads to carry out the work of the municipal government.

Village Government. There are several communities in New Mexico that use the Village Plan of Government. A village government is used when a community has a population of less than fifteen hundred people.

To become a town, two hundred people must request the board of county commissioners to change the charter from a village to a town. The commission provides for an election, and if a majority of the people vote for the request, the village becomes a town. However, the population must reach 1,500 or more before the commission will grant the request.

A Village Government is described as follows:

Elected Officials:
Commissioners
Magistrate Judge
Appointed Officials:
City Manager
Clerk
Treasurer
Police Chief
City Attorney
Other necessary officers

In the village form of government the mayor and the clerk are elected for terms of two years. The trustees are elected for a term of four years each.

The mayor may appoint the village marshal, treasurer, and other officials necessary to carry out governmental procedures; however, his appointments are subject to the approval by the trustees.

The judge (magistrate judge) is elected for two years and presides over the local court when anyone violates a village ordinance (see Judicial Branch).

Since very little money is received from taxes, the board of trustees can do very little. They do provide for a local form of government, which is shared by the people in the community.

Responsibilities of the Citizen

The one important element in our democratic form of government is "The Citizen." He should be eager to involve himself in government no matter what his job requirements are, or what race, creed, or color he may be.

Young people can play a big part in government by obeying laws and being interested in learning about our democratic system. In this way, they prepare themselves to take their place in society when they are ready. Voting is one of the best ways to demonstrate a desire to improve government.

It is the duty and privilege of each citizen to learn, to participate, and to grow with his local, state, and federal governments.

REVIEW ACTIVITIES

1. From outside reading, identify the members of the governor's cabinet. What is the purpose of the cabinet? What are the main duties of the cabinet?
2. Organize the class into a senate. Introduce a bill for passage, taking it through all the necessary steps.
3. Write a paper on the subject "equal protection under the law."
4. Explain the need for government.
5. Why should you study government?
6. Name the major parts of our federal Constitution.
7. What are the "Bill of Rights" in the New Mexico Constitution? Compare them with the "Bill of Rights" in our federal Constitution.
8. Explain the amending process in New Mexico.
9. How may the New Mexico Constitution be revised? How often should the constitution be revised?

10. Who is entitled to vote in the state of New Mexico?
11. What are the qualifications for a member of the House of Representatives in the New Mexico legislature? The Senate?
12. Name the main leaders in the House of Representatives and the Senate. What are their duties?
13. How often does the New Mexico legislature meet?
14. Explain how a bill becomes law.
15. What are the qualifications for governor in the State of New Mexico?
16. What are the duties of the governor? What are his powers?
17. List the other important officials in the executive branch and tell their duties?
18. What are the qualifications for election to the Supreme Court? To the lower courts?
19. How many different courts are there in New Mexico? Explain the duty of each court.
20. Why do we have taxes? Name some of the major taxes levied on the people of New Mexico.
21. What are some of the services provided by our state government?
22. How many forms of local government do we have in New Mexico?
23. Diagram your county government. Diagram your city, town, or village government. Explain the duties of your local government officials.

RECOGNIZE AND UNDERSTAND

amendment
preamble
legislative
executive
judicial
majority rule
bicameral system
precinct
checks and balances
referendum

legislative district
impeachment
rules committee
committee on committees
pardon
reprieve
commissioners
alderman
city council
ordinance

APPENDIX

A JOURNEY THROUGH NEW MEXICO HISTORY

NEW MEXICO

	1536 Cabeza De Vaca and Esteban the Moor reach Culiacàn, Mexico, after being shipwrecked off the coast of Texas in 1528. Beginning of rumors of Cìbola.
	1539 Fray Marcos De Niza and Esteban lead expedition to find Cìbola. Contact made with the Zuni, Esteban killed at the Zuni pueblos.
	1540-42 Coronado expedition to locate Cìbola and Quivira.

UNITED STATES & CANADA

1497-98 John Cabot makes voyage to Newfoundland.	**1524** Varrazano explores the coast of North America from the Carolinas to Nova Scotia.
1498 Ponce De Leon first explores Florida.	**1534-41** Jacques Cartier explores the St. Lawrence River.
	1539-42 Hernando De Soto explores the lower Mississippi River Valley.

LATIN AMERICA

1492 Columbus discovers the New World.	**1500** Cabral discovers Brazil.
1499 Amerigo Vespucci sails along the coast of Venezuela.	**1513** Balboa crosses the Isthmus of Panama, discovers the Pacific Ocean.
	1519-21 Cortéz conquers Mexico.
	1530 Rio De Janeiro, Brazil, founded.
	1532-35 Pizarro conquers Peru.
	1534 Quito, Ecuador, founded.
	1535 Pizarro founds city of Lima, Peru.
	1538 Bogotà, Columbia, founded.
	1540 Chile conquered by Pedro de Valdivia.

EUROPE & ASIA

1453 Constantinople falls to the Turks.	**1509** Henry VIII is King of England.
1469 Marriage of Ferdinand and Isabella.	**1524** Beginning of the Protestant Reformation.
1485 End of the Wars of the Roses in England. First of the Tudor kings comes to power.	**1534** King Henry VIII establishes the Anglican Church.
1486 Vasco Da Gama sails around the Cape of Good Hope.	**1577-80** Sir Francis Drake sails around the world.
1499 Switzerland becomes an independent republic.	

PEOPLE

1452 Leonardo Da Vinci born.	**1508** Michelangelo commissioned to paint the Sistine Chapel at the Vatican.
1483 Raphael (painter) born	**1517** Martin Luther writes his ninety-five theses.
	1541 El Greco born.
	1547 Miguel de Cervantes born.

INVENTIONS

1453-55 First book printed by Gutenberg.	**1500** First pocket watch.
1472-1519 Leonardo Da Vinci devised the following inventions: Breech-loading cannon Rifled firearms Universal joint Link chains Compass Parachute Lamp chimney	**1518** Fire engine.
	1535 Diving bell.
	1539 First astronomical map based on heliocentric theory.
1492 First globe invented.	**1545** Modern surgery developed.

Reprinted by permission of Museum of New Mexico Press.

1550   1600   1650

1580-81 Rodríguez, Espejo and Beltrán expeditions to New Mexico.	**1605** Oñate expedition to the Colorado River visits El Morro, leaves message on Inscription Rock.	**1680** Pueblo Revolt: Spanish forced to flee to El Paso del Norte (present-day Ciudad Juárez).
1598 Juan De Oñate colonizing expedition settles at San Gabriel.	**1608** New Mexico made a royal province. **1608-10** Pedro De Peralta establishes the new capital at Santa Fe; Palace of the Governors built.	**1680-92** Indians rule from the Palace of the Governors. **1692-93** De Vargas reconquers New Mexico.

1565 St. Augustine, Florida, established. **1585** First British colonization attempt at Roanoke Island, North Carolina. **1590** Mysterious end of Roanoke Colony.	**1607** Jamestown, Virginia, established. **1609-10** Henry Hudson discovers bay and river which today bear his name. **1619** House of Burgesses in Virginia established, first legislative body in what is now the United States. **1620** The Mayflower Compact. **1624** Manhattan Island (New York) purchased from local Indians. **1630** Massachusetts colonized. **1634** Ships *Ark* and *Dove* bring the first colonists to Maryland.	**1673** Marquette and Joliet journey down the Mississippi River. **1674** New Amsterdam becomes British by treaty and is renamed New York. **1675** King Philip's War. **1676** Bacon's Rebellion. **1688** La Salle sails down the Mississippi River. **1690's** Salem witch hunts.

1550 Concepción, Chile, founded. **1569** King Philip II establishes the Inquisition in Latin America. **1580** Settlement of Buenos Aires, Argentina. End of continental stage of Spanish expansion.	**1638** British begin to settle Honduras.	

1558 Elizabeth I is Queen of England. **1588** The Spanish Armada sails against England. **1589** The Bourbon dynasty begins in France.	**1618-48** The Thirty Years Wars. **1642-46** Civil war in England. Oliver Cromwell takes control. **1643** Reign of King Louis XIV of France begins. **1638** Japan closed to Europeans (until 1865).	**1658** Cromwell dies. **1682** Peter the Great is Tsar of Russia. **1688** Glorious Revolution in England. Beginning of the reign of William and Mary.

1561 Sir Francis Bacon born. **1564** William Shakespeare born. Galileo born. **1577** Peter Paul Rubens born. **1599** Diego Velásquez born.	**1608** John Milton born. **1632** John Locke, English philosopher, born.	**1685** J.S. Bach born. **1694** Voltaire born.

1550 First suspension bridge built. **1558** Military tank developed. Camera obscura with lens and stop for diaphragm developed. **1565** Lead pencil invented. **1582** Gregorian calendar revised. **1585** Decimal system developed.	**1609** Galileo develops the first law of motion. **1620** Adding machine invented. **1635** First discovery of minute organisms by Leeuwenhoek. **1643** Barometer invented. **1650** Calculating machine invented by Pascal.	**1654** Law of probability stated. **1658** Discovery of red corpuscles in blood. **1666** Mirror telescope devised by Newton. **1667** Cellular structure of plants discovered by Hooke. **1675** Greenwich Observatory founded. **1678** Power loom. **1682** Law of gravitation stated by Newton.

265

A JOURNEY THROUGH NEW MEXICO HISTORY

1700

1750

1800

1706	Albuquerque founded.
1709	Three campaigns made into the Navajo country by Marques De La Pañuela.
1710	San Miguel Church in Santa Fe rebuilt (destroyed earlier during the Pueblo Revolt of 1680).

1776	Dominguez-Escalante expedition explores the West from Santa Fe.
1778	De Anza makes peace with the Comanches.
1793	First school text printed in New Mexico by Antonio José Martinez, priest and schoolteacher of Taos.

1821	Mexico declares its independence from Spain. Santa Fe Trail opened by William Becknell.
1837	Revolt of 1837 by New Mexicans and Indians; Governor Albino Pérez killed.
1841	Texas invasion of New Mexico thwarted by Governor Manuel Armijo.
1846	Mexican War; Kearny raises the U.S. Flag in Santa Fe.
1847	Taos rebellion; Governor Bent killed.

1732	Benjamin Franklin publishes "Poor Richard's Almanac."
1733	Oglethorpe founds colony in Georgia.

1754	The French and Indian War.
1763	Treaty of Paris signed, ending the French and Indian War.
1769	First mission and presidio founded in Upper California: San Diego de Alcala (San Diego, California)
1775-83	The American Revolution.
1776	The Declaration of Independence.
1787	Adoption of the Constitution.
1789-97	George Washington is President of the U.S.

1803	Louisiana Purchase.
1805	Lewis and Clark exploration.
1812	War of 1812.
1819	Florida acquired from Spain.
1836	Texas wins independence.
1847	Salt Lake Valley settled by the Mormons.
1848	Treaty of Guadalupe Hidalgo ends Mexican War.

1719	Viceroyalty of New Granada created, embracing present-day Columbia, Venezuela, Ecúador, Panama.

1767	King Charles III expels the Jesuits from the New World.
1776	La Plata viceroyalty created, embracing present-day Argentina. Uruguay, Paraguay, Bolivia.

1812	Simón Bolívar is hailed as the liberator of Venezuela.
1818	Chile declares its independence.
1819	Bolivar takes Bogotá, sets up a new country, Gran Colombia, embracing present-day Colombia, Venezuela, Ecuador.
1821	Jose De San Martín declares Peru independent. Mexican independence.
1825	Bolivia declares its independence.
1833	Santa Ana becomes president of Mexico.
1839	Spain recognizes Mexico.

1702-13	War of Spanish Succession.
1713	Peace of Utrecht.

1756-63	French and Indian War in North America. Seven Years War in Europe.
1762-96	Catharine the Great is Tsarina of Russia.
1763	Treaty of Paris: France loses her foothold in continental North America.
1789	Fall of the Bastille in Paris.
1789-99	French Revolution, Napoleon comes to power as the First Consul of France.

1815	Battle of Waterloo.
1830	Belgium wins its independence.
1837-1901	Queen Victoria reigns.
1839-42	First Opium War in the Orient.
1848	Communist Manifesto issued by Marx and Engels.

1706	Benjamin Franklin born.
1734	Daniel Boone born.

1756	Mozart born.
1769	Napoleon born.
1770	Beethoven born.
1772	Samuel Taylor Coleridge born.
1783	Washington Irving born.
1789	James Fenimore Cooper born.
1793	Marie Antoinette beheaded during the French Revolution.
1795	Keats born.

1809	Charles Darwin born. Lincoln born. Edgar A. Poe born.
1815	Otto von Bismark born.
1817	Henry David Thoreau born.
1818	Karl Marx born.
1819	Walt Whitman born.
1821	Napoleon dies.
1822	Louis Pasteur born.
1844	Nietzsche born.

1714	Mercury thermometer invented by Fahrenheit.
1733	John Kay invents the fly shuttle, revolutionizing the weaving industry.
1742	Benjamin Franklin invents the Franklin stove.

1752	Franklin conducts his kite experiment.
1763	James Watt invents the first practical steam engine.
1792	Eli Whitney develops the cotton gin.
1798	Jenner discovers a vaccine for smallpox.
1799	Nitrous oxide (laughing gas) first used as an anesthetic.

1802	An English inventor gets patent for a steam locomotive.
1829	First railroad built in the United States. Braille developed.
1834	McCormick reaper invented.
1844	Telegraph invented.
1845	Elias Howe invents the first modern high-speed sewing machine.

266

1850

1850	New Mexico designated a territory but denied statehood.
1861-62	Confederates invade from Texas.
1862	Battle of Glorieta, near Santa Fe.
1862-67	Apaches and Navajos relocated at Bosque Redondo
1878	The railroad comes to New Mexico.
1878-81	Lincoln County War.
1881	Billy the Kid shot by Sheriff Pat Garrett.
1886	Geronimo captured; Indian hostilities in the Southwest cease.

1853	Perry opens trade with Japan.
1855	Gadsden Purchase finalizes continental U.S. borders.
1860	Lincoln elected President.
1861-65	Civil War.
1867	Alaska purchased from Russia. Canada made a dominion.
1898	Spanish-American War.

1862	Archduke Maximilian of Austria sent to Mexico as emperor by Louis Napoleon.
1867	Maximilian surrenders troops at Querétaro and is shot.
1899	Cuba and Puerto Rico win their independence from Spain.

1850-64	Taiping Rebellion in China.
1851	Louis Napoleon of France sets up the Second Empire.
1854-56	The Crimean War.
1860	Garibaldi conquers the kingdom of the Two Sicilies, uniting Italy.
1861	Tsar Alexander II frees all the serfs in Russia.
1870	Franco-Prussian War.
1895-96	Sino-Japanese War.

1865	Lincoln assassinated.
1872	Horace Greeley, famed American journalist, dies.

1859	First oil well drilled.
1861	Gatling machine gun.
1867	Dynamite invented by Nobel.
1876	Telephone invented.
1898	Radium discovered.

1900

1912	New Mexico granted statehood.
1916	Pancho Villa raid on Columbus, N.M.
W.W. I	17,157 men from New Mexico serve.
1923-24	Oil is discovered on the Navajo Reservation.
W.W. II	Heavy losses of New Mexicans at Pearl Harbor, the Philippines, and other engagements. Secret laboratories at Los Alamos produce the first atom bomb.
1945	World's first atomic explosion at Trinity Site, N.M.

1917	U.S. enters World War I.
1929	The Wall Street Crash.
1930-34	The Depression.
1941-45	World War II.

1910	Inauguration of Porfirio Diaz as the president of Mexico.
1913	Pancho Villa takes Juarez.
1914	Zapata and Villa occupy Mexico City.

1900	The Boxer Rebellion in China.
1905	The first Russian revolution.
1914-18	World War I.
1920-46	The League of Nations.
1936	Hitler remilitarizes Germany
1936-38	Spanish Civil War.
1939-45	World War II.
1945	The United Nations established.

1901	President McKinley shot.

1903	First airplane flight.
1907	Tungsten lamp.
1908	Model T Ford.
1910	Gyro compass.
1912	Vitamins discovered.
1920	Radio broadcasting.

APPENDIX
GOVERNORS OF NEW MEXICO
Under Spanish Rule

1598-1608	Don Juan de Oñate
1608-1610	Don Cristobal de Oñate
1610-1614	Don Pedro de Peralta
1614-1618	Admiral Don Bernadino de Ceballos
1618-1625	Don Juan de Eulate
1625-1630	Admiral Don Felipe Sotelo Ossorio
1630-1632	Capt. Don Francisco Manuel de Silva Nieto
1632-1635	Capt. Don Francisco de la Mora y Ceballos
1635-1637	Capt. Don Francisco Martinez de Baeza
1637-1641	Capt. Don Luis de Rosas
1641-	Gen. Don Juan Flores de Sierra y Váldez
1641-1642	Sergeant Francisco Gómez; Cabildo of Santa Fe
1642-1644	Capt. Don Alonzo Pacheco de Herédia
1644-1647	Capt. Don Fernando de Argüello Caravajál
1647-1649	Capt. Don Luis de Guzmán y Figueroa
1649-1653	Capt. Don Hernando de Ugarte y la Concha
1653-1656	Don Juan de Samaniego y Xaca
1656-1659	Capt. Don Juan Mansso de Contreras
1659-1661	Capt. Don Bernardo López de Mendizabal
1661-1664	Capt. Don Diego Dionisio de Peñalosa Briceño y Berdugo
1664-1665	Capt. Don Juan de Durán de Miranda
1665-1668	Capt. Don Fernando de Villanueva
1668-1671	Capt. Don Juan de Medrano y Mesia
1671-1675	Gen. Don Juan Durán de Miranda (2nd term)
1675-1677	Capt. Don Juan Francisco de Treviño
1677-1683	Capt. Don Antonio de Otermin
1683-1686	Capt. Don Domingo Jironza Pétriz de Cruzate
1686-1689	Don Pedro Reneros de Posada
1689-1691	Capt. Don Domingo Jironza Pétriz de Cruzate (2nd term)
1691-1697	Don Diego de Vargas Zapata Lujan Ponce de León y Contreras
1697-1703	Don Pedro Rodríguez Cubero
1703-1704	Diego de Vargas Zapata Lujan Ponce de León y Contreras (Marquez de la Nava Brazinas) (2nd term)
1704-1705	Capt. Don Juan Paéz Hurtado
1705-1707	Don Francisco Cuervo y Villaseñor
1707-1712	Admiral Don Joseph Chacón Medina Salazar y Villaseñor (Marquez de las Peñuelas)
1712-1715	Don Juan Ignacio Flores Mogollón
1715-1717	Capt. Don Felipe Martinez, acting
1717-	Capt. Don Juan Paéz Hurtado, acting
1717-1722	Capt. Don Antonio Valverde y Cossio, acting
1722-1731	Don Juan Domingo de Bustamente
1731-1736	Don Gervasio Cruzat y Gongora

1736-1739	Don Henrique de Olavide y Micheleña
1739-1743	Don Gaspar Domingo de Mendoza
1743-1749	Don Joaquin Codallos y Rabal
1749-1754	Don Tomás Véles Cachupin
1754-1760	Don Francisco Antonio Marin de Valle
1760-	Don Mateo Antonio de Mendoza, acting
1760-1762	Don Manuel de Portillo y Urrisola, acting
1762-1767	Don Tomàs Véles Cachupin (2nd term)
1767-1778	Capt. Don Pedro Fermin de Mendinueta
1778-	Don Francisco Trebol Navarro, acting
1778-1788	Lt. Col. Don Juan Bautista de Anza
1788-1794	Don Fernando de la Concha
1794-1805	Lt. Col. Don Fernando Chacón
1805-1808	Col. Don Joaquin del Real Alencaster, acting
1808-	Don Alberto Máynez, acting
1808-1814	Lt. Col. Don Jose Manrrique, acting
1814-1816	Don Alberto Máynez (2nd term)
1816-1818	Don Pedro Maria de Allande, acting
1818-1821	Capt. Don Facundo Melgares, acting

Under Mexican Rule

1821-1822	Capt. Don Facundo Melgares
1822-	Francisco Xavier Cháves
1822-1823	Col. José Antonio Vizcarra
1823-1825	Bartolomé Baca
1825-1827	Col. Antonio Narbona
1827-1829	Manuel Armijo
1829-1832	José Antonio Chávez
1832-1833	Santiago Abreú
1833-1835	Francisco Sarracino
1835-1837	Col. Albino Pérez (assassinated, Aug. 9)
1837-1844	Manuel Armijo (2nd term)
1844-	Mariano Chávez, acting
1844-	Felipe Sena, acting
1844-1845	Gen. Mariano Martinez de Lejanza
1845-	Jose Chávez y Castillo
1845-1846	Manuel Armijo (3rd term)
1846-	Juan Bautista Vigil y Alarid, acting

United States Occupation, 1846-1850

1846-	Brigadier Gen. Stephen Watts Kearny (Aug.-Sept.)
1846-1847	Charles Bent (assassinated, Jan. 19, 1847)
1847-1848	Donaciano Vigil (Civil)
	Col. Sterling Price (Military)
1848-1849	Col. John M. Washington
1849-1851	Col. John Munroe

APPENDIX
Territorial Government

1851-1852	James S. Calhoun	1875-	William G. Ritch, acting
1852-	John Greiner, acting	1875-1878	Samuel B. Axtell
1852-1853	William Carr Lane	1878-1881	Lew Wallace
1853-	W. S. Messervy, acting	1881-1885	Lionel A. Sheldon
1853-1856	David Meriwether	1885-1889	Edmund G. Ross
1856-1857	W. W. H. Davis, acting	1889-1893	L. Bradford Prince
1857-1861	Abraham Rencher	1893-1897	William T. Thornton
1861-1866	Henry Connelley	1897-1906	Miguel A. Otero
1866-	W. F. M. Arny, acting	1906-1907	Herbert J. Hagerman
1866-1869	Robert B. Mitchell	1907-	J. W. Raynolds, acting
1869-1871	William A. Pile	1907-1910	George Curry
1871-1875	Marsh Giddings	1910-1912	William J. Mills

State Government

1912-1916	William C. McDonald
1917-	Ezéquiel C de Baca (died, Feb. 18)
1917-1918	Washington E. Lindsey
1919-1920	Octaviano A. Larrazolo
1921-1922	Merritt C. Mechem
1923-1924	James F. Hinkle
1925-1926	Arthur T. Hannett
1927-1930	Richard C. Dillon
1931-1933	Arthur Seligman (died, Sept. 25)
1933-1934	A. W. Hockenhull
1935-1938	Clyde Tingley
1939-1942	John E. Miles
1943-1946	John J. Dempsey
1947-1950	Thomas J. Mabry
1951-1954	Edwin L. Mechem
1955-1956	John F. Simms
1957-1958	Edwin L. Mechem
1959-1960	John Burroughs
1961-1962	Edwin L. Mechem (appointed U.S. Senator in Nov.)
1962-	Tom Bolack (Dec.)
1963-1966	Jack M. Campbell
1967-1970	David F. Cargo
1971-1974	Bruce King
1975-1978	Jerry Apodaca
1979-1982	Bruce King
1983-1986	Toney Anaya
1987-1990	Garry Carruthers
1991-	Bruce King

A JOURNEY THROUGH NEW MEXICO HISTORY

FREQUENTLY USED SPANISH PLACE NAMES AND TERMS

(Courtesy of New Mexico Blue Book)

acequia (ah-sa'ke-ah) ------------------------------------Irrigation ditch.

Adobe (a-do-beh) --------------------------------------Sundried brick.

Aqua (ah'wah) ---Water.

Alameda ((Al-lah-meh-dah) ------------------A poplar grove or shaded walk.

Alamogordo (Al-ah-mo-gor'do) -----------------------Large cottonwood.

Albuquerque (Al-boo-kehr'keh) -----------Named for Juan Fernández de la Cueva y
                Enríquez, Duke of Albuquerque and 34th Viceroy of New Spain.

Alcalde Mayor (al-kahl-deh-ma-yor) ----Chief local administrator under Spanish and
                Mexican government.

Algodones (Al-go-don'es) -----------------------------------Cotton plants.

Amigo (ah-me'go) --A friend.

Arroyo Seco (ah-royo Seh'ko) ----------------------------A dry rivulet.

baile (by-leh) --Dance.

caballo (ka-bah-yo) ---Horse.

camino (kah-me'no) --------------------------------Road or highway.

cañoncito (kan-yohn-see'toh) ------------------Little canyon or gorge.

carne (kar'neh) ---Meat.

casa (kah'sah) ---House.

Cebolleta (se-bo-ye-ta) ------------------------------Little wild onion.

chili (che'le) ---Pepper plant.

Cimarron (Se-ma-ron) ----------------------------------Wild or untamed.

conejo (ko-ne-ho) ---Rabbit.

conquistador (kon-kees-tah-dor) --------------Early Spanish "conqueror" of N.M.

culebra (koo-leh'brah) ------------------A snake, especially rattle snake.

Domingo (Doh-mcen'goh) -----------------------------------Sunday.

El Ortiz (El Or-teez') ----------Named for an old and prominent New Mexico family.

El Rito de los Frijoles (El Ree'toh deh lohs Free-hol'lehs) _The little river of beans.

Embudo (Em-boo'do) ----------------------------Funnel shaped cañon.

Encino (En-see'no) --Live oak.

Española (Es-pahn-yoh'lah) --------------------------Spanish woman.

Espiritu Santo (es-pee-ree-tuh Sahn'toh) --------------------Holy Ghost.

Estancia (Es-tahn'cia) ----------------------------------Large estate.

fiesta (Fe-es'ta) -----------------------------A feast or celebration.

gallina (ga-ye-nah) ---Hen.

gato (ga-to) --Cat.

genizaro (Henisaro) --------------Displaced Indians who had lost their tribal identity
                through capture by other tribes.

hondo (on'do) --Deep.

La Bajada (La Bah-hah'dah) -----------------------------The descent.

la bruja (la broo'hah) -----------------------------------The witch.

Laguna (Lah-goo'nah) --Lake.

Las Cruces (Lahs Cru'ses) ------------------------------The crosses.

Las Palomas (Lahs Pa-lo'mas) --------------------------The doves.

Las Vegas (Lahs Veh-gahs) -----------------------------The meadows.

loma (lo'mah) . . . . Long low hill.

Los Alamos (Lohs Ah'lah-mohs) . . . . The poplars.

Los Cerrillos (Lohs Seh-ree'yos) . . . . Little hills.

Los Lunas (Lohs Loo-nahs') . . . . Named for the prominent Luna family.

Manzano (Mahn-zahn'noh) . . . . Apple tree.

Mesa Encantada (Meh-sah Ehn-kahn-tah'dah) . . . . Enchanted mesa.

Mesilla (Meh-see'ya) . . . . Little tableland.

Nochebuena (No'che-bway'nah) . . . . Christmas Eve.

Ojo Caliente (O-ho Cahl-i-en'te) . . . . Hot Springs.

Pajarito (pah-hah-ree'toh) . . . . The bird.

patio (pah'te-o) . . . . Inner court yard.

Peña Blanca (Payn-yah Blahn'kah) . . . . White rock.

Peñasco (Pehn-yas'co) . . . . Large rock.

piñon (pen-yon') . . . . An edible pine nut.

plaza (plah'zah) . . . . Public square; marked place.

primo (pree'mo) . . . . Cousin

Puerto de Luna (Poor-er-to deh Loo-na) . . . . Gateway of moon.

Quemado (Keh-mah'do) . . . . Burned.

Questa (Kwes'tah) . . . . Edge of a long ridge.

Raton (Rah-ton') . . . . Mouse.

Rio Abajo (Ree'oh Ah-bah'ho) . . . . . Lower river; region below La Bajada hill.

Rio Arriba (Ree'oh Ah-re'bah) . . . . . Upper river; region above La Bajada hill.

Rio Puerco (Ree'oh Poo-er'ko) . . . . Very dirty river.

Sandia (Sahn-dee'ah) . . . . Watermelon.

Sangre de Cristo (Sahn'greh deh Krees'toh) . . . . Blood of Christ.

Santa Fe (Sahn-tah Feh') . . . . Holy Faith.

Santo Niño (Sahn'to Neen'yo) . . . . Holy Child.

Socorro (So-cor'ro) . . . . . . Named by conquistadores for Nuestra Señora de la Socorro.

sombrero (som-breh-ro) . . . . Hat.

Tecolote (Teh-koh-loh'teh) . . . . The ground owl.

Tierra Amarilla (Tee-er-ra Ah-ma-ree'ya) . . . . Yellow earth.

Tres Piedras (Tres Pee-eh'dras) . . . . The three rocks.

Truchas (Troo'chas) . . . . Trout.

viga (vee-ga) . . . . Ceiling beam.

viva (vee-vah) . . . . Hurrah!

ORIGIN OF COUNTIES

*BERNALILLO
One of the seven original counties—reorganized in 1852 and named for the town of Bernalillo, then its county seat. In 1854 the county seat was changed to Albuquerque. A companion of Cortés, Bernal Díaz del Castillo, is the namesake for the county.

CATRON
Established in 1921. Named for Thomas B. Catron, United States senator from New Mexico (1912-1917).

CHAVES
Named for the Chaves family, long prominent in New Mexico. The county was established in 1889.

CIBOLA
Established in 1981. Spanish word for buffalo.

COLFAX
Established in 1869. Named for Schuyler Colfax, then vice-president of the United States under President Grant.

CURRY
Established in 1909. Named for George Curry, territorial governor of New Mexico (1907-1910).

DE BACA
It was named for Ezéquiel Cabeza de Baca, governor of New Mexico in 1917. De Baca County was established in 1917.

DOÑA ANA
Established in 1852. Named for a daughter of Colonel Ana, who was captured by Apaches.

EDDY
Established in 1889. It was named for Charles B. Eddy, promoter of the Carlsbad Irrigation project and railroad magnate.

GRANT
Grant County was established in 1868 and named for General (President, 1869-1877) Ulysses S. Grant.

GUADALUPE
The county was established in 1891. It was named for the patron saint of Mexico, Our Lady of Guadalupe.

HARDING
Harding County was established in 1921 and named for President Warren G. Harding (1921-1923).

HIDALGO
It was established in 1919 and named for the town Guadalupe Hidalgo, near Mexico City, where the treaty ending the Mexican War was signed.

LEA
Established in 1917. Named for Joseph C. Lea, a pioneer leader.

LINCOLN
Lincoln County was established in 1869. It was named for the town of Lincoln, which was named for President Abraham Lincoln (1861-1865).

LOS ALAMOS
Los Alamos County was established in 1949 and named for the town, Los Alamos, "the poplars."

LUNA
Established in 1901. Named for Salomon Luna, a prominent political figure of New Mexico's territorial days.

McKINLEY
It was established in 1899 and named for President William McKinley (1897-1901).

MORA
Established in 1860. Named Mora (mulberry) because of the mulberry trees found growing here.

OTERO
Otero County was established in 1899 and named for Miguel A. Otero, then governor of New Mexico (1897-1906).

QUAY
It was established in 1903 and named for Senator Matt Quay of Pennsylvania (1887-1904).

*RIO ARRIBA
Rio Arriba, one of the seven original counties, was reorganized in 1852. The name means "upper river," referring to the upper reaches of the Rio Grande.

ROOSEVELT
Established in 1903. Named for President Theodore Roosevelt (1901-1909).

SANDOVAL
Established in 1903 and named for the Sandoval family.

SAN JUAN
San Juan County was established in 1887. Named for the San Juan River, which was named for Saint John.

*SAN MIGUEL
The county is one of the seven original New Mexico counties. It was established in its present form in 1852. San Miguel was named for the early settlement of San Miguel del Bado, which in turn was named for Saint Michael.

*SANTA FE
Another of the seven original counties. It was reorganized in 1852 and named for the city, Santa Fe (San Francisco de Asís de la Santa Fé).

SIERRA	Established in 1884. Named Sierra (high, sawtooth mountains) because of the mountainous country included in it.
SOCORRO	Established in 1850. Named for the county seat Socorro which means "help." This town was so named by the Spanish in memory of the help received here from the Indians by the Oñate expedition.
*TAOS	This county is one of the seven original counties established under Mexican rule. It was reorganized in 1852, and named for the Taos Indians who occupy Taos Pueblo in the county.
TORRANCE	Established in 1903. Named for Francis J. Torrance, one of the promoters and builders of the New Mexico Central Railroad.
UNION	Established in 1893. Named Union because the people were united in their desire to form a county.
*VALENCIA	One of the seven original counties that was reorganized in 1852. It was named for Juan de Valencia, a seventeenth-century settler.

*Santa Ana County was one of the seven original counties. Part of the county was located in the northeastern portion of Bernalillo County. The county seat was Peña Blanca. Later, Santa Ana County merged with Bernalillo County by act of 1876.

The seven original counties were established before New Mexico became a territory of the United States. After the Mexican War, some of these countries were reorganized or they merged with other counties. The remaining counties retained their original boundaries.

NATIONAL PARKS AND MONUMENTS IN NEW MEXICO

National Park — Carlsbad Caverns
— Chaco Culture National Historical Park

National Monuments

Aztec Ruins	El Malpais	Salinas
Bandelier	El Morro	Pecos
Capulin Mountain	Fort Union	White Sands
	Gila Cliff Dwellings	

NEW MEXICO STATE PARKS AND MONUMENTS

Bluewater Lake	Heron Lake	Pancho Villa
Bottomless Lakes	Hyde Memorial	Percha Dam
Caballo Lake	Indian Petroglyph	Red Rocks
Chicosa Lakes	Jemez State Monument	Rio Grande Gorge
City of Rocks	Kit Carson Memorial	Rock Hound
Clayton Lake	Leasburg Dam	San Gabriel
Conchas Lake	Lincoln State Monument	Santa Fe River
Coronado State Monument	Living Desert	Smokey Bear
Coyote Creek	Manzano	Storrie Lake
Elephant Butte	Morphy Lake	Sumner Lake
El Vado Lake	Navajo Lake (Pine)	Ute Lake
Fort Seldon State Monument	Navajo Lake (Sims Mesa)	Valley of Fires
Fort Sumner State Monument	Oasis	Villanueva

274

BIBLIOGRAPHY

BIBLIOGRAPHY

AGOGINO, GEORGE A.
Archaeological Excavations at Blackwater Draw, Locality Number 1, New Mexico 1963-1964.
National Geographic Society Research Reports, 1963 Projects, pages 1-7. Washington D.C., 1968.
A New Point Type From Hell Gap Valley, Eastern Wyoming. American Antiquity, Volume 26, Number 4, April, 1961.
A Brief History of Early Man in the Western High Plains. Pamphlet, 1968.

BAILEY, R. L. *The Long Walk.* Los Angeles: Westernlore Press, 1964.

BALL, LARRY D. *The United States Marshals of New Mexico and Arizona Territories, 1846-1912.* Albuquerque: University of New Mexico Press, 1978.

BANCROFT, H. H. *History of Arizona and New Mexico.* Albuquerque: Horn and Wallace, 1962. (Reprint).

BANDELIER, ADOLPH F. A.
The Gilded Man. Chicago: The Rio Grande Press, Inc., 1962. (Reprint).
The Delight Makers. New York: Dodd, 1959. (Reprint).

BECK, WARREN A. *New Mexico History of Four Centuries.* Norman: University of Oklahoma Press, 1963.

BECK, WARREN A. and HASS, YNEZ D. *Historical Atlas of New Mexico.* Norman: University of Oklahoma Press, 1969.

BENDER, NORMAN J., ed. *Missionaries, Outlaws, and Indians: Taylor F. Ealy at Lincoln and Zuni 1878-1881.* Albuquerque: University of New Mexico Press, 1984.

BENSON, NANCY C. *Women in New Mexico.* Albuquerque: Museum of Albuquerque, 1976.

BLOOM, LANSING B. and DONNELLY, THOMAS C. *New Mexico History and Civics.* Albuquerque: The University Press, 1933.

BOLTON, HERBERT E. *Coronado, Knight of Pueblos and Plains.* Albuquerque: University of New Mexico Press, 1949.

BROOKS, CLINTON E. and REEVE, FRANK D. *Forts and Forays.* Albuquerque: University of New Mexico Press, 1948.

CHAVEZ, ANGELICO *My Penitente Land.* Albuquerque: University of New Mexico Press, 1974.

CHRISTIANSEN, PAIGE W. and KOTTLOWSKI, FRANK E. *Mosaic of New Mexico Scenery, Rocks, and History.* Albuquerque: University of New Mexico Press, 1964.

CHURCH, PEGGY *The House at Otowi Bridge.* Albuquerque: University of New Mexico Press, 1974.

CLEAVELAND, AGNES MORLEY *No Life for a Lady.* Cambridge: Riverside Press, 1941.

COKE, VAN DEREN
Photography in New Mexico. Albuquerque: University of New Mexico Press, 1979.
Taos and Santa Fe Artists. Albuquerque: University of New Mexico Press, 1962.

COOKE, P. ST. GEORGE *The Conquest of New Mexico and California: An Historical and Personal Narrative.* Albuquerque: Horn and Wallace Publishers, 1964. (Reprint).

COX, E. W. and RICHARDSON, B. J. *Noteworthy Black Women in New Mexico.* No publisher listed, 1977.

CUTTS, JAMES MEDISON *The Conquest of California and New Mexico by the Forces of the United States in the Years 1846-1847.* Albuquerque: Horn & Wallace, 1965. (Reprint).

DAVIS, BRITTON *The Truth About Geronimo.* New Haven: Yale University Press, 1929.

DAVIS, W. W. H. *El Gringo: Or New Mexico and Her People.* Chicago: Rio Grande Press, 1962. (Reprint).

DOBIE, FRANK J. *Up The Trail from Texas.* Eau Claire, Wisconsin: Hale Press, 1955.

DONNELLY, THOMAS C. *The Government of New Mexico.* Albuquerque: University of New Mexico Press, 1953.

DUTTON, DR. BERTHA P.
Indians of New Mexico for New Mexico Department of Development

EMMETT, CHRIS *Fort Union and the Winning of the Southwest.* Norman: University of Oklahoma Press, 1965.

FERGUSSON, ERNA *New Mexico: A Pageant of Three Peoples.* New York: Alfred A. Knopf Inc., 1951.

FITZPATRICK, GEORGE *This is New Mexico.* Albuquerque: Horn and Wallace, 1962.

BIBLIOGRAPHY

FORREST, EARLE R. *Missions and Pueblos of the Old Southwest.* Chicago: Rio Grande Press, 1965. (Reprint).

GANAWAY, LOOMIS MORTON *New Mexico and the Sectional Controversy 1846-1861.* Albuquerque: University of New Mexico Press, 1944.

GARCIA, F. CHRIS, HAIN, PAUL L., and RHODES, HAROLD *State and Local Government in New Mexico.* Albuquerque: University of New Mexico Press, 1979.

GATES, RICHARD *True Book of Conservation.* Chicago: Children's Press, 1959.

GORDON, DOROTHY L. *You and Democracy.* New York: Dutton, 1951.

GREGG, ANDREW K. *New Mexico in the Nineteenth Century.* Albuquerque: University of New Mexico Press, 1968.

HACKETT, CHARLES *Revolt of the Pueblo Indians of New Mexico and Otermin's Attempted Reconquest.* Albuquerque: University of New Mexico Press, 1969.

HALL, MARTIN HARDWICK *Sibley's New Mexico Campaign.* Austin: University of Texas Press, 1960.

HAMMOND, GEORGE P. and DONNELLY, THOMAS C. *The Story of New Mexico, Its History and Government.* Albuquerque: University of New Mexico Press, 1936.

HIBBIN, FRANK C. *The Lost Americans.* New York: Thomas Y. Crowell Co., 1946.

HISTORIC SANTA FE FOUNDATION *Old Santa Fe Today.* Albuquerque: University of New Mexico Press, 1972.

HOLBROOK, STEWART H. *The Golden Age of Railroads.* New York: Random House, 1960.

HOLLON, W. EUGENE *The Southwest Old and New.* New York. Alfred A. Knopf Inc., 1961.

HOLMES, JACK E. *Politics in New Mexico.* Albuquerque: University of New Mexico Press, 1967.

HORGAN, PAUL *Great River.* New York: Holt, Rinehart, and Winston, 1960.

HORN, CALVIN *New Mexico's Troubled Years.* Albuquerque: Horn and Wallace, 1963.

HORN AND WALLACE, ed. *Confederate Victories in the Southwest.* Albuquerque: Horn and Wallace, 1961.

HUGHES, JOHN T. *Doniphan's Expedition, Containing an Account of the Conquest of New Mexico.* Chicago: Rio Grande Press, 1963. (Reprint).

JENKINS, MYRA ELLEN, and SCHROEDER, ALBERT H. *A Brief History of New Mexico.* Albuquerque: University of New Mexico Press, 1974.

JONES, OAKAH L., JR. *Pueblo Warriors and Spanish Conquest.* Norman: University of Oklahoma Press, 1966.

KELEHER, WILLIAM A.
Violence in Lincoln County. Albuquerque: University of New Mexico Press, 1957.
Turmoil in New Mexico 1846-1868. Santa Fe: Rydal Press, 1952.

KIDDER, ALFRED V. *An Introduction to the Study of Southwestern Archaeology.* Connecticut: Yale University Press, 1962.

KLEIN, BERNARD AND ICOLARI, DANIEL, editors. *Encyclopedia of the American Indians.* New York: B. Klein and Co., 1967.

KLUCKHORN, CLYDE AND LEIGHTON, DOROTHEA *The Navaho.* Garden City, New York: Doubleday, 1962.

LA FARGE, OLIVER *Santa Fe, the Autobiography of a Southwestern Town.* Norman: University of Oklahoma Press, 1959.

LAMAR, HOWARD R. *The Far Southwest, 1846-1912.* New York: W. W. Norton, 1970.

LANDES, RUTH *Latin Americans of the Southwest.* New York: McGraw-Hill, 1965.

LARSON, ROBERT W. *New Mexico's Quest for Statehood.* Albuquerque: University of New Mexico Press, 1968.

LAVASH, DONALD R. *Sheriff William Brady: Tragic Hero of the Lincoln County War.* Santa Fe: Sunstone Press, 1985

LAVENDER, DAVID
Bent's Fort. New York: Doubleday, 1952.
Laws of the Territory of New Mexico, Passed by the Legislative Assembly, 1856-1857. Printed at the Office of the Democrat, 1857.
Lew Wallace Papers. Santa Fe: State Records Center.

BIBLIOGRAPHY

LOONEY, RALPH *Haunted Highways.* New York: Hastings House, 1968.

LUMMIS, CHARLES F. *The Spanish Pioneers.* Chicago: Rio Grande Press, 1963. (Reprint).

McGREGOR, JOHN C. *Southwestern Archaeology.* second edition. Urbana: University of Illinois Press, 1965.

MEETER, GEORGE F. *The Holloman Story.* Albuquerque: University of New Mexico Press, 1967.

MOORHEAD, MAX *The Presidio.* Norman: University of Oklahoma Press, 1975.

MURPHY, LAWRENCE R. *Philmont: A History of New Mexico's Cimarron Country.* Albuquerque: University of New Mexico Press, 1976.

NAHM, MILTON C. *Las Vegas and Uncle Joe. The New Mexico I Remember.* Norman: University of Oklahoma Press, 1964.

NASON, THELMA CAMPBELL *Under the Wide Sky.* Chicago: Follett Publishing Co., 1965.

OTERO, NINA *Old Spain in Our Southwest.* Chicago: The Rio Grande Press, 1962 (Reprint).

PEARCE, T. M. *New Mexico Place Names. A Geographical Dictionary.* Albuquerque: The University of New Mexico Press, 1965.

PERRIGO, LYNN I. *Our Spanish Southwest.* Albuquerque: University of New Mexico Press, 1975.

POTTER, R. D. *Young People's Book of Atomic Energy.* New York: Dodd-Mead Press, 1953.

PRICE, EUGENE H. *Open Range Ranching.* Clarendon, Texas: Clarendon Press, 1967.

PRINCE, L. BRADFORD
A Concise History of New Mexico. Cedar Rapids: Torch Press, 1912.
Historical Sketches of New Mexico from the Earliest Records to the American Occupation. Kansas City: Ramsey, Millet, and Hudson, 1883.
New Mexico's Struggle for Statehood, Sixty Years of Effort to Obtain Self Government. Santa Fe: New Mexico Printing Co., 1910.

REEVE, FRANK D. *History of New Mexico.* Volume I, II, III. New York: Lewis Historical Publishing Co. Inc., 1961.
New Mexico. Denver: Sage Books, 1964.

RICHARDSON, BARBARA J. *Black Directory of New Mexico.* Rio Rancho: Panorama Press, 1976.

RITTENHOUSE, JACK D. *New Mexico Civil War Bibliography 1861 - 1865; an annotated checklist of books and pamphlets.* Houston: Stagecoach Press, 1960.

SAUNDERS, LYLE *A Guide to Materials Bearing on Cultural Relations in New Mexico.* Albuquerque: University of New Mexico Press, 1944.

SHERMAN, JAMES E. and BARBARA H. *Ghost Towns and Mining Camps of New Mexico.* Norman: University of Oklahoma Press, 1975.

SIMMONS, MARC *New Mexico, A History.* New York: W. W. Norton, 1977.
Spanish Government in New Mexico. Albuquerque: University of New Mexico Press, 1968.

SONNICHSEN, C. L. *The Mescalero Apache.* Norman: University of Oklahoma Press, 1958.

STANLEY, F. *The Jicarilla Apache.* Pampa: Pampa Print Shop, 1967.

STOUTENBURGH, JOHN L., JR. *Dictionary of American Indians.* New York: Crown Publishers Inc., 1969.

TATE, BILL *The Penitentes of the Sangre de Cristo.* Española: The Rio Grande Sun Press, 1973.

THEISEN, GERALD *Guide to New Mexico History.* Santa Fe: Museum of New Mexico, 1977.

THOMAS, ALFRED BARNABY *After Coronado.* Norman: University of Oklahoma Press, 1966.

TWITCHELL, RALPH EMERSON *The Leading Facts of New Mexico History.* Volume I, II. Albuquerque: Horn and Wallace, 1963. (Reprint).

VILLAGRA, GASPAR PEREZ DE *History of New Mexico.* Alcalá de Henares: 1610. Translated by Gilberto Espinosa. Introduction and notes by F. W. Hodges. New York: Arno Publishing Company, 1967. (Reprint).

WARREN, R. P. *Remember the Alamo.* New York: Random House, 1958.

BIBLIOGRAPHY

WEBB, WALTER PRESCOTT *The Great Plains.* Boston: Ginn and Company, 1931.

WEBER, DAVID J. *Taos Trappers.* Norman: University of Oklahoma Press, 1971.

WEIGLE, MARTA *Brothers of Light, Brothers of Blood: The Penitentes of the Southwest.* Albuquerque: University of New Mexico Press, 1976.

WELLMAN, PAUL I. *Glory, God, and Gold.* Garden City, New York: Doubleday, 1954.

WILLIAMS, C. IRWIN
Contribution to Southwestern Pre-History. Eastern New Mexico University, Paleo-Indian Institute. Volume I, Number 1, 1968.
Picosa: The Elementary Southwestern Culture. American Antiquity, Volume 32, Number 4, 1967.

WILLIAMS, C. IRWIN AND TOMPKINS, S. *Excavations at En Medio Shelter, New Mexico.* Eastern New Mexico University, Paleo-Indian Institute. Volume I, Number 2, 1968.

WORMINGTON, H. M. *Ancient Man in North America.* fourth edition. Denver: Peerless Printing Co., 1957.

ZUNI PEOPLE, trans. ALVINA GUAM, *The Zunis: Self Portrayals.* Albuquerque: University of New Mexico Press, 1974.

NEW MEXICO LITERATURE

ANAYA, RUDOLFO. *Bless Me, Ultima* (1975).

BRADFORD, RICHARD. *Red Sky at Morning* (1968).

CABEZA DE BACA, FABIOLA. *We Fed Them Cactus* (1979).

CATHER, WILLA. *Death Comes for the Archbishop* (1971).

CORLE, EDWIN. *Billy the Kid* (1979).

DOBIE, J. FRANK. *Apache Gold and Yaqui Silver* (1976).

FERGUSSON, HARVEY.
The Conquest of Don Pedro (1974).
Grant of Kingdom (1975).

HORGAN, PAUL. *Far From Cibola* (1974).

LA FARGE, OLIVER. *The Enemy Gods* (1975).

MOMADAY, N. SCOTT. *House Made of Dawn* (1968).

OTIS, RAYMOND. *Miguel of the Bright Mountain* (1977).

SUGGESTED AVAILABLE AUDIO-VISUAL AIDS

Hispanic Weaving in New Mexico — 2 parts, Spanish and English narration on cassette with filmstrip. Part I: The history of Rio Grande weaving; Part II: The craft of weaving as practiced by Spanish families. (purchase)

Lifeways — A series of films and slide/tape programs that explore contemporary Hispanic life and culture in the Southwestern United States. (rental or purchase)

Look What We've Done to the Land — 16mm color/sound film and videocassette. Identifies the Four Corners power production complex, and the effects of mining operations on the Navajo and Hopi Indians living in the area. (rental or purchase)

Los Santeros — 16mm color/sound film and videocassette. This film traces the history of the Santeros' art in New Mexico and shows the woodcarving and painting techniques employed to realize their creations. (rental or purchase)

Madrid, New Mexico — 16mm color/sound film and videocassette. Filmed at daybreak in a deserted coal mining town. The voices of a husband and wife evoke the moods and feelings of their hard life, far from their original home in Ohio. (rental or purchase)

Spanish Colonial Life in the Southwest — Spanish and English narration on cassette. This filmstrip recreates the daily life and activities in a Southwestern Spanish colonial village. (purchase)

Rio Grande — 16mm color/sound film and videocassette. This film ties together the people, culture, landscape, and history of New Mexico.

The above films are available from: Blue Sky Productions
P.O. Box 548
Santa Fe, New Mexico 87501

New Mexico, An Enchanted Land — 80 color slides, script cassette. (free loan)
Available from: New Mexico Travel Division C&ID
Bataan Bldg.
Santa Fe, New Mexico 87503

SUGGESTED AVAILABLE AUDIO-VISUAL AIDS

El Rancho de Las Golondrinas: A Living Museum — 80 color slides. (free loan)

For information	Old Cienega Village Museum
on above materials	Rt. 214
contact:	Santa Fe, New Mexico 87501

History of New Mexico — Three half-hour shows on the development and history of New Mexico. A KNME videotape production. (free print)

Lincoln: The People, The Pageant — The annual Lincoln pageant acted out on stage. A KNEW videotape production. (free print)

For information	Materials Resource Center
on above materials	State Department of Education
contact:	Santa Fe, New Mexico 87503

Comparative Cultures: Japan, Navajo Indians, and Mexico — 16mm color sound film. Two programs each on Japan, Navajo Indians and Mexico. Focus: The physical environment of each group and how it influences the lifestyles of each culture. (rental or purchase)

Mesa Verde: Mystery of the Silent Cities — 16mm color sound film. Presents the Mesa Verde civilization; it depicts housing carved out from sheer canyon walls and multi-storied buildings. (rental or purchase)

Santa Fe — 16mm color/sound film. A lyrical interpretation of the culture in the capital city. (rental or purchase)

The Hands of Maria — 16mm color/sound film. A film on San Ildefonso's potter, Maria. (rental or purchase)

For information on above	Materials Resource Center
materials contact:	State Department of Education
	Santa Fe, New Mexico 87503

Where Edges Meet — 16 mm color/sound film. Mixes glimpses of New Mexico's geographic, cultural, ethnic, and historical aspects. (free loan)

For information	Materials Resource Center
on above materials	State Department of Education
contact:	Santa Fe, New Mexico 87503

Rio Grande — 16mm color/sound film. Explores the history, cultures, traditions, and landscape of the state. (free loan)

Available from:	New Mexico State Park and Recreation Commission
	Box 1147
	Santa Fe, New Mexico 87503

Conquistadores Trail — 16mm color/sound film. Retraces the trails the Conquistadores blazed through New Mexico, Arizona, and Texas. (free loan)

It's a Whole New World — 16mm color/sound film. New Mexico's cultures — highly visible in all the arts, professions, and history. (free loan)

Wildlife World — 16mm color/sound film. Surveys New Mexico's varied wildlife from elk and mountain sheep to trout. (free loan)

The three films are available from:	Film Librarian, C&ID
	Bataan Bldg.
	Santa Fe, New Mexico 87503

Teaching about New Mexico History and Culture (Otero) — An activity book with objectives, grade levels for which activity is suitable, time allowed each activity, materials required, procedures to follow and evaluation. (printed material — purchase)

Available from:	Materials Resource Center
	Center for the Teaching of International Relations (CTIR)
	University of Denver
	Denver, Colorado 80208

New Mexico Map Skills Program (Newmann) — The program includes individual student sets of graphic learning materials lithographed in color on heavy-duty card stock. Student activities and evaluation are developed around each unit of study. (printed material — purchase)

Available from:	American Media
Listed in the New	1204 East Secretariat Dr.
Mexico catalogue of	Tempe, Arizona 85284
adopted materials.	

INDEX

INDEX

A JOURNEY THROUGH NEW MEXICO HISTORY
PHOTO CREDITS

PHOTO CREDITS